Fragments from the History of Loss

AnthropoScene
THE SLSA BOOK SERIES

Lucinda Cole and Robert Markley, General Editors

Advisory Board:
Stacy Alaimo (University of Texas at Arlington)
Ron Broglio (Arizona State University)
Carol Colatrella (Georgia Institute of Technology)
Heidi Hutner (Stony Brook University)
Stephanie LeMenager (University of Oregon)
Christopher Morris (University of Texas at Arlington)
Laura Otis (Emory University)
Will Potter (Washington, D.C.)
Ronald Schleifer (University of Oklahoma)
Susan Squier (Pennsylvania State University)
Rajani Sudan (Southern Methodist University)
Kari Weil (Wesleyan University)

Published in collaboration with the Society for Literature, Science, and the Arts, AnthropoScene presents books that examine relationships and points of intersection among the natural, biological, and applied sciences and the literary, visual, and performing arts. Books in the series promote new kinds of cross-disciplinary thinking arising from the idea that humans are changing the planet and its environments in radical and irreversible ways.

Fragments from the History of Loss

The Nature Industry and the Postcolony

Louise Green

The Pennsylvania State
University Press
University Park,
Pennsylvania

Library of Congress Cataloging-in-Publication Data

Names: Green, Louise, 1968– author.
Title: Fragments from the history of loss : the nature industry and the postcolony / Louise Green.
Other titles: AnthropoScene.
Description: University Park, Pennsylvania : The Pennsylvania State University Press, [2020] | Series: AnthropoScene: the SLSA book series | Includes bibliographical references and index.
Summary: "Examines the theoretical framing of 'nature' in South Africa and beyond. Analyzes myths and fantasies that have brought the world to a point of climate catastrophe and continue to shape the narratives through which it is understood"—Provided by publisher.
Identifiers: LCCN 2019059729 | ISBN 9780271087016 (hardback)
Subjects: LCSH: Nature—Effect of human beings on. | Nature—Effect of human beings on—South Africa. | Climatic changes—Social aspects. | Climatic changes—Social aspects—South Africa.
Classification: LCC GF75 .G74 2020 | DDC 304.2—dc23
LC record available at https://lccn.loc.gov/2019059729

Copyright © 2020 Louise Green
All rights reserved
Printed in the United States of America.
Published by The Pennsylvania State University Press,
University Park, PA 16802-1003

The Pennsylvania State University Press is a member of the Association of University Presses.

It is the policy of The Pennsylvania State University Press to use acid-free paper. Publications on uncoated stock satisfy the minimum requirements of American National Standard for Information Sciences—Permanence of Paper for Printed Library Material, ANSI Z39.48-1992.

Material in chapter 5 appeared as "Apartheid's Wolves: Political Animals and Animal Politics," *Critical African Studies* 8, no. 2 (2016): 146–60, DOI: 10.1080/21681392.2016.1209873. Copyright © Centre of African Studies, University of Edinburgh, reprinted by permission of Informa UK Limited trading as Taylor & Francis Ltd., http://www.tandfonline.com, on behalf of Centre of African Studies, University of Edinburgh. Material in chapter 6 appeared as "A Landscape with Objects: Private Game Reserves, Game Lodges and the 'New Safari,'" *Social Dynamics* 36, no. 2 (2010): 288–301, DOI: 10.1080/02533951003794381, https://www.tandfonline.com.

Contents

List of Illustrations | vii

Acknowledgments | ix

1. The Nature Industry | 1

2. Nature in Fragments | 27

3. Living in the Subjunctive | 54

4. The Primitive Accumulation of Nature | 74

5. The Cult of the Wild | 103

6. Privatizing Nature | 125

7. Living at the End of Nature | 150

Notes | 161

References | 171

Index | 183

Illustrations

1. The Hall of Biodiversity, American Museum of Natural History. Photo: François Olivier. | 38

2. The Rain Forest and Mediterranean Biomes in the Eden Project. Photo: Louise Green. | 43

3. Part of the West Africa rain forest exhibit in the Eden Project. Photo: Louise Green. | 46

4. The Kimberley Club. Photo © Africana Library, Kimberley. | 79

5. De Beers mine. Photo © Africana Library, Kimberley. | 85

6. De Beers compound. Photo © Africana Library, Kimberley. | 89

7. "Hunting with Mr Rhodes." Photo © Africana Library, Kimberley. | 99

Acknowledgments

The writing of this book has been a long-term project, and a great many people have contributed to it in various ways. I am grateful to the National Research Foundation of South Africa and to Stellenbosch University for their financial support of the research included in this book. Thanks also to Bernice Nagel and the staff of the Kimberley Africana Research Library for their guidance during my visit.

The ongoing encouragement and generosity of a number of colleagues have sustained me over the years. I would like to thank all the members of the Stellenbosch English Department for their support and encouragement. Special thanks are due to the lift club, Tina Steiner, Riaan Oppelt, Megan Jones, Uhuru Phalafala, and Nadia Sanger, for the many lively conversations and especially for their forbearance with me in the final stages of the project. Also to Dawid de Villiers, who has been a sympathetic listener as I wrestled with the final revisions. Thanks also to my coeditors at *Social Dynamics*, Bernard Dubbeld and Chris Ouma, for their support and to Noelle Koeries for her excellent work managing the journal.

I am not a solitary writer, and I would like to thank the many people, individuals, and members of reading and writing groups I have been part of who have provided an important intellectual community in which to formulate my ideas. In the early stages of this project, John Higgins, Kylie Thomas, Meg Samuelson, and Sandra Young were all valued readers and commentators. Premesh Lalu and Sarah Nuttall also enriched my reading and provided critical insights on early pieces of work that ultimately formed part of this book. I would also like to thank Tilla Slabbert and Eckard Smuts and the other members of the Nature Critical reading group, especially Philip Aghoghovwia, Eve Nabulya, and Francois Olivier, who have challenged me and extended my own thinking about environmental issues over the years. Noeleen Murray, Leslie Wits, Tina Steiner, Gabeba Baderoon, and Brenda Cooper were a necessary part of imagining the book in its final form. In the final stages, Stephanie Newell's wit and encouragement helped sustain my momentum. Special thanks are due to Brenda Cooper for her insight and enthusiasm and for her patient but forthright insistence on completion.

I am deeply indebted to Dorn Hetzel and Gabeba Baderoon for many, many things: for giving me a place to stay on my visits to State College that is beautiful, comfortable, and full of books, good conversation, and delicious vegetarian food and for their enduring support and friendship. While at Penn State University, Jonathan Marks, Rose Jolly, and the participants in the Bioethics Colloquium provided valuable comments and suggestions on individual chapters. I am particularly grateful to Susan Squier for her thoughtful suggestion regarding publication and to my editor at Penn State University Press, Kendra Boileau, for her support of the project.

In a book about the particular texture of the everyday, it would be remiss not to mention those friends and family who have provided practical and emotional support both directly and indirectly related to the writing of the book: Lena and Elizabeth Green, Sharon Hughes, Shannon Neill, Kris Kelly, Nina Hattingh, and Imraan Jardine have all contributed in important ways. I am grateful to the many breakfast-time conversations with Ute Kuhlmann, Craig Mason-Jones, and Andrew Marquard. Lena, Ute, and Sharon provided invaluable help with proofreading and the preparation of the final manuscript. Thanks also to all the staff of the Superette in Woodstock, where much of this book was written. I am grateful too to all at Cape Town Aikido for keeping me sane while writing this book.

Special thanks go to Tina Steiner and Gabeba Baderoon, my most longstanding writing companions, for the many hours spent writing together in various, diverse locations around the world and for your insights and encouragement. Finally, I feel much gratitude for those other supportive longtime companions, Neo, Riley, and Mira, who are not interested in books at all but who take me out of the house and into the open air.

The Nature Industry

Paysage—The shortcoming of the American landscape is not so much, as romantic illusion would have it, the absence of historical memories, as that it bears no traces of the human hand. This applies not only to the lack of arable land, the uncultivated woods often no higher than scrub, but above all to the roads. These are always inserted directly in the landscape, and the more impressively smooth and broad they are, the more unrelated and violent their gleaming track appears against its wild, overgrown surroundings. They are expressionless. Just as they know no marks of foot or wheel, no soft path along their edges as a transition to vegetation, no trails leading off into the valleys, so they are without the mild, soothing, un-angular quality of things that have felt the touch of hands or their immediate implements. It is as if no-one has ever passed their hand over the landscape's hair. It is uncomforted and comfortless. And it is perceived in a corresponding way. For what the hurrying eye has seen merely from the car it cannot retain, and the vanishing landscape leaves no more traces behind than it bears upon itself.

—Adorno

The more reified the world becomes, the thicker the veil cast upon nature, the more the thinking that weaves that veil in its turn claims ideologically to be nature, primordial experience.

—Adorno

The Weight of Water

In the era of privatized natural resources, the public spring in Cape Town is a strange remnant of a different relation to the natural world. As a free resource, it is an anomaly, an anachronism. It offers an apparently limitless supply of fresh mineral-rich water filtered down through Table Mountain's multiple layers of rock. It is always sparklingly clear, exuberantly lively, and irresistibly delicious. For many years, it could be collected from outside the South African Brewery in Newlands—one of the middle-class, formerly whites-only suburbs that lie close to the foot of the mountain—where it ran continuously from three copper outlet pipes.

In the summer of 2018, the dams providing water to the city of Cape Town almost ran dry. Water restrictions, always in place, became increasingly severe. Water allocation was gradually reduced to fifty liters per person per day, and as the rain continued to stay away, plans were made for what appeared inevitable—the day the municipal water would be turned off. When the city announced the plans for day zero—an allocation of twenty-five liters to be collected at water points around the city—supermarkets ran out of bottled water. The city experienced the limit of a natural resource that directly affected the texture of everyday life. For a brief moment, it was confronted with the terrifying yet utopian possibility of an egalitarian distribution of resources. Many people in South Africa still do not have access to municipal water. Fetching water from shared taps is still a common experience. Yet almost immediately the capitalist machine responded to the new demand, bottled water was imported, five-liter plastic bottles of water lined supermarket aisles, and the hierarchy of access was reimposed.

What makes this example singular is the way in which it made visible and called into question a certain "technique of life."[1] This technique of life is in no way uniformly experienced by all city dwellers. But it is implicit in Cape Town's image of itself as a "modern" city, in which a functioning infrastructure separates those with resources from directly experiencing the work of maintaining everyday existence. Many have written about how failures in infrastructure make things visible that have been deliberately backgrounded by the particular form of life associated with modernity. In the particular case of Cape Town's water crisis, this shift in perspectival logic went further. The causes of infrastructure failure are complex and entangled, but its effect was to make tangible the abstract idea of climate change as something that directly impacts everyday life. The natural world could no longer be conceived of as a set of documented "environmental factors" that influence human settlement, a background against which human history unfolds. Rather, as rain clouds repeatedly gathered and then drifted out to sea, it appeared as an unstable and unpredictable historical agent.

Fragments from the History of Loss

During the crisis, the queues at the spring became increasingly long, and the increased traffic created problems for the brewery that managed the outlet. Eventually, the collection point was closed, and the water was rerouted to a new point a few kilometers away on a little piece of wasteland between some shops and the Newlands public swimming pool. Distributed among sixteen taps now, the spring was resituated within a fenced and paved yard presided over by a guard. The winter rains in 2018 came slowly with few of the usual downpours, but gradually the dams refilled. The moment of panic receded, though weather patterns continued to appear strange. Fetching water from the spring, usually late at night to try to avoid the still lengthy queues, and standing in the wind and the at times wild, wind-borne rain, I have found my carrying capacity. It is not large: two ten-liter bottles, one in each hand. A small industry has sprung up of water carriers who offer to ease the labor of carrying water for a low price.

I choose not to accept their service despite their mild irritation that I, a white, car-owning South African, could obviously afford to pay. I like to feel the weight of my drinking water, the labor it costs me to fill my two bottles and carry them to the car, to take my next two bottles and rejoin the back of the queue. It is a kind of discipline, an enforced slowness, a repetitive ritual. People are sometimes silent, sometimes communicative. Practices have developed that conflict with the official notice attached to the fence, which states, "Maximum of 25 liters per person at a time." After hours, someone tells me, you can now take fifty. The guard controls access, closing the gate and opening it to regulate the flow of people to the taps. People step out of the queue to have a cigarette, leaving their bottles to keep their place. The wind begins to shift them, and the person behind anchors them with a foot or a knee. At the taps, each person performs the same action, first rinsing his or her bottle in the freshwater and then standing it in place and waiting for it to fill, adjusting it to the exuberant flow of water, and then when the task is completed, shouting "Next" to indicate to the person at the front of the queue that the tap is now free.

Despite the queues and the expenditure of effort after the day's work is done, there is a pleasure in fetching water from the spring that has something to do with contact—contact with the water that splashes so energetically from the taps, contact with others engaged in a similar task, contact with the necessity of survival and the limits of your own ability. Although it is a form of consumption that is outside the logic of exchange, it is not an entirely innocent pleasure. Water is heavy, and carrying it away requires some kind of technology—sometimes a cart or trolley but in most cases a motor car. Fetching water requires certain resources of transport, time, energy, and physical strength. The existence of the guard is a reminder of the fragility of such resources and the possibility of their exploitation. Yet despite this, the spring remains a strangely open space—in the privatized city, it has given rise to and sustains a small enclosure of common ground.

Unlike earlier decolonial struggles that took place in the 1960s, South Africa's delayed liberation in 1994 took place at the very moment when the egalitarian promise of democracy—that the benefits of modernity accrue to all citizens instead of the tiny white elite—collided with a global narrative of environmental limits.[2] Reviewing the municipal water system from the perspective of its near failure, the wastefulness of using fresh drinking water to move sewage through the sanitation system became apparent. The flush toilet appeared suddenly as an unwarranted luxury even as people in informal settlements, who had been forced all their lives to contend with various forms of inadequate sanitation, protested against the shared chemical toilets that are the city's "temporary" response to these areas' lack of access to the formal sewage system. The lack of access to municipal sanitation is not a consequence of the water shortage caused by the drought. Rather, it was the result of colonialism and apartheid's long history of entrenched inequalities and the city's slow development of infrastructure, especially in poor areas. But the juxtaposition of these two events happening at the same time meant that the usually invisible texture of everyday domestic experience became visible as a confrontation between the aspiration to a "modern" lifestyle and the anticipated environmental transformations predicted by climate change.

"Modernity" is a difficult condition to quantify. It is associated with a certain rational control of the environment and a form of life not limited by the immediate demands of survival, although the precise form such an organization of everyday life might take is in a state of constant revision. Yet despite its uncertain and shifting definition, it has exerted a powerful influence on the way humans inhabit the world. Through the narrative of progress, it has justified massive and often violent forms of social transformation. It has become what distinguishes everyday life in England, Europe, and North America from life in Africa and other previously colonized places. Held up as the often-elusive goal of projects of development, it directs flows of money and resources. Beyond its precise definition, modernity has come to describe a condition of being protected from the everyday work of surviving and the freedom to work for profit and to access a high standard of living—a lifestyle dependent on the consumption of fossil fuels and access to goods from all over the world.

While the carbon emissions generated by the African continent are negligible compared to those of North America, Europe, and China, within Africa, South Africa is one of the biggest contributors to global warming. With its coal-fueled power stations, its reliance on road transportation, and its attachment to imported commodities, it ties into global patterns of consumption. Yet it is also a product of uneven development. Alongside its ports, with their sophisticated intermodal transport technologies, lie settlements with very tenuous links to modern techniques of life and world markets. The colonial project was contradictory, invested both in destroying indigenous techniques of life to create a modern workforce and modern consumers and in maintaining the colony as wild open space, distinct from the rapidly industrializing metropolitan centers.

In Africa in particular, the natural world acquired value as the domain in which, freed from constraints of everyday domestic life in the metropole, the white colonial hero and occasional heroine could test their mettle through various profitable exploits—exploring, hunting, and mining. These exploits conferred a certain glamour on the ruthless exploitation of Africa's abundant natural resources. The history of South Africa provides one iteration of how these contradictory impulses continue to configure the global landscape even in the twenty-first century. If nature in the era of climate change now appears in a new form, as a fragile, even evanescent afterimage of earlier plenitude, it is one that continues to be profoundly, perhaps even unconsciously, shaped by this long imperial history.

Although the material I gather here is drawn predominantly from South Africa, I have adopted the term *postcolony* as a collective noun to reference a wider experience, to describe a particular position in the world based on the historical transformation wrought by a violent imposition of modernity—an organization of society based on industrialization and the production and distribution of consumer goods. It is deployed as a reminder of the historical forces that have produced the current situation and that threaten to be elided by the universalizing narrative of the Anthropocene. Fractured by the unfinished project of liberation, mesmerized by the promise of capitalism, South Africa offers an exposed surface for reading the set of contradictions that the current confrontation between capitalist modernity and environmental limit has driven to the surface. But it is not unique. I offer these particular moments in the history of the production of nature in South Africa, Africa, and beyond as part of the necessary project of analyzing the complex myths and fantasies that have brought the world to this point of crisis and continue to shape the narratives through which it is understood.

The Alibi of Nature

In the era of environmental crisis, nature has become the subject of an intense, almost obsessive scrutiny. In this book, I argue that, within these myths and fantasies, "nature" has come to occupy the position of an alibi. Holding the promise of a value separate from the vicissitudes of culture and politics, it has become the perfect elsewhere. Yet to view nature this way is to neglect the way in which the environmental crisis is itself imbricated in a broader crisis of modernity.

Nature is a word that invites the form of the present tense—the form for expressing general, unchanging truths about the world. In this book, I am interested in how the narratives that have emerged to describe the current crisis facilitate or limit what can be said about nature and its relation to history, how nature is complicated by the particularities of time and place. The work of this book is to make these forms visible not through a systematic analysis of the diverse discourses through which nature is daily revealed (a potentially endless task) but through a strategic and selective juxtaposition of different orders of knowledge and experience.

In the subtitle, the phrase *the nature industry* is linked to the term *postcolony* with the conjunction *and*. On the surface, *and* is the most neutral and unexpressive of conjunctions, since it merely adds one thing to another without suggesting anything about their relationship. In this, it resembles the rhetorical device *parataxis*. The term *parataxis* comes from the Greek and indicates the act of placing things side by side. It is a grammatical form that assigns an equal relationship between the various words or phrases linked together. One thing is not subsumed by another. Placing the nature industry and the postcolony in juxtaposition, I explore how each concept configures the other.

There is a long tradition of writing about nature that favors observation, fact, and documentation. I propose a different approach, one that can encompass different orders of knowledge in a nonhierarchical arrangement. The book employs a synecdochic logic. *Synecdoche* is a figure of speech in which the part stands for the whole or the whole for the part. Following the logic of the synecdochic figure allows movement back and forth between the part and the whole, the specific and the general, and the material and the thing itself. Through this operation of substitution, which works both ways, the form permits the most abstract ideas to be anchored in historical particularity. Refusing the separation of theory and experience, it acts to concretize abstract processes, finding in the most insignificant features of everyday life exemplary fragments of the whole.

In order to interpret these fragments, I have chosen to follow a particular intellectual trajectory. I make the claim that thinking about nature in the postcolony might best be achieved by following a tradition and a form of critique developed in another moment of extreme uncertainty, the period of the Second World War and its immediate aftermath. The approach outlined by Walter Benjamin and Theodor Adorno offers a uniquely flexible set of critical practices for articulating the diverse elements of the current crisis. While Adorno's work does not directly address the problematic at the center of this book—the particular configurations that emerge from considering the nature industry and the postcolony in juxtaposition—he does provide a compelling form for considering complex concepts, ones that circulate through diverse conceptual domains. The particular, he asserts, should not be subsumed within the general but rather should be placed alongside the general category in a way that might disturb the system as a whole. Experience, the contingent, and the ephemeral are all relevant for a study that takes seriously the demands of the subject under investigation. This is particularly true when considering the many narratives that emerge in response to climate change. Documenting carbon emissions involves measuring almost all aspects of everyday life, from the use of cars to the way myriad electrical devices structure life and the effects of industrial processes that underlie big infrastructural projects.

Through making constellations drawing on elements from art, local histories, politics, popular culture, consumer culture, and environmental writing of various kinds, I consider the cultural and philosophical implications of living under the sign of imminent geophysical change. The term *constellation* to describe a particular methodological practice of combination was first proposed in the work of Benjamin and Adorno. As a method, it is useful because it offers a way of resisting the apparent immediacy of the concept of nature.[3] "Knowledge," Adorno notes, "comes to us through a network of prejudices, opinions, innervations, self-corrections, presuppositions and exaggerations, in short through the dense, firmly founded but by no means uniformly transparent medium of experience" (Adorno 1978, 80). The constellation offers a way of assembling some of these diverse forms of knowledge so as to reveal the manner in which they structure our understanding of and response to the transformations produced by climate change.

The current environmental crisis exists not only as an event in the world but also in a pervasive texturing of contemporary consciousness. It exists not only as scientific data but also as a reordering of the social around a new set of coordinates. For sociologist Ulrich Beck, what characterizes the current phase of modernity is the proliferation of unpredictable and unwanted side effects of modernization.[4] Climate change represents perhaps the most comprehensive of these damaging side effects. While the phrase *global warming* has become part of the shorthand of public discourse, the precise dimensions of this crisis, its complexity, and its strangeness are often obscured by the frequency of its iteration. This is in part because it occurs at an unprecedented level of abstraction. This is not to say that the effects of global warming and other forms of environmental degradation do not impact peoples' lives in very direct and intimate ways. Rather, it is to draw attention to the fact that what defines this crisis, its globalness, is precisely what is most difficult to bring into consciousness. The mystifying complexity of this new totality requires thinking not only in different scales of time and space but also in shifts between intimate everyday practices and great impersonal earth systems. In the face of the manifest impossibility of what is needed—a theory of everything—the work of this book, which is a gathering or assembling, a placing of things side by side, allows for the production of temporary and contingent relationships that refuse the division of the world into discrete sectors and scholarship into compartmentalized disciplinary logics. Such arrangements are deliberate works of interpretation designed to bring certain details into the domain of attention in a new way.

The Nature Industry

The phrase in the subtitle of this book, *The Nature Industry*, repeats and adapts the title of Adorno and Horkheimer's famous critical intervention *The Culture Industry*, written in the 1940s while both were in exile in California. *The Culture Industry* describes the way in which, in the era of mass production, culture becomes subjected to the logic of capitalist production to the extent that it loses any autonomous existence. Adorno brings the two words *culture* and *industry* into contact to generate a shock—one brought about by the forced combination of two incommensurable concepts—but it is a shock that we can no longer experience. In his essay "The Exact Sense in Which the Culture Industry No Longer Exists," Adorno scholar Robert Hullot-Kentor argues that the precise meaning of Adorno's phrase has been irrevocably lost, as the words themselves have become absorbed into the everyday language of commerce. The phrase continues to circulate in the contemporary "frictionless vernacular" (Hullot-Kentor 2010, 9) but as a description of a legitimate domain of commercial transaction, not as critique. The word *industry* affixed to almost any human activity reduces it to a generalizable enactment for the purposes of profit.[5]

Recognizing the pervasiveness of the word *industry*, my choice of the phrase *the nature industry* for the subtitle both acknowledges the existence of such a commercial flattening and engages in the work of disaggregating the seamlessness of the fit. While *nature* has unquestionably become subsumed within the instrumental logic of capitalist production,[6] it is also now, in the light of the extent of environmental crisis, subject to a certain haunting. The commodification and the loss exist together in one breath, its precise value as an object of commerce being its precarious evanescence.

For Adorno, culture had, in the past, held the potential to offer a critique of society. Art held the residue of autonomy in an increasingly administered world. In a similar way, nature seems to contain some residue of utopian promise. It seems to offer a way of imagining the whole, of reintegrating the fragmented elements of modern life. Yet nature, like culture, to which it is frequently opposed, is a term of immense complexity and ambiguity.[7] In some ways, the setting up of this opposition between nature and culture masks the fact that the two terms are not commensurable. Culture, as a set of human practices that includes the classification and demarcation of the world, always contains nature as one of its categories.[8] From this point of view, nature can never escape into pure materiality, and the ways in which it has been categorized means that for many theorists, it is too fundamentally implicated in the legitimation of a variety of oppressive practices to be useful.[9]

Yet the ubiquity of the term *nature* in contemporary life means that it is impossible simply to dismiss it as irrelevant. It continues to exert pressure on the terms through which the current crisis is described. In another conceptual juxtaposition, Adorno proposes the combination of nature and history as a means of allowing the pressure of the material to enter narrative. However, it is clear that he does not believe nature can do this in any straightforward way. "The Idea of Natural History" is a lecture Adorno presented to the *Kant-Gesellschaft* on July 15, 1932.[10] While it is primarily a philosophical intervention, directed at countering the phenomenological claims of Husserl and Heidegger, its staging of the complex interaction of nature and history provides a valuable guide to a mode of thinking that might reach beyond the current obsessive reiteration of nature as the domain of unmediated experience. What emerges instead is the idea of *second nature*, a phrase that aptly captures the way in which habits and conventions have become raised to the status of mythic inevitability. By twisting the articulation of the two terms *nature* and *history*, Adorno elicits a recognition of the limits of a form of thinking that simply describes and justifies the world as it is and, in doing so, covertly confirms the inevitability of a particular technique of life. Most importantly for this study, it describes a particular optics or adjustment of the gaze that might be deployed to bring the technique of life of consumer society into focus in a new way.

To describe this approach, Adorno uses the phrase *natural history* but wrenches it from its conventional meaning as describing the (prescientific) study of nature through observation. Instead, he proposes bringing these two terms together to generate a disturbance of both categories—a conceptual shock. At the beginning of the lecture, Adorno explains the two concepts that he hopes to overcome. The one is nature as myth, as that "fatefully-arranged and predetermined being that underlies history"; the other, history as the "mode of conduct established by tradition that is characterized primarily by the occurrence of the qualitatively new" (Adorno 1984, 111). Yet he resists an attempt to define how the concept of "natural history" exceeds or transforms the terms it contains. Instead, he suggests that the juxtaposition of the terms enables an analysis that pushes "these concepts to a point where they are mediated by their apparent difference" (111).

Adorno first approaches the question from the standpoint of neo-ontological thought—in which, through a formulation of the concept of being, historicity itself is naturalized—and then shifts to a reading of the philosophy of history in which the historical being of nature is revealed.[11] For Adorno, the problem with Heidegger's embrace of historicity is that it translates history as concrete details into something entirely abstract. Historicity as the condition of the possibility of being itself no longer has any connection to historical contingency, to the facticity of particular phenomena. Naturalizing historicity as the condition of possibility of being itself is ultimately an ideological move that elevates the existent, the material conditions at a particular historical moment, to the ground for philosophical speculation. The loss of the real, the impression of the existent as something foreign, which, for Adorno, constitutes a specific historical condition—the condition of capitalist estrangement—becomes the basis for a philosophical position.

Instead, Adorno locates a new way of formulating the question in the work of Benjamin and Georg Lukács. For Lukács, the lost world of the real constitutes what he refers to as second nature, the world of conventions. He writes that "the world of conventions, a world from whose all-embracing power only the innermost recesses of the soul are exempt, a world which is present everywhere in a multiplicity of forms too complex for understanding. . . . It is second nature, and, like nature (first nature), it is determinable only as the embodiment of recognised but senseless necessities and therefore is incomprehensible, unknowable in its real substance" (1978, 62).

Confronted by the world of second nature, Adorno writes, "The problem of natural history presents itself in the first place as the question of how it is possible to know and interpret this alienated, reified, dead world" (1984, 118). For Lukács, at this stage of his thinking, the problem of awakening this world is conceived in metaphysical terms, as a form of "theological resurrection," a notion that persists today in ecological theories that seek to "re-enchant the world."

For Benjamin, the project of awakening is part of the task of philosophical interpretation and can best be understood through the mode of allegory. Adorno writes, "Allegory is usually taken to mean the presentation of a concept as an image and therefore it is labeled abstract and accidental. The relationship of allegory to its meaning is not accidental signification, but the playing out of a particularity; it is expression. What is expressed in the allegorical sphere is nothing but a historical relationship" (1984, 119).

Allegory as Benjamin defines it, Adorno suggests, provides "a presentiment of the procedure that could succeed in interpreting concrete history" (1984, 121). This procedure, which is the project of natural history, involves a different conceptual approach to that which is "based on a project whose foundation is constituted by a general conceptual structure" (120). What Adorno is describing here is the "constellation." The constellation does not aim at the definition and clarification of terms but rather provides a form that holds them in a particular relation to one another. Max Pensky explains that constellations "are not to be regarded as providing 'solutions' to problems posed by the assemblage of recovered cultural material. Rather, such solutions are to be regarded as directions toward a political practice that would seek to dissolve the puzzle-like character of the real, rather than merely solving it" (2004, 234).

Constellations become the mode of illuminating not fixed coordinates but the ever-shifting ground of historical facticity so that in the moment of their juxtaposition, they are temporarily released from their solidification in second nature. Nature in its transience constantly invokes the historical and thus works against the seemingly fixed character of second nature. Adorno explains that "for radical natural-historical thought, however, everything transforms itself into ruins and fragments, into just such a charnel house where signification is discovered, in which nature and history interweave and the philosophy of history is assigned the task of their intentional interpretation" (1984, 121). The charnel house, an image taken from Lukács, becomes the figure for understanding the reified world not as a totality but as a collection of fragments ceremoniously housed together but constantly in a process of decay.[12] Philosophy, confronted with the world as a charnel house, finds its own impulse, "the urge to be at home everywhere in the world" turned against itself. To be at home in a charnel house is to belong there, to be one of the dead. The task of philosophy thus needs, Adorno suggests, to be redefined so that it does not become merely the legitimation of the given—the task of making the charnel house more homely.

The justification of the existent takes many forms, but what underlies all of these is an appeal to the notion of the inevitable. The real presents itself as something that cannot be avoided, something separate from subjective apprehension and providing an exact and preordained limit. The real, whether manifested in the ineluctable workings of market forces, the inevitability of capitalism as a system, or the unthinkability of a life not propped up with consumer goods and services, becomes the point at which critical thought must give way before something more solid. It is against this real—empirically supported by a host of institutions, statistics, scholarly papers, policy documents, and vested interests—that ideas collide when alternative economies and techniques of life are proposed. To describe something as second nature is to point to an absence of thought. It refers to an action that is habitual to such an extent that it vanishes as a deliberate activity and becomes inevitable, something that merely gives form to the real. It is precisely the automatic nature of such actions and interactions that gives the world of conventions the character, for Lukács, of a "charnel house." No longer attached to the fulfillment of actual social interaction, they constitute a kind of "senseless necessity."

An allegorical reading becomes the means by which to disturb this world of conventions and reified traditions. Subject to the optic of natural history, these "fragments and ruins" are displaced, shaken up, and reconstituted as constellations. The surface of the real decomposes into multiple incommensurable and discontinuous pieces no longer lined up in the service of mythic inevitability. Instead of a guarantee of authority, nature testifies to the transience not only of living things but also of knowledge itself. The optic of natural history provides a way of approaching climate change and the postcolony weighted by a specific materiality and by something less tangible as well—an affective texture or mode of inhabiting the world.

A Theory of Everything

Before the recognition of global warming, environmental damage had always been attached to particular localities.[13] In the nineteenth century, intense forms of environmental damage surrounded Britain's rapidly industrializing north.[14] The manufactories produced both "the plague of smoke" and the goods that generated the wealth that approximately one hundred years later was able to rehabilitate the landscape. It also produced, as an invisible side effect, the carbon dioxide that is currently still accumulating in the atmosphere. In the contemporary "geography of capitalism" (Smith 1984, 7), a complex checkerwork of spaces, industrial, industrializing, and postindustrial, emerges where the most evident damage tends to occur in prolonged, intense encounters with capital that then moves on, taking with it all the paraphernalia of visibility—media attention, publicity, and expert personnel. The current mobility of capital disperses the sites of damage more widely, but what makes the crisis global is not simply the extension of damage into previously nonindustrial space; it is the evidence of the damage reflected back from the atmosphere, the invisible but increasingly significant rise in carbon dioxide levels. In the 1990s, when scientific evidence of global warming first began to enter the public domain, it provoked an anxiety not just about the practical consequences of this change to the biochemistry of the planet but also about its philosophical implications. Because climate change affects all aspects of the natural world, it undermines the possibility of a nature independent of human activities. "The end of nature"[15] signifies the condition of environmental damage but also a painful psychic loss. Nature can no longer be regarded as a numinous presence, offering the possibility of escape from human society, and appears instead as attenuated and haunted by loss. Chapter 2 addresses this moment of loss, arranging its constellation around two public displays that attempt to offer advice about the proper response to nature in an era of predicted scarcity. Global warming, unlike other forms of environmental destruction, requires not only an awareness of damage done in a series of displaced elsewheres but also a recognition of damage being done in another time, in that most strange of locations—the future. The evidence of damage read in the material of the earth emerges as the teleological end point of our current trajectory. It presents a moral critique of modernity and the progress of human societies toward a particular "standard of living"—and a refutation of certain cultural and epistemological assumptions.

In 2000, this conceptual shift was formalized in the proposal, made by chemist Paul Crutzen, that the current geological age be renamed the "Anthropocene" to signify the impact of human activities on the geological and ecological substrate of the earth. In 2004, the International Geosphere-Biosphere Programme (IGBP) published a series of graphs that represent statistically the massive increase in consumption that has taken place since the 1950s.[16] This series of graphs, which has come to be known as the Great Acceleration graphs, juxtaposes graphs showing increases in human consumption with graphs showing changes in earth systems. All graphs show an exponential rise in the period since 1950 and are designed to show unequivocally the correlation between human activity and changes to the earth's physical, chemical, and biological processes. Chapter 3 engages with this moment of naming and accounting in which scientific nomenclature enters general public circulation and a set of graphs establishes a new measure for charting the relation between nature and history. This act of naming is a response to the crisis in knowledge and certainty that climate change inaugurates. I am not talking here about the "production of doubt" characteristic of climate change denialists.[17] Even those convinced of the accuracy of accounts of global warming are subject to uncertainty about the degree of increase and the precise effects of climate change. Despite sophisticated and detailed scientific research into change over time, the immense complexity of earth systems means that predictions about the future proliferate. The subjunctive mood describes a grammatical form used to talk about events we are not certain will happen. It reflects perfectly the condition of confronting climate change, the unpredictability heralded by the phrase "If temperatures were to rise by four degrees . . ." and the difficulty of responding to a crisis that is happening in the future. By claiming that we live in the subjunctive, I wish not to undermine the claims made by climate change scientists but rather to draw attention to the fact that accepting climate change science (inevitably an incomplete and ongoing set of experiments, models, and predictions) means accepting the unpredictability of its effects and the uncertainty of the future.

The Great Acceleration graphs document the connection between the culture of consumption and the science of climate change. They invite into intimate proximity very different orders of knowledge. They place in a single conceptual frame the concrete everyday world of traffic and cell phone use, the culture of modernity embodied in glossy advertisements for new cars and cell phone networks alongside the abstract knowledge of rising global levels of carbon dioxide and the increase in the earth's surface temperature. Yet climate change is a crisis that is occurring while concurrently, the everyday life of consumer capitalism appears to continue unaffected. Climate change occupies the space of the early twenty-first century even as other crises—in world political configurations, in economics and the distribution of debt, and in global distributions of violence—continue to take place. In the past, the climate, as a relatively stable natural phenomenon, would be considered part of the background to human activity. Yet in the era of climate change, it is background that increasingly exerts pressure on the foreground.

In chapters 2 and 3, the technique of life I am interested in is one in which consumption is driven not—or not mainly—by the need to sustain life but, more urgently, by the network of social practices that define a certain mode of living as valuable. David Bellamy Foster and Brett Clark have argued that "what people are taught to value and consume in today's acquisitive society are not use values, reflecting genuine needs that have limits, but symbolic values, which are by nature unlimited" (2010, 124). This is not to argue that highly disposable commodities such as mobile phones and computers do not have a use value but rather that the precise nature of their functionality is not what drives the desire for replacement. In fact, these objects are seldom used to their full capacity, which for most users exists only as an attractive potentiality. Deyan Sudjic, the director of the London Design Museum, begins his book *The Language of Things* with the following claim: "Never have more of us had more possessions than we have now, even as we make less and less use of them" (2009, 7). He is referring, of course, to populations of developed countries. Yet a set of expectations about goods branded as valuable and their relation to what constitutes a life worth living, a life of value, circulates around the world through the global culture industry. The crisis of global warming cannot be separated from these more ephemeral transformations in modes of human activity taking place at the level of culture.

Although the phrase *conspicuous consumption* seems particularly suited to describe the activities of contemporary consumer society, it was first used more than one hundred years ago in relation to a very different society, although one that contained elements that have intensified in the past century. In 1899, American sociologist Thorstein Veblen published his anatomy of contemporary society, locating it within a historical trajectory starting with the archaic hunter and warrior and moving through feudal lord and monarch to the individual of the modern industrial age. He used the phrase *conspicuous consumption* to describe a form of consumption designed to enhance status. Veblen's basic argument locates the impulse to consume in "invidious comparison," used, he explains, in its technical sense to describe "a comparison of persons with a view to rating and grading them in respect of relative worth or value" (1943, 34). Consumption attributes value to the consumer because it takes place not in isolation (an individual consuming something in order to meet a basic need) but within a social context, one in which comparison with others forms the fundamental basis for establishing a sense of self-worth. Drawing on an evolutionary narrative, Veblen identifies a continuity between the distribution of value in traditional societies and those in modern societies—in both, he suggests, certain activities not linked to productive labor like warfare and hunting are associated with honor and status while others, including the drudgery of everyday survival, are associated with debasement and a lack of status. In all forms of human society, the impulse to consume beyond what is necessary for survival is driven by the principle of "pecuniary emulation," or the desire of the individual to prove his or her worth in relation to others through activities that display his or her worth—conspicuous leisure and consumption.

In a prescient way, Veblen provides a vocabulary for describing the role of consumption in the global circulation of value between objects and people in the late twentieth and twenty-first centuries. He provides a way of addressing the mysterious power of commodities to signify value beyond their immediate usefulness. "Under Veblen's gloomy gaze," Adorno notes, "lawn and walking stick, umpire and domestic animals become revealing allegories of the barbarism of culture" (1981, 76). Modern industrial society alters the form and extent of consumption and introduces new "canons of taste," but its logic is not different from or more rational than earlier social forms. Although at times

Veblen's analysis seems a relentless reiteration of his central point, that the real reason for consumption is its indirect impact on others, his attention to the minute surface detail of everyday experience allows for a form of reading that is both minutely detailed and nuanced.

Adorno, like Veblen, is concerned with reading the social forms that manifest in everyday situations. As well as offering a form for articulating incommensurable orders of knowledge, his work also offers a particularly acute and detailed study of the culture of consumption. Fredric Jameson suggested in 1990 that Adorno, though writing from the 1930s to the 1960s, may turn out to be, presciently, the best analyst of the late twentieth and early twenty-first century, "which he did not live to see, and in which late capitalism has all but succeeded in eliminating the final loopholes of nature and the Unconscious, of subversion and the aesthetic, of individual and collective praxis alike, and with a final fillip, in eliminating any memory trace of what thereby no longer existed in the henceforth postmodern landscape" (Jameson 1990, 5). He argues that Adorno's critique of positivism translates with peculiar ease into a critique of consumer culture, despite the fact that the glossy outward manifestations of contemporary consuming practices are apparently so different from the nineteenth-century petty-bourgeois philosophy of science out of which contemporary consumerist society emerges. Positivism becomes postmodernism, Jameson suggests, after it has fulfilled its own logic, one aspect of which is the abolition of the subjective—the "hesitations, deliberations and civilities" (Adorno 1978, 40) that form the material of subjective engagement.

If in the early twenty-first century, the term *postmodern* has lost currency, this is at least partly because of the insistent return of the real signaled by climate change and environmental crisis. Reading across the surface of cultural practices, this return of the real has taken many forms, from the popular attachment to reality television programs and nature documentaries to the sharp rejection within the academy of poststructuralist theories of social construction and the rise in status of personal engagements with nature and theories of materialism. That *postmodern* is superseded by the term *global* as the signifier for the contemporary moment testifies to a shift in conceptual orientation. The fragile earth becomes the new totality, a serious and unavoidable reality that undermines the postmodern celebration of relativity and fluidity. Ecology thus redeems realism and demands that the geophysical be taken seriously. Yet at the same time, the cause of the crisis lies in the ephemeral realm of culture—lifestyle, habit, modes of consumption, the articulation and pursuit of desire, what counts as value—those intangible yet powerful motive forces that economists refer to as "public sentiment."

The first set of acceleration graphs used the number of McDonald's restaurants worldwide as the measure of globalization. While this was changed in the 2010 version of the charts to the less suggestive category "foreign direct investment," the implication remains that what the graphs depict is primarily the scale of human consumption. What persists despite the change in terminology is the centrality of the culture of consumption itself and the extension of commodification into all areas of life, including "nature" itself.

The Postcolony

In the reconfiguring of the world that is being brought about by globalization and climate change, the terms *colony* and *postcolony* may seem like a method of designation from an earlier world order. Perhaps in the future, a new set of categories need to be developed relating specifically to carbon emissions, dividing the world into those whose emissions are above or below a certain point.[18] Yet for the purposes of this book, *postcolony* remains an important term because of how it draws attention to the particular way in which various countries enter this new global configuration.

Invoking the postcolony is an act of naming that draws attention to the fact that the defining character of this collective identification is history, not geography.[19] It allows me to extrapolate from the thick description and detailed analysis of particular instances to the larger global arrangement of the world in the condition of environmental crisis. My concern is with the distribution of a technique of life that crosses geographical localities but that is also determined by specific local conditions. Within the synecdochic logic deployed by this book, the postcolony is both a general concept, encompassing countries with multiple different historical trajectories, and an exemplary fragment, a specific part that stands against and disrupts the whole.

Achille Mbembe, who first outlined the notion of the postcolony in an article published in 1992, proposes the term as an alternative to *postcolonial* to develop a different way of thinking about the operation of time. Unlike the postcolonial, which forecasts a time after colonialism, the postcolony invokes a sense of stasis, the interruption of the temporal overcoming promised by national liberation. While postcolony refers to geographical location primarily in terms of its position in a particular historical trajectory, it also offers a collective noun for identifying elements of common experience. Mbembe's primary interest is in the specific character of political power and violence that emerges in Cameroon and elsewhere in Africa after independence as it plays out at the level of everyday acts of signification. The postcolony provides a means of assembling some of these fragments of common experience. Like Mbembe, I do not suggest a uniformity or homogeneity across those countries that experienced colonial conquest, nor do I wish to annihilate differences in the way these global forces act in each individual case. Instead, in my argument, the term *postcolony* is used to denote a particular kind of specificity, a reminder that the world is not uniform in relation to environmental damage.

Because of the particular history of economic development in the colonies, the commodification of nature follows a different trajectory from the one it took in countries such as the United Kingdom and the United States. The colony was imagined as a discontinuous geography of valuable sites separate from their surroundings. These spaces were valued because of what could be extracted from them—their raw materials. Colonial mining projects generated enclaves around these spaces of natural value, constituting them as a different kind of ground. At an African Union summit in 2006, Hugo Chávez asserted Latin America and Africa's potential for development by identifying Africa's natural resources: "Africa is not a poor continent. . . . How can Africa be poor having oil, diamonds, cobalt, wide forests, all kinds of minerals?" (2006). Yet natural resources in African countries have an ambiguous status. In 1993, British economist Richard Auty coined the phrase *resource curse* to describe the curious effect of natural resources on developing economies, suggesting that in many cases, instead of generating wealth, mineral resources distort economies and lead to instability and conflict.[20]

In this book, I argue that Marx's phrase *primitive accumulation* has particular resonance for an investigation of the nature industry and the postcolony. Marx uses the phrase *primitive accumulation* to describe a particular moment in the prehistory of capitalism when accumulation takes place through violent dispossession. Chapter 4 presents such a moment of appropriation, generating a constellation around a particular instance of mineral resource extraction—the diamond rush in Kimberley. The constellation seeks to illuminate the way the primitive accumulation of this artifact of nature provokes a rearrangement of human activities and a redistribution of social status. In a short chapter in *Capital* called "The Secret of Primitive Accumulation," Marx describes the mythical past imagined by political economists as including two sorts of people: "the diligent, intelligent and above all frugal elite" and "the other lazy rascals, spending their substance, and more, in riotous living" (1976, 873). He continues in a sarcastic tone, "And from this original sin dates the poverty of the great majority who, despite all their labor, have up till now nothing to sell but themselves, and the wealth of the few that increases constantly, although they have long since ceased to work" (873). In place of this mythical process of "natural" selection in which the elites accumulate capital through the diligence of their own labor, Marx offers an account of the actual history of accumulation—"the history of expropriation . . . written in the annals of mankind in letters of blood and fire" (875). He draws his empirical evidence for this from a moment in British history—the enclosure of the commons. In order for capitalism to appear as a noncoercive system of free labor, the violence of this expropriation, which is the foundation of the capitalist class, has to be forgotten. Thus the need for the mythical past presented by political economists.

Subsequent theorists have suggested that instead of locating primitive accumulation in the past, it should be recognized as an ongoing part of the capitalist system—in particular, of imperial expansion. Rosa Luxemburg, one of the first to develop this idea, argues that capitalism requires "the existence of non-capitalist forms of production" (1951, 368) as a market for its surplus, as a source of raw materials for production, and as a resource of potential wage labor. She argues that "a natural economy thus confronts capitalism at every turn with rigid barriers. Capitalism must therefore always and everywhere fight a battle of annihilation against every form of natural economy that it encounters. . . . The principal methods in this struggle are political force (revolution, war), oppressive taxation by the state, and cheap goods" (369).

In his article "Disaggregating Primitive Accumulation," Robert Nichols suggests that instead of seeing land simply as a commodity like any other (although clearly it can be bought, sold, or stolen like other commodities), Marx saw land as also located in nature, an instrument of purposeful labor, not simply an object on which labor was performed. Dispossession thus involves not simply the theft of land but something more complex. Nichols writes, "Marx's focus on land is the particular expression of a generalizable insight, namely that dispossession entails the appropriation of, and consolidated class monopoly in, the mediated 'metabolic interaction' of humanity and the productive resources of the earth" (2015, 26). Nichols suggests that the term *dispossession* is more precise and concludes that it "comes to name a distinct logic of capitalist development grounded in the appropriation and monopolization of the productive powers of the natural world in a manner that orders (but does not directly determine) social pathologies related to dislocation, class stratification and/or exploitation while simultaneously converting the planet into a homogenous and universal means of production" (27). Although Nichols prefers the term *dispossession*, I argue that *primitive accumulation* has a particular relevance for describing what happens to nature in the postcolony. Through the settlers' refusal to recognize any form of property except private ownership, nature in the colony is cast as a wilderness uniquely available for accumulation. I investigate the diamond industry in South Africa as an exemplary fragment of the primitive accumulation of nature, a *fantastic* project of value extraction. The discovery of diamonds precipitated the reorganization of the economy and the landscape of the colony and provided the ground for the emergence of an elite whose wealth depended on a complex management of value through the promotion or interruption of the flow of this natural artifact.

The idea of development that emerges after World War II constructs a model for historical progress and incorporates colonized and formerly colonized countries into this model at a temporally earlier stage. Colonial countries were subjected to a compulsion to modernize that addressed itself specifically to the form of everyday life. The introduction of commodities was key to this process.[21] Gustavo Esteva identifies the founding moment in the history of the idea of development in a speech by Truman in 1949 in which the U.S. president deliberately distances himself from "the old imperialism" and affirms a "program of development based on the concept of democratic fair dealing" (quoted in Esteva 1992, 6). The notion of development assumes that the historical trajectory of a very few nations can provide the model for defining and judging the value of techniques of life elsewhere. Development implies a condition of lack that must be improved by intervention. In the most general terms, it is associated with more efficient systems, a growing economy, industrialization, and a stable government. But it also contains the promise of a certain lifestyle of consumption and freedom of choice in which the aspiration and target are particular standards of living. In South Africa during apartheid, the discourse of development was modified to accommodate the idea of "separate development," a different trajectory for black and white South Africans. This racially inflected interpretation of the idea promoted a particular standard of living among the small white population while advocating a different set of conditions for black South Africans. Yet these carefully calibrated distinctions had to be maintained through force. Chapter 5 reflects on a moment of rational calculation in which a fundamentally instrumental attitude toward nature gives rise to bizarre experiments. In a strange collision of rational science and irrational fantasy, nature is conceived of as a resource of primitive violence to be crafted and deployed in defense of a particular way of life.

The narrative of development presupposes a linear temporality. The temporality of the postcolony is very different from this gradual progress toward an established goal. For Achille Mbembe, "the postcolony encloses multiple *durées* made up of discontinuities, reversals, inertias, and swings that overlay one another, interpenetrate one another, and envelop one another: an *entanglement*" (2001, 14). This entangled time places the postcolony in a very different relation to history than the one opened up for the former colonies by the narrative of development. Instead of occupying an earlier moment in a general world history, the postcolony describes a condition of inhabiting different times at the same time, disrupting any notion of a linear progression toward a predefined end point. The postcolony emerges as a consequence of a violent but also incomplete imposition of a particular technique of life. The postcolony describes the resulting site of discontinuous and competing regimes of value.

In the era of environmental crisis, nature in Africa assumes a new global importance. In this narrative, it is precisely Africa's lack of development that makes it a valuable repository of nature. Yet even though Africa's contribution to global carbon emissions is negligible, the postcolony is nevertheless a space that is disproportionately subject to the social and environmental costs of global production. Rob Nixon uses the phrase *slow violence* to describe "a violence that occurs gradually and out of sight, a violence of delayed destruction that is dispersed over time and space, an attritional violence that is typically not viewed as violence at all" (2011, 2). Typically, effects are divorced from causes by a displacement across time and space. It is, he notes, "a violence that is neither spectacular or instantaneous, but rather incremental and accretive, its calamitous repercussions playing out across temporal scales" (2). Slow violence, he suggests, is a particularly important concept for understanding environmental damage and the "unintended consequences" or side effects of extraction, production, and even military invasions in a range of different contexts. The difficulty with slow violence, he observes, is that unlike spectacular violence, it is difficult to bring into and hold within the public imagination. It requires sustained attention, something that the contemporary culture of "accelerated connectivity" (13) tends to erode. Nixon's careful reading of texts by writer activists Wangari Maathai and Ken Saro Wiwa demonstrates one way of bringing into the foreground these elusive threads of damage. These writers reflect on local depredations wrought by the nature industry in Africa—despite the low levels of industrialization, the damage of deforestation and mineral extraction are extreme. In his book *The Social Costs of Production* (1971), Karl William Kapp, an economist briefly associated with the Frankfurt School in New York, argues that in working out the cost of production, those factors designated as "externalities" are, in fact, costs borne by the society as a whole. "Capitalism," he notes, "must be regarded as an economy of unpaid costs, 'unpaid' in so far as a substantial portion of the actual cost of production remain unaccounted for in entrepreneurial outlay" (231). The postcolony, I argue, describes a space particularly burdened by such costs. This is evidenced, for instance, in the different responses by oil companies to oil spills in American and Nigerian waterways.[22]

These spaces of mineral exploitation exist alongside different kinds of enclosures—fragments of untouched nature that provided the ground for exploits such as hunting and for demonstrations of wealth and status. Upmarket reserves directed toward the international tourist industry, owned often by large corporations, frame their ownership of land in Africa in terms of a global duty to preserve "nature" and the environment. James Ferguson notes how these often exist as independent entities linked into the global economy through technology but separate from the surrounding land and society.[23] Chapter 6 reflects on a moment of sequestration in which nature, entirely dominated, is produced as a scarce resource and privatized for its own protection. Set aside from everyday experience, enclaved nature is crafted to recall the exploits of past encounters. In a work of dispossession that is both material and metaphysical, nature in the postcolony appears always to be produced for the benefit of others.

Conversations about climate change are characterized by a perceived acceptance of the inevitability of capitalism and the sanctity of "life as we know it" or the culture of consumption. Acts to mitigate the effects of climate change are framed as necessary in order to maintain an already existing lifestyle. Yet the style in which we live is not inevitable. It is a complex negotiation of desire, choice, necessity, attitude, culture, history, and innovation. It is an orientation toward the world and to other people, a conscious and unconscious distribution of what is considered valuable. The following chapters track some of this fractured landscape of desires and habits through which world nature is constituted as valuable. As a resistance to the promise of totality offered by the global and the earth as a system, I put together fragments of specific habits of consumption and fantasies about style and the possibilities and impossibilities of imagining a different technique of life.

They include certain awkward, strange, and at times uncomfortable gatherings of historical incident, artistic projects, consumer choices, and cultural ephemera in which nature is found to be a decisive element. Chapter 2 brings together exhibitions from the American Museum of Natural History in New York—dinosaurs, the Akeley Hall of African Mammals, and the Hall of Biodiversity's Dzanga-Sangha rain forest—the Rain Forest Biome at the Eden Project in Cornwall, and the fate of the banana as iconic instances of nature under threat. In chapter 3, I take the totality proposed by the name Anthropocene and break it down into parts that do not quite add up to the whole—rhetoric and science, cell phone contracts and carbon emissions, the promise of development, the rise of advertising, and the impossibility of satisfaction. Both of these chapters bring into focus the fragmentary references to forms of consumption in order to reveal what lies submerged in these narratives—the centrality of a particular technique of life based on the conspicuous consumption of goods and energy. At the same time, I trace the way in which, throughout these responses to climate change, traditional imperial narratives continue to surface as reminders of a past not superseded by this new crisis. The following three chapters reflect in more detail on these traditional imperial and colonial narratives by offering moments from the backstory of the technique of life based on consumption inflected through the history of South Africa's entry into capitalist modernity. The discoveries of first diamonds and then gold in the late nineteenth century are crucial to the story of South Africa's modernity. Chapter 4 offers four photographs of Kimberley in the 1880s—the gentleman's club, the mine, the labor compound, and the hunt—as tableaux of social distinction, setting these alongside the memoir of a diamond smuggler and a massively successful advertising campaign. Chapter 5 confronts a strange moment in the history of the production of nature in South Africa—the South African Defence Force's wolf dog breeding program. It brings together Truth and Reconciliation Commission (TRC) transcripts from hearings on chemical and biological warfare and two self-published border war memoirs to explore these wolves' ambiguous position, caught between nature and history. Gathering together a controversial Land Rover advertisement, modernist game lodges, golden wildebeest, and a dead lion with a big international following, chapter 6 investigates the proliferation of high-end private game reserves in

Africa as the manifestation of an emerging economic but also symbolic and emotional investment in the value of nature. Placed within constellations, all these small, diverse details become points of access for decoding nature in the current moment of crisis.

In his most literary text, *Minima Moralia*, Adorno employs the aphorism to consider, in a unique way, problems of experience and subjectivity. Written in the mid-1940s while Adorno was in exile in California, the text is a sustained reflection on the ethics of form and the possibilities opened up by juxtaposition as a combinatory practice. Composed as a series of fragments, *Minima Moralia* reflects upon those minute details of everyday experience that give form to contemporary life. In the preface, Adorno writes, "He who wishes to know the truth about life in its immediacy must scrutinize it in its estranged form, the objective powers that determine individual existence even in its most hidden recesses" (1978, 15). Although the objects of scrutiny here are the "objective powers," in a sense, it is the "hidden recesses" that seem to engage Adorno's attention most thoroughly. What Adorno's text takes as its object is not the discovery of the hidden "intentions" of reality, the identification of a concealed meaning or order, but rather the analysis of overlooked moments of reality, unguarded moments of what Adorno calls "unintentional reality." *Paysage*, the aphorism quoted at the start of this chapter, describes a fragment of experience from life in its estranged form. The car, an emblematic fragment of what Jennifer Wenzel calls the "petromodern," is part of the unintentional reality of life in contemporary consumer society (2017, 10). Traveling by car habituates the body to a certain kind of perception—the hurried glimpse. Reducing the passing landscape to a background, it enables a detachment from the world so that "it is as if no one had passed their hands over the landscape's hair. It is uncomforted and comfortless" (Adorno 1978, 48). This missing gesture, this gentle yet expressive touch, offers a metaphor for an interpretative project that involves not a rigid separation of subject and object but rather a delicate sensory engagement with the object—a conceptual feeling through the body. The work of the chapters that follow is to feel through the accumulation of details, the fissures and rough edges that the long history of colonial exploitation has impressed on the world.

The concept of the Anthropocene, with its invocation of a singular-subject "humanity" responsible for global warming and its urgent message about imminent disaster, invites us to forget about history and to focus on the present as it careens into an unthinkable future. Thinking about climate change and the

Anthropocene from the perspective of South Africa means interrupting this increasingly popular global narrative to offer instead an account that is neither exemplary nor representative but that as a collection of fragments of the damaged whole nonetheless has the power to illuminate something beyond its own particular history.

Fragments from the History of Loss

2
Nature in Fragments

Mammoth—... The zoological gardens in their authentic form are products of nineteenth-century colonial imperialism. They flourished since the opening-up of wild regions of Africa and Central Asia, which paid symbolic tribute in the shape of animals. The value of the tributes was measured by their exoticism, their inaccessibility. The development of technology has put an end to this and abolished the exotic.

—Adorno

Artifacts of Nature

Fragments of African nature can be found in many places in the world. The list is potentially endless: living animals in zoos and menageries, embalmed or stuffed animals in museums, plants in botanical gardens and scientific herbaria, and more obliquely minerals in industrial processes and as luxury commodities such as diamonds, gold, and tanzanite. In the early twenty-first century, these displaced fragments assume a new form. Plants and animals are exported no longer as signs of exotic nature but rather as specimens of a disappearing nature. Zoos take on a new role as barriers against extinction, justifying their existence with the proud but urgent claim that they house the last breeding pair of a particular species. The environmental crisis at the end of the twentieth and the beginning of the twenty-first centuries produces nature in a new form—as the object of nostalgia. Yet it is nostalgia of a very particular kind. It is nostalgia for what is still present but that appears as a shadow of itself, a mirage, a form that has been emptied of content. In this chapter, I consider two contemporary cultural artifacts that are themselves synecdochic instances of nature as it is produced by the current environmental crisis. These cultural artifacts, which I call *natural installations*, are both pieces of nature produced inside public spaces, one in the American Museum of Natural History in New York and one at the Eden Project in Cornwall.

The first natural installation, housed in the Hall of Biodiversity in the American Museum of Natural History, is a re-creation of a segment of the Central African Republic's Dzanga-Sangha rain forest.[1] Partially screened off behind glass but crowding assertively out of this containment, it is situated in the center of the exhibition hall. On the sidewall of the exhibition hall is a brightly lit display of animal specimens from moths to mammals. The Hall of Biodiversity is, as its name suggests, devoted to educating people about species extinctions and loss of biodiversity, and in one corner, a documentary loop describes the destructive effects of industrialization and population expansion on the environment.

The second natural installation forms part of the Eden Project, one of a number of projects worldwide to use technology to create artificial environments that house not individual animals or plants but whole biomes. Developed as part of a regeneration plan for previously industrial sites and situated in a worked-out clay pit in Cornwall near St Austell, the project describes its main aim as environmental education. While the entire site has been reworked as a garden, the site's main attractions are its two massive domes containing the Rain Forest Biome and the Mediterranean Biome. In each, fragments of nature from other parts of the world are assembled into a living museum. The broad path leading through the Rain Forest Biome takes the visitor through South Asia, West Africa, and South America. In each area, there are displays providing information, usually through art installations, about plants and environmental issues relating to these regions. South Asia contains a "traditional" grass house; West Africa has a set of totem sculptures by artist El Antsui made from wood recycled from Falmouth jetty, originally built from West African hardwood. High up against the side of the fifty-meter-high dome, a waterfall emerges, and a stream splashes down through the various areas represented. It is, the Eden Project brochure proudly proclaims, "the largest rainforest in captivity."[2]

These fragments of nature away from home are a response to actual and anticipated loss. The two installations are both educational tools designed to give advice about the proper response to the anticipated effects of environmental destruction and climate change. Yet this advice is, I argue, circumscribed by the particular way in which each exhibit formulates nature as its object. They attempt to address the scale and complexity of the anticipated end of nature that climate change presages through assembling certain natural artifacts. Reading these fragments as material objects that are invited to concretize the abstract idea of environmental crisis, the chapter explores what these natural installations can tell us about the forms through which environmental crisis is being materialized in the global imagination. In each of these exhibitions, a particular part—the rain forest—acquires significance for the whole. Through focusing on the way in which the rain forest is exhibited, I track the place of Africa in these works of disassembly and reassembly.

The exhibitions are public interventions, put together in response to the social, epistemological, and even philosophical crises that widespread environmental destruction and climate change inaugurate. The transformations to the material environment provoke certain intractable questions: How might it be possible to assemble research from different orders of knowledge to address a crisis that brings into proximity geophysics, history, habit, culture, and capital? How might it be possible to imagine a future not as an extension of the present but as discontinuous with contemporary experience? How is it possible to live with a future made strange, even uncanny, by a radical unpredictability? In the next chapter, I will discuss in more detail this situation of living in the subjunctive—a situation in which the future can only be imagined as radically contingent on urgent but undefined action in the present. In this chapter, I focus on the problem of formulating advice in conditions of radical uncertainty.

As discussed in the previous chapter, Adorno's notion of the constellation, or "historical image," enables the assembly of diverse material, fragments that cannot be accounted for in a single system of knowledge. It allows for an arrangement of personal experience, public desires, political events, and concrete scientific data in a conceptual, three-dimensional space, not in the mode of a hierarchical or explanatory diagram, but so as to reveal the way each element exerts a gravitational pull on the others. Formulating a constellation allows me to place these exhibitions in relation to diverse other texts—earlier exhibitions, other public responses to climate change, and the objects and texts that are either included or excluded but nevertheless crowd about them—in order to mark out the limitations of their production of nature as a response to environmental crisis. Starting from a single aphorism from *Minimal Moralia*, I take Adorno's historical image of nature circa 1945 and trace the lines of continuity and the shifting intensities that emerge when these elements are reanimated in the twenty-first century.

The aphorism from *Minima Moralia* I discuss in this chapter, *Mammoth* addresses in a very particular way the question of nature. It takes as its starting point a news article announcing the discovery of a "well-preserved dinosaur in Utah" and places this archaeological find in relation to a constellation of cultural forms: King Kong, the Loch Ness Monster, tigers, zoos, and Karl Hagenbeck, the animal dealer who designed one of the first "open zoos" in Hamburg in 1907. This aphorism, I suggest, offers an interesting way of considering how it might be possible to talk about nature at the current historical moment, a moment in which anxiety about the environment is everywhere and environmental crisis often seems to supersede, even obliterate other forms of crisis. I want to use this aphorism to think about the way form holds certain conversations about nature at bay and facilitates others and to consider the aphorism as a form that permits or enables the holding together of different orders of knowledge.

For literary critic Gary Saul Morson, the aphorism should be considered in relation to other forms that fall within the category of quotations. In a distinctly aphoristic style, Morson makes a number of claims about the similarities and differences between the various short forms that fall within this category. Along with maxims, dicta, witticisms, and anecdotes, the aphorism refers to something already spoken, a wisdom that is at once startling and familiar, both strikingly singular in expression yet part of a general public knowledge. As distinct from maxims and dicta, Morson suggests the aphorism does not claim to express a generalizable self-evident truth, the solution to a mystery, but rather "asserts the essential mysteriousness of the world" (2006, 221). Aphorisms, he suggests, consist not in "solving puzzles but in deepening questions" (221). He also asserts that aphorisms seek a specific occasion, and that occasion is typically at "a conventional end point that now does not close but opens onto more mysteries" (222).

Morson uses the term *wisdom* to indicate the aphorism's tendency to occupy itself with ethical questions, with questions of conduct. He does not discuss what I think is one of the most interesting aspects of the aphorism, which is its tendency to cross between different orders of knowledge. Crossing the conceptual territory of science, traditional knowledge, conventional wisdom, and cliché, the aphorism makes statements about ethical conduct and personal experience without insisting on universalizing principles. It offers instead a kind of shorthand, everyday form for provisional ethical judgment, one that engages directly with experience and action or conduct.

In a fascinating article, scholar of German literature Jakob Norberg suggests that *Minima Moralia* conforms to but also subverts the genre of advice literature that was very popular in Germany and the United States at the time of its first publication in the 1940s. This form enables Adorno to consider the relation among experience, conduct, and social structures in a way that opens experience to critical reflection. For Adorno, Norberg notes, "individual experience can be relevant to a theorist of the social world, and not everything the individual does is entirely subservient or perfectly fitted to the inexorable work of vast collective structures. Yet one can illuminate moments of insight and incongruence without denying the individual subject's social history" (2011, 402). The moments of insight and incongruence emerge in precisely those areas where the individual fails to perform his or her "scripted role" or comes up against an intractable problem of conduct (403).[3]

In discussing Adorno's writing in relation to the production of an ethics within discourse, Bernstein links the form of the aphorism to that of the essay. "Aphorism and essay," he explains, "both begin 'in the middle' with a cultural artifact or practice that is imbued with history, including the history of what has been said about it. For this focus to be maintained, aphorism and essay must dispense with definitions, grounds, first principles; but equally they must dispense with the syntactic markers through which the legal rational authority of first principles and logical rules is transmitted to what falls under them" (2001, 356). The cultural artifact is composed in part by what is said about it, the historical layers of utterances that seek to embed the object within a particular discursive genre. Taking a particular moment as a starting point, which is not the object's origin or definition, the aphorism or essay mimics in its syntax the kind of relations it wishes to produce in the world. In other words, juxtaposition replaces hierarchy as a method of apprehension and as a way of composing and arranging sentences.

Adorno uses the term *constellation* to describe the particular way in which his aphorisms juxtapose elements from different orders of knowledge, refusing a hierarchical ordering of the general and the particular. The idea of the constellation as a form through which phenomena might be understood originates with Walter Benjamin and is first articulated in *The Origin of Tragic Drama*.[4] Adorno scholar Brian O'Connor writes that "Benjamin's theory posits the idea of constellations, a metaphor which expresses the practice of philosophical truth. In this practice the subject mediates phenomena, striving to arrange them in such a way, in 'constellations,' that they might reveal their idea. Importantly ideas are neither generalizations nor subjective reconstructions in that they are the very intelligibility and truth of phenomena. . . . In a constellation particular phenomena are not subsumed under universals. Rather the meaning of any phenomenon can emerge only when the phenomenon is understood as configured with certain other phenomena" (2000, 4).

What is significant about Benjamin's conceptualization of the constellation is its emphasis on an arrangement of phenomena that avoids hierarchical ordering. The particular is never simply an example of a general rule. Phenomena instead become intelligible only in relation to other phenomena. The constellation allows seemingly incommensurable things to be placed alongside each other without reducing them to a relationship of equivalence. It makes visible the contradictory aspect of the real, introducing awkward material complexity into the smooth logic of any systematic organization.

Constellations of phenomena are always provisional, unlike stellar constellations that appear from the perspective of historical time to be eternal and unchanging. The elements are constantly rearranged until the moment when the image emerges. The historical image introduces what Fredric Jameson refers to as a "pseudo-totality." He writes,

> Pseudo-totality: the illusion of the total system is aroused and encouraged by the systematic links and cross references established between a range of concepts, while the baleful spell of the system itself is then abruptly exorcised by the realization that the order of presentation is non-binding, that it might have been arranged in an utterly different fashion, so that, as in a divinatory cast, all the elements are present but the form of their juxtapositions, the shape of their falling out, is merely occasional. This kind of *Darstellung*, which seeks specifically to undermine its own provisional architectonic, Benjamin called configuration or constellation. (1990, 50)

In Adorno's formulation in 1931, he favors the term *historical image* over Benjamin's notion of the "idea" (Buck-Morss 1977, 102). *Historical image* emphasizes both the contingent and the material quality of whatever might emerge from the constellation as well as the fact that the image itself is not intuitive or metaphysical but rather produced by human subjects through analysis.

The phenomenal elements that make up the constellation are, Susan Buck-Morss suggests, "codes" or "ciphers" of social reality, seemingly insignificant things like a popular song, fleeting events such as a concert, and easily overlooked details such as certain fragments, images, or metaphors in a philosophical text. In themselves, she explains, such phenomenal elements have no fixed value. They might be judged positive in one constellation and negative in another (1977, 99). They become meaningful only in relation to the other elements in the constellation.

Mammoth as Historical Image

In 2013, the discovery of a well-preserved woolly mammoth in the Siberian permafrost led to ambitious claims from scientists about the possibility of re-creating this extinct animal. For instance, the *Huffington Post Canada* headlines read, "Woolly Mammoth Clone Now Possible, Say Scientists," and the article begins with the following statement: "Scientists now say they've got enough blood and bone to bring an Ice Age icon kicking and stomping into the modern age" (Cotroneo 2014). In the months following this statement, the scientific challenges facing such a project emerged—the difficulty of extracting sufficient viable DNA, the problem of incubating a zygote if one could be created—and gradually undermined the initial optimism. One of the key questions to emerge was an ethical one. Was the cloning project legitimate? Where and with whom (i.e., with what animal community) would the cloned mammoth, supposing a viable birth could be achieved, live? Even in the *Huffington Post* article, some hesitation is expressed about the purpose of such a scientific project. Radik Khayrullin of the Russian Association of Medical Anthropologists is quoted as saying, "We must have a reason to do this, as it is one thing to clone it for scientific purpose, and another to clone for the sake of curiosity" (Cotroneo 2014).

Although Adorno's aphorism makes no mention of an actual mammoth, the discovery of the mammoth in Siberia repeats with interesting difference the opening gambit of the constellation. The aphorism *mammoth* begins with a reference to a piece of scientific knowledge reported in "American newspapers": the discovery of a well-preserved dinosaur in the state of Utah. The publicity around the dinosaur, which Adorno links to the "repulsive humoristic craze" surrounding the Loch Ness Monster and King Kong, is offered as a puzzle or conceptual irritant.

In the decades since Adorno read about and puzzled over the publicity surrounding the discovery, the fascination with dinosaurs has grown exponentially.

Art historian and cultural critic W. J. T. Mitchell takes this strange attraction as the subject for his wry, humorous reflection on contemporary culture, *The Last Dinosaur Book*. The dinosaur is, he argues, "a powerful cultural symbol" of modernity, and "its cultural status is entwined with—that is, both driven and influenced by—its scientific status" (1998, 282). Dinosaurs exist both as fossil remains and as myths, metaphors, and images. The dinosaur is a creature that brings into close proximity different orders of knowledge. Like Adorno (whom he references at several points), Mitchell argues that fascination with the dinosaur is in part to do with its size. The existence of these animals, even only as trace and fantasy, defamiliarizes the world adjusted to a human scale. For Adorno, the fascination with the unthinkably large is a "collective projection of the monstrous total state," an attempt to "assimilate to experience what defies experience" (Mitchell 1998, 115). Mitchell suggests a division of what he calls "Dinosaurology" into three distinct periods: Victorian (1840–1900), modern (1900–1960), and postmodern (1960–present). The image of the dinosaur of the 1940s was of a living organism, "an engine or machine that moved in space and evolved over time. It was a creature of thermodynamics, a motor that consumed energy, reproduced itself and finally died out" (208). When Adorno was writing in the 1940s, the mechanical dinosaur, associated with the steam engine and later the automobile, offered a way of constructing at the level of fantasy the experience of human smallness and impotence in relation to the indifference of large institutions pursuing their own aims.

In contemporary culture, Mitchell argues, the dinosaur means something different. They are no longer imagined with the clumsy indifference of mechanical objects but rather possess the uncanny agility of cybernetic organisms. *Jurassic Park* is the text that perhaps most clearly reflects this shift in the imaging of the dinosaur. In *Jurassic Park*, dinosaurs have been cloned using blood found in a mosquito preserved in amber. This conceit, which surely inspired (and perhaps also cautioned) the scientists unearthing the mammoth remains, enables a de-extinction narrative that goes horribly wrong for the human creators, whose hubris is the belief that they can control nature.

For Sarah Franklin, *Jurassic Park* and its many cultural spin-offs can be read as a sign of "a wider social process of redefining the natural, the global, and the future" (2000, 223). Coinciding with the release of the film, the American Museum of Natural History opened a new exhibit titled "The Dinosaurs of *Jurassic Park*." For the museum, the film provided a means of drawing public attention to its scientific work; scientists at the museum had developed the technique of extracting paleo-DNA from insects trapped in amber. It offered a fiction that could reinvigorate public interest in the real. What is significant about dinosaurs in the twenty-first century is not so much their size as their alien intelligence. The dinosaurs of *Jurassic Park* interrupt the history of nature as framed by the narrative of evolution and instead propose nature as itself disaggregated into its component parts—genetic material—which can be assembled through scientific technique.

The fact that dinosaurs continue to circulate, through new fossil discoveries, children's toys, museum displays, and remakes of *Jurassic Park*, suggests that their potency as cultural icons is not yet exhausted. This is perhaps partly because they activate two other narratives that have gained currency in response to climate change and environmental crisis—extinction and deep or geological time. In Adorno's aphorism, the dinosaur is not only to be read allegorically as reflecting something about popular anxieties about the state; it is also to be read metonymically as a representative of nature. Adorno writes, "The desire for the presence of the most ancient is a hope that animal creation might survive the wrong man has done it, if not man himself, and give rise to a better species, one that finally makes a success of life. Zoological gardens stem from the same hope. They are laid out on the pattern of Noah's ark, for since their inception the bourgeois class has been waiting for the flood" (1978, 115).

The "hope" that dinosaurs and zoological gardens inspire, Adorno suggests, relates to the sense—dimly acknowledged but not rationally accepted (at least not in the 1940s)—of the damage done to nature in order to make possible the lifestyle of industrial capitalism. In this hoped-for future, "man" would be sidelined (animal creation would survive the wrong man has done), and a better species would emerge that "finally makes a success of life" (1978, 115). In a typically Adornian fashion, the slightly mocking judgment is contained in the qualifying subclause, the idea that animal creation might even survive "man himself." If August 1945 marks the inauguration of the intense anxiety about the possibility of human extinction consequent on the dropping of the two nuclear bombs on Hiroshima and Nagasaki, the ideas contained in this aphorism seem closer to the contemporary attachment to the idea of extinction as a judgment on human actions. Human extinction has become not only a popular topic for books across a range of disciplines but also a desired destiny of groups such as the Voluntary Extinction Movement, who propose the cessation of human reproduction with the ultimate aim of total human extinction as a response to the human-induced environmental crises.[5] Extinction, hovering between feared threat and desired fantasy, refigures the idea of human teleology to flirt with the idea of a literal end of history.[6]

In the aphorism, the zoo and the ark can be seen as allegories for animal creation reduced merely to specimens or mating pairs, preserved against a disaster. Yet to see disaster in terms of the extinction of species misses what for Adorno is the important point, which is that the management of nature—its preservation and transplantation as well as its reduction to species or specimens—is already a loss, even a disaster. A form of thinking that subsumes animals under the general categories of species allows them to enter the discussion only as representatives of a category, as abstractions. Unlike the tiger pacing furiously or in bewilderment in the cage, these specimens cannot challenge human conduct, cannot reflect back anything of what Adorno terms at this point *humanity*. In an article published in 2009, historian Dipesh Chakrabarty suggests that climate change represents a challenge to existing explanatory or analytic frameworks for understanding history. It introduces into the domain of history a requirement to think again at the level of the species. While there is ample evidence that industrialization has been responsible for the conditions that have led to climate change, a critique of capitalism, he suggests, is no longer adequate to the sort of crisis that is emerging. He writes,

> It seems true that the crisis of climate change has been necessitated by the high-energy consuming models of society that capitalist industrialization has created and promoted, but the current crisis has brought into view certain other conditions for the existence of life in the human form that have no intrinsic connection to the logics of capitalist, nationalist, or socialist identities. They are connected rather to the history of life on this planet, the way different life-forms connect to one another, and the way the mass extinction of one species could spell danger for another. Without such a history of life, the crisis of climate change has no human "meaning." (217)

The difficulty of thinking together the two narratives of globalization and global warming, human history and natural history, is a result of their incommensurability. They operate according to different epistemological frameworks with different orders of time as well as with different conceptions of agency, event, and causation. The disciplines concerned with the history of nature traditionally study deep time; climate change seems to reflect an acceleration in the slow movement of nature so that changes in the natural substrate or background, previously irrelevant to the study of historical events, become suddenly part of historical time. Extinction becomes an event in history.

Yet Chakrabarty rightly identifies that the construction of a new collective defined in terms of its species operates at a level of abstraction that is difficult to assimilate into historical narratives. "We humans," he suggests, "never experience ourselves as a species. We can only intellectually comprehend or infer the existence of the human species but never experience it as such. There could be no phenomenology of us as a species. Even if we were to emotionally identify with a word like *mankind*, we would not know what being a species is, for, in species history, humans are only an instance of the concept species as indeed would be any other life form. But one never experiences being a concept" (2009, 220).

The problem with the concept of a species is that it operates at a level of abstraction that precludes experience. Although on one level, it allows us to consider the human in relation to other species—as a species that, according to Adorno, has not "made a success of life"—at another, it inserts into the domain of history a category strangely at odds with human agency. In the long duration of deep time, a species could do things slowly, primarily evolve. The category *species* creates a collective from which each individual is necessarily alienated. It invites a level of "scientific" detachment that makes it conceivable to bring the possibility of human extinction into historical time with a certain nonchalance.

Mammoth as aphorism or historical image addresses the problem of nature at a historical moment that bears a strange resemblance to our own. Although extinctions nowadays crowd everyday representations of nature, and diminishing numbers of animals are listed on reusable supermarket shopping bags (like the wild dog shopping bag that states that only 450 wild dogs still exist in South Africa), this aphoristic critique of the conceptual limitation of thinking about nature as a simple concept is one that still seems relevant.

A Rain Forest in the Museum

The Hall of Biodiversity, my first natural installation, is preeminently concerned with species and extinctions and represents one example of a knot or entanglement of scientific knowledge, public desire, and global sentiment relating to nature in the era of crisis. On the surface, the museum (with its assembly

Fig. 1 The Hall of Biodiversity, American Museum of Natural History. Photo: François Olivier.

of different halls juxtaposing exhibitions from different historical periods and very different philosophies of collection and display) bears some resemblance to a constellation. Yet the work of juxtaposition undertaken by the museum tends to erase rather than make visible the different kinds of knowledge on display. The museum presents a smooth and enduring surface in which the exhibitions are separated from their histories and the particular ideological moments of their inception.

The Hall of Biodiversity was developed for the museum by Ralph Appelbaum and Associates (RAA), an international museum design firm, as part of the museum's new "issues" halls in 1997. According to the RAA website, the exhibition is designed to "alert . . . the public to the ecological crisis we face and the part humans are playing in the Sixth Mass Extinction—the current massive loss of biodiversity" (Ralph Appelbaum and Associates n.d.). The Hall of Biodiversity includes, on one side, a backlit wall showing a range of individual species. In the center of the room, there is an "immersive diorama" of a section of rain forest, partly surrounded by glass walls but open so as to give the impression that the visitor is entering the forest. The rain forest is a replica of a piece of the Dzanga-Sangha rain forest located on the borders of the Central African Republic, Congo, and Cameroon. The RAA website claims that the exhibit shows "a hundred and sixty species of plants, animals, and insects" and that its "digital imaging and environmental effects are combined with traditional techniques to create an advanced, vivid new kind of diorama."

One floor above the Hall of Biodiversity in the central part of the museum is located one of the museum's most celebrated permanent exhibitions—the Akeley Hall of African Mammals. In *Primate Visions* (1989), Donna Haraway identifies this exhibition as defining a particular moment in the history of the production of nature at the American Museum of Natural History. Although the hall was only opened in 1936 after his death, the exhibit represents Carl Akeley's dream of using taxidermy to create a "Garden of Eden"—a series of dioramas depicting mammals in family groups in their natural habitat.[7] Throughout his adult life, Akeley undertook expeditions to Africa to collect specimens for his dioramas. Even as he was shooting animals and sending their remains back to be "immortalized" through resurrection in his mammal dioramas, he was, Haraway notes, lamenting the loss of African nature. Yet as Haraway points out, "Akeley sees himself as an advocate for 'nature' in which 'man' is the enemy, the intruder, the dealer of death. His own exploits in the hunt stand in ironic juxtaposition only if the reader [of his biography] evades their true meaning—the tales of a pure man whose danger in a pursuit of a noble cause brings him into communion with nature through the beasts he kills" (1989, 48). Referring to the Roosevelt African Hall at the museum, Akeley remarks, "In this, which we hope will be an everlasting monument to the Africa that was, the Africa that is fast disappearing, I hope to place the elephant on a pedestal in the centre of the hall—the rightful place for the first among them" (quoted in Haraway 1989, 48).

For Haraway, what is of significance is the way in which race and gender underpin the apparently objective scientific project of selecting and preserving specimens of African wildlife. African men are, in Akeley's account of his "safaris," incapable of the noble communion with African animals that characterizes his own hunt guided by the pure intentions of conservation. Although Africans provide all the material conditions needed to facilitate the hunt, from portering goods to expert knowledge of terrain and tracking, the courageous performance of masculinity embodied in the hunt is reserved for white men. During the early part of the twentieth century, the high point of colonial fervor, Haraway comments, "African human life had the status of wildlife in the Age of Mammals. That was the logic of 'protection'—the ultimate justification for domination" (1989, 46). Although the anticolonial struggles of the middle part of the century and the assertions of negritude and black consciousness fundamentally disrupted this particular self-serving Western construction, Africa continues to hold an ambiguous place in narratives about environmental crisis. Reading Akeley's account, what becomes apparent is that what it completely fails to register is the experience of the rain forest not as adventure hedged around—even crowded by—the security of things (guns, cameras, tents, food) but as everyday life, as habitual and repeated encounters. African nature is always encountered as an exceptional space, temporarily inhabited, regretfully abandoned for the real business of life that takes place elsewhere. Africa as the terrain of expeditions becomes defined by fragmentary encounters, parts that come to stand for the whole.

Although from the perspective of the 1990s, Akeley's position seems obviously ideological, something to be superseded by newer modes of collecting and display, Africa in the museum continues to be produced through the work of such temporary encounters. Preparing for the rain forest exhibition at the museum also involved an expedition to Africa to ensure that the diorama met with the requisite standards of realism. In the preface to *Inside the Dzanga-Sangha Rainforest*, Francesca Lyman explains that "it would take 20 scientists, artists, and filmmakers 6 weeks in a tropical rain forest to research and collect the necessary materials" (1998, 7). *Inside the Dzanga-Sangha Rainforest*, an account of the making of the exhibition aimed at children, involves a series of short chapters that combine scientific information with a description of the experience of gathering material for the exhibition. She explains that "we organized everything by drawing maps of different forest areas, then dividing them into grids and numbering them. That way, we'd know where to find a certain tree or nest again" (64). They are assisted in this project by guides drawn from the local inhabitants—the Baka people. She notes that "although today most people farm or work in the lumber mill or with the conservation project, all still depend on the natural resources of the forest. Like their ancestors before them, the Baka rely heavily on hunting and gathering for their daily needs" (74). The chapter titled "The People of the Rainforest" describes some of these practices, including the eating of raw caterpillars. Although, unlike Akeley, the tone of her description of the local inhabitants is carefully respectful, the expedition itself in many ways resembles these earlier collection adventures. Although no large mammals were shot, the aim was to collect specimens and to return with them to New York. More than ten thousand pounds of material was collected and shipped back to the United States. The exhibition was then built first as a three-dimensional model and then as a life-size diorama, using casts of bark created from impressions made in the rain forest. Actual leaves collected in the Dzanga-Sangha forest were spread on the ground and coated with paste so as to make them look wet. Film footage was then used to create the backdrop of the diorama and to give the impression of life and movement. The vast and costly expedition introduces experts into the rain forest in order to record and capture it accurately before returning to New York to replicate it in the museum. It is an experience of the exotic in which modern individuals are confronted with alien practices such as the eating of raw caterpillars (a cultural practice the author admits she was never able to try) while pursuing scientific knowledge for the purposes of education.

The sign at the entrance to the rain forest exhibit provides the following description: "Like tropical forests everywhere, the Dzanga-Sangha is threatened by human activities. Overseas corporations extract timber and diamonds. Local people clear forest for agriculture and use the forest for other basic needs. These uses jeopardize the region's biological diversity, and the future of its people."

Although the careful neutrality of the language avoids assigning blame, the logic of the sentences sets up an opposition between humanity or human activities and nature. Corporations and locals alike are the cause of the destruction of the rain forest. Halfway along the diorama, a red board with white writing is affixed to the glass: "Today we face a crisis: the loss of perhaps 30,000 species a year as the human population and resource demand explodes and habitats are destroyed." The idea of an "exploding" population is one that haunts environmental discourse. The increase in human populations is seen as a threat to the earth's "carrying capacity." Humans, through their consumption of resources, are seen to be displacing nature.

Although the Hall of Biodiversity seems to repeat Akeley's anxiety about loss, it does so in a different register. It is no longer individual animals as types that come to stand for their disappearing kin but rather habitats or biomes that have become the focus of attention. Instead of continental or national boundaries, nature is divided into terrains, ecosystems, and biomes. The notice boards, images, and documentary film all have an overtly educational intention—the rain forest is there to supplement the concept of a rain forest, to make real in some sense the loss that is being described. The rain forest installation is produced for the species as a metonymic reference to nature as universal, but it is a nature that is already, as a consequence of human action, lost. Nature in the form of the rain forest is produced as an affective marker, as a texture to supplement the concept of nature.

One striking aspect of the Hall of Biodiversity is the lighting. Compared to the brilliantly lit animal dioramas in the Akeley Hall of African Mammals, the rain forest diorama is so dimly lit that it is difficult to read the signage. The backlit wall of species provides the largest source of lighting, throwing the displayed specimens into harsh silhouette. The rain forest itself is in semidarkness, and although a screen at the back of the diorama provides a flickering backdrop, it is still difficult to see the forest clearly.

The well-lit displays in the Akeley Hall of African Mammals seem to suggest a confidence and clarity that is missing from the more murky Hall of Biodiversity. Yet the presence of these animals who died for Akeley's grand project of conservation—considered as individuals, not merely as examples or specimens—seems to haunt the Hall of Biodiversity. Like the dinosaurs two floors above, they are a reminder of the history of nature, both the deep history of extinctions and the shallower history of human practices. Akeley's project of preservation now appears disturbingly like carnage, an assembly line of dead animals, subject to a science of resurrection that in the age of mammal extinctions seems scarily wasteful.

"The Largest Rainforest in Captivity"

The Eden Project, the second natural installation, is also engaged in the work of remaking nature for the purposes of environmental education. Unlike the Hall of Biodiversity, it is not part of an established institution. Instead, the initial impetus for the idea came from a very different discipline : gardening. More specifically, it came from the idea of the greenhouse, a space in which the environment might be controlled for the purposes of the propagation of plants. The cofounder and chief executive of the project, Tim Smit, describes how the idea for a transformative garden emerged from his sense of the centrality of plants to contemporary existence and the fear that with climate change and habitat destruction, many species were in the process of being lost.[8] The project was established as an educational trust funded through the Millennium Commission, private donors, and other public funding organizations such as

Fig. 2 The Rain Forest and Mediterranean Biomes in the Eden Project. Photo: Louise Green.

the European Union and Southwest Regional Development Agency, and the Eden Project site opened in 2000.

Taxidermy and photography were the key technologies for the reproduction of nature in the museum of the early part of the twentieth century. The Hall of Biodiversity uses these along with the additional immersive possibilities offered by digital imaging and effects. In the Eden Project architecture, landscape design, engineering, and horticulture become the new technologies for the creation of a very different kind of museum of nature.

It is difficult to resist Tim Smit's engaging and suspenseful narrative of the genesis of the Eden Project in his book available for sale at the Eden Project shop in the visitors' center. His enthusiasm for the idea is infectious, as is the story of struggle against tremendous odds, of drawing more and more talented and well-connected people into the magical circle of the project, of people working without payment, of people investing both money and time when there was no concrete evidence that the project would be realized, of working through the night to meet funding proposals, of disappointments, of serendipitous meetings on the train, of unprecedented community support, of generosity and goodwill and unswerving commitment to the idea. While part of this enthusiasm seems linked to the specific locality and an investment in the regeneration of Cornwall, Smit makes it clear that the idea extends beyond local upliftment to a wider commitment to the transformation of relations between humanity and the environment. The project is at once a practical plan for a garden and a much more ambitious vision for the future. The ambitious nature of the project becomes evident in Smit's reflection on the act of naming. He explains, "We came up with the name somewhat tentatively because of the religious connotations, but it made sense as a symbol of Mankind in harmony with bounteous Nature. I also enjoyed the conceit that we had been thrown out of Paradise for eating from the tree of knowledge; perhaps only now, through the gathering of greater knowledge could we return" (2011, 80).

The Eden Project thus represents a return to nature, but not the sort of nature encountered in the surrounding fields and hedgerows of Cornwall. Instead, it appears as nature intensified, designed, landscaped, augmented, and concentrated—the assembled nature of the world. The repeated theme throughout the interpretative signage is the contrast between "before," the bleak postindustrial landscape, and "after," the spectacular display of natural abundance.

At the announcement that the project's bid for U.K. Lottery Millennium funding was successful, the Millennium commissioner present, Heather Couper, praised the project, saying, "The scale is absolutely mind-boggling, it's the most breathtaking thing I've ever heard of, a unique facility which will benefit not just the ecological movement but the whole world. It's a truly grandiose mission" (quoted in Smit 2011, 121).

The idea that the project holds deep significance not only as a local attraction but for "the ecological movement" and "the whole world" (leaving aside the accuracy of the statement) suggests something about the affective force of nature in the era of climate change and environmental crisis. The project becomes the physical form through which the utopian possibilities of nature are articulated—life, abundance, food, locality, authenticity—as opposed to the alienated world of global modernity, whose ultimate trajectory now appears to be global warming and extinctions.

A particular kind of realism is at work in the production of nature in the Eden Project. In the Hall of Biodiversity, the aim is to create an exact copy through painstaking attention to scientific detail. In the Rain Forest Biome, the possibility of such a direct replication is dismissed as impossible. Instead, the

Rain Forest Biome becomes itself a form of representation. The living plants extracted from the rain forest and carefully cultivated guarantee the reality of this representation. They represent themselves but are assembled in such a way as to tell the specific story the Eden Project wishes to tell. Smit explains, "We quickly squashed the idea that we could recreate ecosystems, which would be a nonsense and scientifically impossible. We intended to represent and interpret climate zones which exhibited the maximum impact of man on the environment, thus providing a canvas on which to explore the widest range of issues. We wished to recreate certain habitats to inform and entertain the public about human dependence on plants, and in doing so create a predisposition to effect or support positive changes in the way we live" (2011, 129).

The highly managed experience of Eden; the drama of the approach, with its carefully staged signs inviting the visitor to participate in a new future; the minute attention to detail, from the authentic mud wall in the visitors' center to the carefully chosen artworks; the use of natural local ingredients in the various restaurants; the intensive landscaping; and the assembly of plants from various parts of the world generate a vast expectation of significance. Yet the precise nature of this significance remains elusive. Smit articulates this as creating "a predisposition to effect or support positive changes in the way we live." At the center of this hugely ambitious and capital-intensive project, there is this vagueness—the possibility of changes in habit, conduct, "the way we live." The pronoun itself contributes to the indefiniteness of reference, suggesting as it does a common human form of life, a "species life." Yet it is precisely at the level of habit, of technique of life, that the differential impact of individuals and groups on the environment makes itself felt.

Although in his narrative, Smit acknowledges that "the world is now being interpreted in a post-imperial way" (2011, 180), Africa continues to figure in the project in very specific ways. In describing the effect the project sought to produce on its visitors, Smit writes, "We wanted them to be first awestruck by the sheer bravura of the architecture and landscape design, and then, all cynicism put aside for a moment, wonder why we did it. They had to be David Livingstone to our Victoria Falls; 'scenes so lovely must have been gazed on by angels in their flight' was what he had said on first seeing them. Under these circumstances maybe, just maybe, people would be in the right frame of mind to be humbled by the power of plants to shape our destiny" (183).

In this evocation of Livingstone, Smit recalls the Africa of Akeley and the expedition—the exceptional space of European encounters with African

Fig. 3 Part of the West Africa rain forest exhibit in the Eden Project. Photo: Louise Green.

nature. Victoria Falls, a site of dramatic natural beauty, becomes the model for the Eden Project's effect. Africa figures as an exceptional space of abundant nature but also inevitably as loss. In the West Africa section of the biome is a small logged and burned area with the following accompanying signage: "Now you see it . . . An area of primary forest the size of this biome is lost every ten seconds."

Fragments from the History of Loss

The rain forest is itself presented as a kind of Eden in which the Baka people live in harmony with nature. In the Rain Forest Biome, the slice of West African rain forest is anchored by a narrative that repeats with minimal difference the long history of Africa's association with nature. For instance, the guide includes the following statement: "The Baka people from the rainforest of Cameroon, the Congo basin and Gabon are deeply connected with nature. The forest is their mother, father and guardian, providing their food, medicines and shelter. They have hunted and gathered, led a very low-impact life and sung and played their way through life for thousands of years" (Elsworthy 2015, 26). The rain forest people are celebrated as "the original tropical ecologists" (Sir Ghillean Prance quoted in Elsworthy 2015, 26), and the low-impact lives of the Baka people are described with some reverence. Yet they are also represented as living in a kind of apolitical and unchanging condition following the temporal rhythms of nature, not history. Eating berries, nuts, fish, termites, and honey, the men hunting, the women cultivating the land, the signage associated with this section of the rain forest presents them as curious remnants of a premodern world. And one that is currently under threat. The guide explains, "Today their way of life, superb listening skills, deep forest knowledge and the forest itself are under threat" (Elsworthy 2015, 26).

Although low-impact lives are presumably the goal of environmental education, what this formulation does is repeat the romantic and exotic picture of Africa as a continent without history. The Baka may be described admiringly for their technique of life, but in this exhibition, they are not held up as model global citizens. Instead, they, like the rain forest itself, are passive victims of destructive commercial practices, and like nature, they are under threat. What is also under threat (although this is implied rather than directly stated) is a particular technique of life based on the products of deforestation. The statement "To ensure our future survival we need to help the forests survive" (Elsworthy 2015, 27) seems to be addressed to a consuming public, as the pieces of advice make clear.

The Plant Takeaway installation in the visitors' center shows a family of life-sized puppets with a dog and a cat about to sit down for a meal. Gradually everything dependent on plant matter is withdrawn—food, clothes, furniture—and the puppets, including the dog and cat, collapse. Although a humorous response, the installation gestures toward the new sense of environmental threat signified by the possibility of human extinction. For the Eden Project, the key point of intervention is to educate people about the intimate interdependence of people and plants. Smit explains, "What had begun as a project to exhibit plants from around the world and show how we had domesticated them developed into a far deeper strategy to use plants as the common backcloth against which all human life is led" (2011, 172). The exhibitions in the biomes focus on returning everyday objects such as rubber, spices, chocolate, coffee, and bananas to their points of origins, making the link between these products and the environments within which these crops are cultivated. Reconnecting products to their point of origin could work to counter the reification of commodities that seeks to erase information about a product's fabrication from its value. Here, although some mention is made about methods of extraction, the fundamental project is to relocate these products in nature—to draw attention to nature as the substrate of contemporary everyday life. Using the alibi of nature, these exhibits avoid the economic and political entanglement of these products as commodities that circulate within capitalist structures of exchange. Erasing the social and indeed the environmental costs of their cultivation, these products appear in the abstract, as global resources of nature rather than integrated into the particular histories of agricultural developments in colonial and postcolonial countries. These products, so integral to the modern technique of life, emerge instead as artifacts of nature.

The two natural installations are both responses to climate crisis as, in part, a crisis of human agency. Confronted with the scientific evidence of environmental destruction and climate change, they attempt to bring into being a new active, environmentally aware public. In keeping with the project's determination to foreground human agency, the Eden Project offers the following suggestions as a response to this information about deforestation: "Share what you discover about how forests keep us alive; Support charities and organisations working to save the forest; Shop for products which look after the forest; Write letters on rainforest issues to politicians; Volunteer for a rainforest charity" (Elsworthy 2015, 27). In their determination to return agency to the individual rather than overwhelm him or her with loss, the Eden Project offers a form of advice literature for the twenty-first century. The end of the Eden Project booklet, *The Guide*, includes a list of abbreviated pieces of advice. The precise terms of the Eden Project's revision of the relationship between nature and humanity become evident in these eleven statements or slogans: "Do Stuff, Be Hopeful, Learn about your Life, Increase your reach, Be angry at things you cannot change, Imagine things differently, Give gifts and give thanks, Get out more, Forgive yourself (and others), Have fun, Be the change you wish to see"

(Elsworthy 2015, 60–61). What is offered is a kind of ecological self-help for living with an ending that has not yet registered and that might still be averted, although no one can offer a coherent framework for how this might be achieved.

What, in fact, emerges is precisely the difficulty of offering advice in a situation in which the past is no guide to the future and in which the scale and complexity of the problem remain far beyond individual human experience. As Erik Swyngedouw points out, the effect of the discourse of climate change is not to produce people as "heterogeneous political subjects, but as universal victims, suffering from processes beyond their control" (2010, 221). The advice offered reveals the difficulty of framing a political response to environmental crisis that goes beyond small adjustments to individual acts of consumption.

In the meantime, the Eden Project provides nature as a solace. A recent article in *National Geographic*, titled "This Is Your Brain on Nature," describes several studies that show that "spending time in nature relieves the stress and mental fatigue caused by the 'directed attention' that work and city life require" (Williams 2016, 56). Experiencing nature changes the blood flow in the brain and the quality of brain activity. Like the Eden Project, this article presents nature as a resource for modern life, a health-giving escape and a way of restoring the brain's capacity for the kind of directed attention needed for work. The article, describing the work of Greg Bratman, a researcher from Stanford who did brain scans on volunteers before and after a ninety-minute walk in a large park, notes that "Bratman believes that being outside in a pleasant environment (and not the kind where you're eaten alive by gnats or pummeled with hail) takes us outside of ourselves in a good way" (67).

In the Eden Project, the contradictions of the contemporary attitude toward nature coalesce. Visiting Eden feels pleasurable precisely because it has overlaid the destroyed industrial landscape of the clay mine with a "pleasant environment," an arrangement of nature with careful detailing to imply abundance and modest statements about impending loss. By framing the experience as part of an ethical revisioning of human relations with nature, it offers the pleasure of consuming nature without guilt. The reality of destruction is present but managed, and even the heat of the Rain Forest Biome is mitigated by the inclusion of a "cool room" in case visitors are made to feel uncomfortable by the temperature and humidity.

Writing in 1995, Bruno Latour proposed "ecologizing" as an alternative to "modernizing." Yet he admitted that the precise dimension of the imperative to ecologize remains unclear: "The range of attitudes, prescriptions, warnings, restrictions, summons, sermons, and threats that go with ecology seem to be strangely out of sync with the magnitude of the changes expected from all of us, the demands that appear to impinge on each and every detail of our material existence. It is as if the rather apocalyptic injunction 'your entire way of life must be modified or else you will disappear as a civilization' has overwhelmed the narrow set of passions and calculations that go under the name of 'ecological consciousness'" (2009, 462).

Twenty years later, the Eden Project's advice offers an oblique attempt to address the difficulty of "ecologizing." By bringing nature inside, they create a magical space of plenitude and agency. Yet in their passionate defense of nature, they invest in a particular concept of nature as if it can stand in for the whole. Despite the luxurious feeling of plenitude the site creates, what it represents is an abstraction. The nature in the project is without ground, or rather the ground for it has been carefully acquired and landscaped. The total management extends beyond the landscaping to the experience itself, and its particular satisfaction is precisely the accuracy with which it assembles objects, animate and inanimate, to fulfill the desire produced by its narrative of loss. It is an investment in nature as a symbolic value, with the rain forest deposited in its biome as a guarantee of future value.

Photographing Bananas

If the Hall of Biodiversity is haunted by the embalmed dead mammals and the bones of the extinct dinosaurs above it, the Eden Project is subject to a different kind of haunting. The encircling parking lots, named after fruit and carefully landscaped, are at once a practical response to the world as it is and a part of the unintentional reality that produces cars as a side effect of this engagement with nature. While the Eden Project offers discounts for those who arrive by public transport, it is clear that the car, excluded at the entrance gate, is a precondition for Eden, a necessary adjunct.

Adorno ends the aphorism *mammoth* with a claim that works strongly against the grain of contemporary environmental calls for a transformed relation between humanity and nature: "Only in the irrationality of civilization itself, in the nooks and crannies of the cities, to which the walls, towers, bastions of the zoo wedged among them are only an addition, can nature be conserved.

The rationalization of culture, in opening its doors to nature, eliminates with difference the principle of culture, the possibility of reconciliation" (1978, 116).

Advice literature as a genre provides guidance about conduct. In its most common form, the self-help book, it promises personal transformation, a mode of being in the world that creates greater wealth, success, and happiness. It presupposes a dysfunctionality, an inability to align personal desires with the demands of collective institutions. In *Minima Moralia*, the form is subverted to show how the dysfunction is located not in the individual who must be helped to integrate more fully into his scripted role but rather in the contradictory demands of estranged consumer society. Adorno's version of advice is determinedly unhelpful in practical terms, but it does allow a deepening of the question. It makes it possible to see how the Hall of Biodiversity and the Eden Project, which each in different ways want to reenvision humanity's relation with nature, are themselves caught in a force field that ties them to the world as it is and reduces their laudable intentions to a few bare gestures—an abundance of nature and money in the first world representing the regrettable loss of nature (and absence of money) in the third world. As a form of advice literature themselves, these interpretative exhibitions offer numbers, species, populations, and extinctions but cannot directly address the problem of conduct, since they have no language to disassemble the technique of life. Hidden behind the phrase "an explosion of resource demand," the reason offered for the destruction of the rain forest in the Hall of Biodiversity diorama is the simple fact of uneven consumption—the huge gap between represented Africa meticulously reconstructed and the absent Africa registering only (despite technological advances) as exotic, aesthetic fantasy and loss.

As I have suggested in the introduction, the narrative of environmental crisis appears to demand realism—simple declarative sentences, facts about human activities, statistics about losses. I argue that such realism can only ever repeat the world as it is. It cannot articulate nature as a complex object, irrevocably entangled in advance with human judgments. In the Rain Forest Biome at the Eden Project, visitors line up to take their photographs with a large cluster of bananas hanging from a banana plant. The bunch hangs on a low branch at roughly adult-head height and has vaguely human dimensions. In keeping with the display's commitment to presenting the rain forest through the products that form part of everyday experience, the variety of the banana included is the Cavendish banana. Next to the banana plant is information about its cultivation and its use and also its vulnerability. Global banana production is currently under threat from Panama disease, caused by a single clone of the fusarium fungus, known as Tropical Race 4. The fungus exists in the soil and from there enters the plant, causing it to wilt and eventually die. Presented in this way, in the context of environmental crisis, the Cavendish banana appears as another example of an endangered species, vulnerable to extinction. It is easy to read this single object as a synecdochic instance of the wider loss of nature, a sign of the fact that everyday experience, instantiated in the products that we encounter in the supermarket, is on the verge of total reorganization. The threat posed by the potential loss of the banana is intimate; it seems extremely close to home.

It is difficult to assess the actual dimensions of the threat. While Panama disease is clearly affecting banana production on a large scale, this crisis is a repeat of an earlier crisis with another banana variety, the Gros Michel, which suffered a similar affliction in the 1950s. The Cavendish was introduced to replace the Gros Michel because of its resistance to the fungus. Since the 1990s, a new strain of the fungus has emerged to which the Cavendish banana in turn is susceptible.[9]

In the late nineteenth century, it is the banana that initiates the development of the "fruit industry."[10] According to Dan Koeppel, the commercial success of the banana gave rise to big fruit companies and caused the development of refrigeration technologies and the building of rail and communication networks in South and North America. The commercial exploitation of bananas created economies reliant on a single export commodity and became the metonymic sign for characterizing politically unstable countries dominated by foreign companies—the banana republics. Bananas are today, Koeppel notes, the world's largest fruit crop and the fourth-largest product grown after wheat, rice, and corn. The banana as an artifact of nature is a point of intersection where what is most intimate—the sensual experience of taste—is brought into contact with nature as industry.

Banana researchers claim that there is no cultivar that could easily replace the Cavendish.[11] The fact that only a single banana variety is produced for the global market contributes to the banana's commercial success, but it is also the cause of its vulnerability. The uniformity of the commercial banana and its reliability have been part of the education of consumer desire.

Since its invention, the photograph has performed a dual function of recording the real and signifying its absence or loss. Although utterly familiar, the banana displayed in its "natural habitat" is something made strange, an exotic fragment of elsewhere. Far from what might pass as a home for a banana, it embodies the contradictory impulses of nature nostalgia, abundance and loss, concentrated in a familiar form made strange by its place in the museum of vanishing nature.

3

Living in the Subjunctive

The constellation illuminates the specific side of the object which to a classifying procedure is either a matter of indifference or a burden.

—Adorno

We must rid ourselves of the delusion that it is the major events which have the most decisive influence on us. We are much more deeply and continuously influenced by the tiny catastrophes that make up daily life.

—Kracauer

The Subjunctive Mood

Mood as a grammatical form indicates the orientation of the speaker toward the subject. The subjunctive is the mood indicated in conditions of uncertainty. Within the form of the verb, it codes hesitation, doubt, vagueness, insecurity, and indecision. It accurately describes the mood produced by the temporality of nature in the era of climate change—no longer reassuring, cyclical, and stable but unpredictable and unknowable. In the previous chapter, I argued that the aphoristic form offered a way of approaching the subject of nature not as a totality but as a complex concept, one that, in the context of environmental crisis, is itself reproduced in fragments. Within the Eden Project's Rain Forest Biome, the banana is a material object that in the context of the exhibition becomes a sign of imminent loss. In my synecdochal reading, the banana takes on a different meaning. As part of the global fruit industry, it is a commodity that signifies a particular mode of consumption. *Its social life, its movement from cultivation to consumption, makes it an exemplary instance of the technique of life of capitalist modernity.* It stands less for the loss of nature than for the loss of capitalist life as we know it.

If the Eden Project represents an abstraction concealed by the work of detailing and the deceptive materiality of the exhibits, *Anthropocene* as a term engages in a similar work of concealment. By introducing the idea of "humanity" as the agent responsible for global warming, the Anthropocene effaces the particular nature of the activities that cause carbon emissions. Generating a powerful but vague causal explanation, it is an act of naming that at once challenges and paralyzes.

In this chapter, I consider what it might mean to consider the Anthropocene historically rather than geologically and at the same time what anthropogenic influence on nature or earth systems might mean for history. I argue that we have to do two apparently contradictory things: First, we have to accept the Anthropocene as rhetoric but refuse it as science. By this I mean accept that globally, the concept holds a rhetorical force that may be able to change public perception and to exert political pressure on government policy. It is, however, also important to recognize that the concept itself as an expression of a new global totality does not have "scientific authority." Instead, it is a response to an anxiety about the universalization of consumption and the consequent universalization of damage. Second, we would need to accept it as science and refuse it as rhetoric. By this I mean that we have to accept the scientific research that has portioned off and measured aspects of the earth systems and that provides piecemeal evidence of changes—accretions, losses, instabilities—in what was previously considered to be a self-regulating system. Yet the sum of this research is not the "Anthropocene," which makes a leap from science to history through the alibi of geology. Although it is called an epoch, it more closely resembles a historical period. To refuse the Anthropocene as rhetoric is to refuse its diffusion of responsibility from consumers to humanity as a whole.

The Anthropocene as an inclusive act of naming presents a particular problem for the postcolony. Within Africa, the preservation of nature is often considered a luxury that struggling postcolonial states cannot afford; outside of Africa, the continent is seen as a reserve of nature that must be protected "for the good of humanity" or as an open, "underpolluted space" for the disposal of the waste of consumer society.[1] In the grand rhetorical gesture that the naming of the Anthropocene represents, the postcolony is an awkward and unruly part that cannot easily be subsumed into the whole.

Living in the Subjunctive

In 1990, ten years before the concept of the Anthropocene entered public circulation, two books were published—Michel Serres's *Le Contrat Naturel* and Bill McKibben's *The End of Nature*[2]—that provide early formulations of the narrative of environmental crisis before it becomes formalized and overtaken by the expert knowledge of science. Central to both these narratives is the ephemeral and intangible quality of experience, the importance of bodies on which the abstract knowledge of climate change registers. The naming of the "Anthropocene" introduces instead of individual bodies a new concept of the "human," one very different from the free and autonomous subject of the Enlightenment. Emerging from the scientific research conducted by the International Geosphere-Biosphere Programme (IGBP) the term reframes the end of nature as a scientific category. The publication of the Great Acceleration graphs in 2004 provided a visual record of some of the scientific research carried out by the program set alongside statistics from a variety of sources as indicators of "human enterprise." They give confirmation of the entanglement of the "physical, chemical and biological cycles and processes" of the earth and "social and economic dimensions."[3]

The Anthropocene and the Great Acceleration graphs represent one response to the condition of living in the subjunctive inaugurated by climate change and environmental crisis—a work of naming and accounting. But frequent repetition has allowed them to generate their own narrative of mythic inevitability. Without wanting to discount their importance, I suggest that they echo, with difference, the narrative of loss described in the previous chapter.

By placing the Anthropocene back into historical time, I investigate what gets lost as a result of the popularity of this ambitious word with its now iconic graphic corroboration. To see both the value of the term and its shortcomings involves the narrative equivalent of a trick of the eye, the simultaneous employment of variable focal lengths that results in a diffuse gaze. It is an optics designed to shift beyond what might in the past have been background nature with a foreground of human activity but that now might place nature in the foreground with an accompanying backgrounding of the particularity of human practices and culture. Such a mode of looking might reveal the remainder that this particular response to the uncertainty generated by climate change produces. Looking at the graphs not as signs of human activity as a whole but as the record of particular activities, I consider some of the chosen indicators as commodities whose circulation gives form to contemporary society. Deploying a synecdochic logic, I use these details to disrupt the stability of the concepts that describe the whole. Attention to these details suggests an alternative response—to accept the condition of living in the subjunctive as an invitation to a radical reconsideration of the technique of life of capitalist modernity.

Big and Small Catastrophes

In painting, the background is the ground or surface behind the objects or figures that are the focus of attention. Serres begins his book *The Natural Contract* with a discussion of a painting by Francisco Goya, *Fighting with Cudgels*. The picture represents two men fighting, both sunk to their knees in quicksand. The intent focus of the opponents means that the real danger—the enveloping mud—is ignored. *Fighting with Cudgels* is one of Goya's enigmatic "Black" paintings, murals he did on the walls of his house near the Manzanares River in 1819 that form "a compendium of the human foibles writ large that had been the subject of his works for almost thirty years" (Stepanak and Ilchman n.d., 48). For Serres, what is significant about this painting is its intellectual conceit. The painting draws attention to the absurdity of a human conflict that is blind to the conditions of its possibility. The fighting men, in their desire to triumph over each other, miss the instability of the ground on which they are standing. For Serres, the painting holds a particular relevance for philosophical thought in the age of environmental crisis. It draws our attention to a shift that is occurring between foreground and background. "Global history," he writes, "enters nature; global nature enters history: this is something utterly new in philosophy" (1995, 4). The material world, previously imagined to be merely the stage for human activity, has become an actor in the unfolding drama of historical time.

McKibben's work reproduces a generalization familiar to the Western philosophical tradition: nature and the human. The end of nature for McKibben is not an apocalyptic vision of the end of the world, although he argues that substantial changes to the physical environment are imminent. It is rather the end of a particular frame of reference, a particular way of understanding people's place in the world. He writes, "We have changed atmosphere, and thus we are changing the weather. By changing the weather, we make every spot on this earth man-made and artificial. We have deprived nature of its independence and that is fatal to its meaning" (1990, 54). McKibben's use of the term *nature* to refer to wild nature is one with peculiarly North American resonances. The celebration of the "untouched land" is part of America's pastoral tradition, from the early naturalists like William Bartram through Emerson, to the predominantly North American deep ecology movement. It locates in nature untouched by human intervention a source of value.[4] It is this resource that is in danger of being lost.

McKibben's anxiety about the end of nature is linked to the extension of the culture of consumption—in particular, the extension of a lifestyle based on motor vehicle transport to developing countries. "It does not take much imagination," he writes, "to foresee the results for the atmosphere if the same percentage of Kenyans and Germans drive cars, much less Indians or Chinese, or even half the percentage, or even a quarter" (1990, 185). McKibben is not actually advocating poverty in the developing world, although there is something slightly panicky about the structure of his statement. In fact, he points out that the logical environmental response would be a redistribution of wealth so that everyone would consume less. However, even as he is making this suggestion, he is noting its impossibility. "This sort of talk," he says, "would erode what support environmentalism enjoys among the privileged" (186). This approach to the political and then withdrawal from it draws attention to one of the contradictions of ecology and the postcolony. If the logical trajectory of the narrative of ecology is, to use Latour's phrase, that "the planet will no longer be modernized," those aspects of modernity associated with development, which have for so long been held up as the goal of developing countries, become suddenly an excess that the planet cannot support.

In the decades after the publication of McKibben's book, the narrative of climate change has become a pervasive element of public discourse. His concern about meaning has in some senses been overwhelmed by more dire predictions relating to rising sea levels, desertification, and crop failures. Although these apocalyptic visions have become a standard point of reference within public discourse, they have been incorporated in a way that tends to evacuate their political content.

Politics presupposes disagreement and the negotiation of different interests. The current postpolitical condition, described by Žižek, Ranciere, and others, is one in which disagreement has been replaced by consensus. Political demands are turned into problems of administration, and experts are assigned to draw up policy documents to affect a resolution. It resembles in many ways what Adorno describes as "administered society," in which all aspects of life are subject to careful technocratic management. Political geographer Erik Swyngedouw argues that the narrative of climate change performs an important rhetorical function in the production of the postpolitical. In his article "Apocalypse Forever: Post-political Populism and the Spectre of Climate Change," he describes how framing the current crisis as a threat to humanity as a whole produces a populist concept of "the people" that is "not constituted as heterogeneous political subjects, but as universal victims, suffering from processes beyond their control" (2010, 221). He suggests, "The presentation of climate change as a global humanitarian cause produces a thoroughly depoliticized imaginary, one that does not revolve around choosing one trajectory rather than another, one that is not articulated with specific political programs or socio-ecological project or revolutions" (219). While there is currently widespread consensus about the seriousness of climate change, the solution to the crisis is seen as the application of expert technological knowledge rather than political intervention. The invention of a new commodity in the form of carbon credit makes the crisis commensurable with the market economy and subordinates actual geophysical transformations to the familiar operations of the capitalist system. "An extraordinary techno-managerial apparatus is under way," Swyngedouw notes, "ranging from new eco-technologies of a variety of kinds to unruly complex managerial and institutional configurations, with a view to producing a socio-ecological fix to make sure nothing really changes. Stabilizing the climate seems to be a condition for capitalist life as we know it to continue" (222).

The key phrase here is "capitalist life as we know it." The anxiety generated by climate change is a suppressed anxiety about class, about lifestyle, about the decline of the promise of Western civilization that is the freedom to consume, to enjoy the proceeds of hard work, to grow, to expand. If the end of nature is a result of the historical trajectory of modernity as the transformation of the world through industrialization, technological advances, and the cultures of consumption that sustain them, then this path of capitalist growth must be interrupted. Instead of being extended to the world as part of the civilizing effects of commerce and consumption, the extension of the lifestyle of modernity is itself the problem. Is this what it means for global nature to enter history? From this point on, nature as a finite resource undoes the project of modernity. One response to the anxiety generated by this question has been an act of naming.

The term *Anthropocene* emerges as a response to the growing scientific evidence of damage to the earth systems previously believed to be independently self-regulating. In 1987, an international organization was formed to "coordinate international research on global-scale and regional-scale interactions between Earth's biological, chemical and physical processes and their interactions with human systems" (www.igbp.net). The name *Anthropocene* was first proposed by Paul Crutzen and Eugene Stoermer in the IGBP newsletter in 2000. Crutzen, an atmospheric chemist and science Nobel laureate, and Stoermer, a biologist, suggested that considering the "major and still growing impacts of human activities on earth and atmosphere . . . at all, including global, scales, it seems to us more than appropriate to emphasize the central role of mankind in geology and ecology by proposing to use the term 'anthropocene' for the current geological epoch" (2000, 17). Although Crutzen proposes *Anthropocene* as the name for a geological epoch, its significance is not primarily for the discipline of geology. Instead, Crutzen's act of naming, which was reiterated in his article "The Geology of Mankind" published in the journal *Nature* in 2002, invites a new orientation toward time, a bringing together of two orders of temporality—the geological and the historical.[5] While its status within the discipline of geology remains uncertain, it has been enthusiastically adopted both within the media and within the humanities and social sciences as a term that describes not so much a new geological period but a new intellectual field and a new orientation toward knowledge.[6]

The Anthropocene has had what Andreas Malm and Alf Hornberg describe as "a truly meteoric career" (2014, 62). In their critical reflection on the term, Malm and Hornberg draw attention to the strange and paradoxical fact that "acknowledgement of the impact of societal forces on the biosphere should be couched in terms of a narrative so completely dominated by natural science" (63). In order for the name to hold explanatory force, they argue, the narrative of the Anthropocene must locate the origins of the epoch in something innately human, because "if the dynamics were of a more contingent character, the narrative of an entire species—the *anthropos* as such—ascending to biospheric supremacy would be difficult to uphold: 'the geology of mankind' must have its roots in the properties of that being" (63). Yet a close reflection on the history of fossil fuels as a driver of modern society shows that to invoke human nature (such as the human ability to manipulate fire) as the cause of social transformation confuses the category of necessary precondition with causation. The ability to manipulate fire might be necessary, but it is certainly not a sufficient condition to explain the exploitation of fossil fuels, the specific form of which occurs as a result of unequal interaction between groups within the species. This uneven distribution, Malm and Hornberg argue, "is a condition for *the very existence* of modern, fossil-fuel technology. The affluence of high-tech modernity cannot possibly be universalized—become an asset of the species—because it is predicated on a global division of labor that is geared precisely to abysmal price and wage differences between populations" (64). Even the rise in world population, which theorists of the Anthropocene tend to regard as one of the key factors determining rising fossil fuel use, can be shown to be based on a general prediction rather than specific research into actual populations. Malm and Hornberg cite a range of research undertaken in disciplines such as economics, sociology, and human geography that shows the flawed reasoning that follows from imagining humanity as a single agent. Social research, such as that undertaken by the International Institute for Environment and Development, reveals that rising populations do not necessarily correlate with rising CO_2 emissions. David Satterthwaite's work, for instance, reveals that low-income countries such as those in Sub-Saharan Africa have a growing population but a stable or decreasing CO_2 emission rate. Instead, he argues that what is significant is consumption patterns. "The dominant underlying cause of global warming," he writes, "is the consumption of goods and services who draw on resources for their fabrication, distribution, sale and whose use (and, for goods, disposal) causes the emission of GHGs [greenhouse gases]. Of course, consideration also needs to be given to the (now heavily globalized) production systems that serve this (and that do so much to encourage high consumption). **Thus, for any individual or household to contribute to global warming, they have to consume goods and services that generate greenhouse gas emissions**" (2009, 547; bold in the original). "Standard of living" is a vague measurement used to define and compare modes of living. Although the official measure of the standard of living is real income, what this implies in most cases is access to goods and services. A high standard of living is associated with the ease and comfort provided by access to commodities.

The Anthropocene interrupts the development narrative by making the extension of a mode of living based on high levels of consumption itself a problem. Development as a political and economic project directed at poor countries by wealthy countries emerges after the Second World War. Arturo Escobar describes "development" as a discourse, a whole set of ideas, institutions, and practices that acted in concert to produce both a subject, the underdeveloped South, and a certain effect—the transformation of societies and economies in line with the goals of modernity. Escobar notes, "The aim of all the countries that emerged with this new status in the global concert of nations was invariably the same: the creation of a society equipped with the material and organizational factors required to pave the way for rapid access to the forms of life created by industrial civilization" (1995, 429). These forms of life are energy intensive and defined by high levels of consumption.[7] Even if the promise of such forms of life is to some extent an illusion—even in wealthy countries, not everyone enjoys a high standard of living—it is an important illusion for the plausibility of the narrative of development. The idea of an ecological limit calls into question what development should mean for the part of the world previously known as the third world but is now redefined as part of a single geopolitical world by the concept of the Anthropocene. What does it mean for "development" if the promise of development—the freedom to consume goods, to achieve a particular "standard of living"—is itself called into question?

The popularity of the term *Anthropocene* testifies to its ability to condense into a single authoritative word the diffuse anxieties and complex conceptual field opened up by claims about climate change and the end of nature. A scientific term is evoked to name a social and political predicament. Yet in invoking the authority of science to define a new organization of the world, the Anthropocene superimposes a new discursive framework on the relation between poor and wealthy countries. Postcolonial subjects are invited to join the category of the human precisely at the moment when the category no longer holds the Enlightenment and developmental promise of comfort, freedom, and autonomy but rather articulates a global burden of responsibility.

The Great Acceleration

The period following the Second World War, in which the discourse of development is defining relations between poor and wealthy countries, is also the period identified in environmental writing as the "Great Acceleration." In 2004, in response to Crutzen's article on the Anthropocene, the IGBP synthesis team produced a set of twenty-four graphs, twelve relating to human enterprise and twelve relating to changes to earth systems in the period from 1750 to 2000.

These graphs represent visually a series of increases in human activity and place them alongside a series of changes in earth systems. Crutzen had suggested that the Anthropocene could be dated from the end of the eighteenth century, proposing that the invention of the steam engine by James Watt in 1774 provided the crucial impetus. The synthesis project chose the date 1750 as "the starting date for our trajectories to ensure that we captured the beginning of the industrial revolution and the changes that it wrought" (Steffen et al. 2015, 82). The earth system measures draw on records about changes in the chemical composition of firn and ice core samples (increases in carbon dioxide, nitrous oxide, methane); the decline of the ozone layer; global temperature anomalies; ocean acidification; global marine fish capture; global aquaculture shrimp production as a "proxy" for coastal modification; model-calculated human-induced perturbation flux of nitrogen into the coastal margin (riverine flux, sewage, and atmospheric deposition); the loss of tropical forest; the increase in agricultural area; and the decrease in species abundance relative to "abundance in undisturbed ecosystems as an approximation for degradation of the terrestrial biosphere." What these measures provide is a series of indicators or signs of transformation of nature—some directly related to human activity (e.g., shrimp aquaculture, marine fish capture, the loss of forest, the spread of agriculture), while others are more indirectly related (e.g., changes in the chemical composition of core ice samples, temperature anomalies, and ocean acidification). The graphs condense a vast body of scientific research into a set of signs that provide a visual narrative of profound transformation. Set alongside these are another set of twelve graphs measuring "human enterprise":[8] global population (with figures before 1950 modeled); global real gross domestic product; the number of McDonald's restaurants worldwide as a measure of globalization; global urban population; world primary energy use; global fertilizer (nitrogen, phosphate, and potassium) consumption; global water use as the sum of irrigation, domestic manufacturing, and electricity water, with livestock water consumption added from 1961; global paper production; global number of new cars per year, including passenger cars, buses and coaches, goods vehicles, tractors, vans, lorries, motorcycles, and mopeds; global sum of fixed landlines (1950–2010) and mobile phone subscriptions (1980–2010); and international tourism through measuring the number of international arrivals per year.[9]

The placing of these two sets of graphs alongside each other is an interesting attempt to bring to the foreground both nature and history. Through the act of graphic plotting, the two are made commensurable and part of a single narrative. But what these schematic renderings of human lives leave out is the way this production of buses and coaches, goods vehicles, tractors, vans, lorries, motorcycles, and mopeds translates into practices of consumption and experiences of modernity. The use of fossil fuel, McKibben notes in 1990, is intimately bound up with the structure of industrial society at every level. He writes that "at least in the West, the system that produces excess carbon dioxide is not only huge and growing, it is also psychologically all-encompassing. It makes no sense to talk about cars and power plants and so on as if they were something apart from our lives—they are our lives" (132). And what will happen, he adds, if they become part of the life of the growing populations outside of North America, outside of the already vehicle-saturated countries of the developed world? Imagine the levels of environmental destruction if what might be called "the lifestyle of modernity" were to be universalized.

In fact, the economic trajectory followed by African countries during the period of the Great Acceleration is exactly the opposite of those followed by the economically developed north. Alain de Botton, in his philosophical reflection on the secret life of consumer society, *Status Anxiety*, tells an anecdote about U.S. Vice President Richard Nixon's visit to the USSR in 1959 to open the American National Exhibition in Sokolniki Park. The exhibit consisted of a whole house filled with labor-saving and recreational devices, and it was something Nixon claimed all Americans could afford. Nixon's gesture testifies to America's economic growth and stability but also to a confidence and investment in consumption as the sign of national well-being. Describing the post-1940s period in Africa, historian Frederick Cooper presents a very different picture. Although there are obviously regional differences, countries in the last years of colonial rule and after liberation had none of the infrastructural resources to embark on large-scale industrial manufacturing projects (with the exception, to a limited extent, of South Africa). In the colonies too, commodities were introduced as ideological devices to transform African societies from self-sufficient to dependent on the monetary economy so as to encourage people to work in agriculture or on the mines. British advertising and commercial interest in the nineteenth century engaged in substantial efforts to discipline Africans into habits of consumption of mass-produced goods.[10]

Yet following the Second World War, economies in Africa did not enter a period of accelerated development. Cooper, in reflecting on the lack of economic growth during this period, suggests,

> Let's look first at economic change, a process subject not only to the rhythms generated in the African continent itself, but to the shifting tendencies in the world economy. These patterns do not fit a break point coinciding with political independence. Rather, they suggest a break a decade later, in the mid-1970s, when modest progress turned into prolonged crisis. The period 1940–73 can be dubbed the development era. The initiatives, as noted earlier, began with colonial regimes, first Britain and then France, trying to make conflict-ridden colonies both productive and legitimate. Portugal and Belgium, and even more so South Africa and Rhodesia, gave little thought to the standard of living of most Africans, but in their own ways used state authority to foster production. (2002, 85–86)

After liberation, Cooper explains, a "nationalist vision of development" continued to shape policies of African governments with some success until the oil prices rose in the 1970s, after which economic development declined, and indebted countries were forced to make "structural adjustments" in order to meet the conditions imposed by international financial institutions. Cooper describes *development* as "a protean word, subject to conflicting interpretations. Its simplest meaning conveys a down-to-earth aspiration: to have clean water; decent schools and health facilities; to produce larger harvests and more manufactured goods; to have access to the consumer goods which people elsewhere consider a normal part of life" (2002, 91).

I am introducing these admittedly somewhat abbreviated historical details in order to insist on the materiality of "human enterprise" and to track behind the abstract "scientific" claims of the Anthropocene and the Great Acceleration the everyday presence of the manufactured commodity. The Great Acceleration graphs imply that to desire the end of poverty, to imagine the development of industry and infrastructure in Africa, is to invite a crisis of global proportions. The juxtaposition of the Great Acceleration graphs implies a correlation between the different indicators, but this is deceptive. Africa registers in the graph showing the increase in population but "disappears" in the graph showing the increase in emissions, leading to the inaccurate conclusion that increasing populations (primarily in the third world) are the cause of rising CO_2 emissions.

It is possible to challenge this implied narrative numerically, as Satterthwaite does, by drawing attention to the extent of existing discrepancies between the greenhouse gas (GHG) emissions produced by average citizens of low-income and high-income countries. After a careful statistical comparison across a range of countries, he concludes that even if those living in poverty in Sub-Saharan countries increase their consumption, their GHG emissions are likely to still be far below "fair share" levels.[11] What is more, he argues,

> even if a significant proportion of the future increase in GHG emissions is from certain nations with rapid population growth, if this is in nations below the "fair share" level for average per capita emissions, it cannot be judged as comparable to that in nations above the "fair share" level. More to the point, a growth in GHG emissions per capita among those individuals or households below the "fair share" level (whatever the wealth of that nation) should be considered as qualitatively different from any growth in GHG emissions per capita among individuals or households above the "fair share" level. (2009, 558)

Satterthwaite insists on the importance of recognizing both that emissions are produced by individuals and households and that an increase in emissions cannot be measured in the abstract without taking into account the baseline from which emission increases are measured. The Great Acceleration graphs offer one way of representing a history of nature and a history of society as intertwined though the abstraction promised by statistical measurement. Satterthwaite, through a different marshaling of statistical information, provides a way of disaggregating "humanity" into nations and, perhaps more important, into consuming subjects.[12]

The Great Acceleration graphs represent the entanglement of the history of nature and the history of society through a process of measurement and an act of juxtaposition. Rhetorically powerful as a visual rendering of transformation across a range of social and natural systems, they nevertheless operate to obscure certain relationships. The general claim comes to dominate the geographical and historical particularity of human activity so that Africa can be at once visible and invisible—visible as contributing to population increase but invisible when not contributing to the acceleration of carbon emissions.

The Paradox of Consumption

The small catastrophes with which I began this chapter are those invisible customs of consumer society—the ziplock bag for preserving food,[13] the new mobile phone, the sports utility vehicle—that structure everyday life and in some indefinable way make life worth living. These objects act as synecdochal instances of consumption as a vector of satisfaction. Consumer culture appears to be the natural outcome of successful capitalist growth, a lifestyle that is the just reward for hard work. In 1992, Alan Durning, the founder and director of Sightline, an environmental nonprofit organization based in Seattle, published a book titled *How Much Is Enough?*[14] The book criticized consumer culture as both unsustainable and unfulfilling. In an article based on the book, Durning suggests, "The wildfire spread of the consumer life-style around the world marks the most rapid and fundamental change in day-to-day existence the human species has ever experienced. Over a few short generations we have become car drivers, television watchers, mall shoppers, and throw-away buyers. The tragic irony of this momentous transition is that the historic rise of the consumer society has been quite effective in harming the environment, but not in providing the people with a fulfilling life" (1993, 177).

The paradox of consumption is that while it operates always as the sign of plenty at the level of society, within the individual, it is predicated on the production of lack. To compare the extension of a consumer lifestyle to the spread of a "wildfire" as Durning does is misleading. Consumer society should instead be recognized as an invention. It was produced as a carefully calculated response on the part of companies after the Second World War to the fear of overproduction—a condition in which supply would exceed demand and manufactured goods would accumulate unsold and, as a result, lose value.[15]

Creating consumers was the stated aim of advertising and publicity in the twentieth century, with the objective of both increasing the velocity of sales and creating stability among the working class. A great weight of commodities was seen to form a kind of ballast against political action. This vast project of recalibrating public opinion mobilized psychoanalytic theories to access the affective dimension of human life—those emotional responses that work below the level of consciousness and organize bodily experience.[16] What Durning describes as a "tragic irony"—the failure of consumer society to provide people with fulfilling lives—can be read rather as the structural precondition of consumer society. An unfulfilled life is a necessary precondition for the sort of desire that would repeatedly invest commodities with value.

The circulation of objects is not, or not only, the result of individual choice. They are part of a culture of consumption indicated by the phrases "standard of living," "lifestyle," and "quality of life." There is, as Foster and Clark point out, a danger of making the individual consumer responsible for environmental crisis. Today's economic Malthusianism, they suggest, "is all about making mass consumption and hence the ordinary consumer (not the wealthy few) the culprit. It insists the average consumer be encouraged to restrain his/her shopping or else that it be rechanneled to beneficial ends: green shopping. It is thus the masses of spendthrift consumers in rich countries and the teeming masses of emerging consumers in China and India that are the source of environmental peril" (2010, 115).

What this interpretation misses, they argue, is the degree to which income has become concentrated in the hands of a small elite; "conspicuous consumption" is becoming increasingly the domain of the wealthy, not the masses. What it also misses is that the extension of the culture of consumption is a political project, not only because of the profitability of new markets, but also because it confirms the legitimacy of the values already assigned to commodities and to forms of life. It implies a universal and therefore inherent value to things currently circulating and sustains the always fragile agreement that exists between producers and consumers about what things are worth.

At the same time, globally, what makes a particular technique of life, surrounded by commodities, valuable is in part that it confers distinction. Approximately ninety years before the publication of Bourdieu's *Distinction*, Veblen offers a set of terms for understanding consumption as a social performance, not an individual act—a relationship between people, not a relationship between person and objects. The intensification of consumption that characterizes the second half of the twentieth century, the period described by climate scientists as the "Great Acceleration," is also the period in which the work of "invidious comparison" is formalized and itself becomes a profitable industry. The expansion of the scope and effectiveness of advertising, its development as a system of judgments about value, its intimate integration into new technological development (first film and later social media), and its extension into personal presentation through the work of publicity are all refined in the period following the Second World War. The massive increase in this kind of human enterprise is not included in the Great Acceleration graphs. This production of desire, which could have been indicated through, for instance, tracking the rise in the number of marketing firms or the proportion of total costs assigned to advertising, remains invisible.

Durning's description of the worldwide attachment to consumer goods confirms, even as it denounces it as unsatisfying, the status of Western modernity as a model for the world. A world in which status is demonstrated through things requires that there is differential distribution of things around the world. If at one the level, commodities must be constantly sold to produce a profit, at another level, they must also be withheld so as to exclude some people from the distinction of ownership. To choose not to consume or to consume better becomes one more sign of distinction, the luxury of living in plenitude.

The culture of consumption is inextricably bound up with the continuation of "capitalist life as we know it." Malm and Hornberg argue that we need to follow "climate science out of nature" and that "we should dare to probe the depths of social history: not relapse into the false certitude of another natural inevitability" (2014, 66). I argue that we need to follow climate change even further into the particular details of the everyday to recognize the invisible impact of the commodities that structure our experience of the world. Without denying the pleasures of certain commodities or their ability to act as signs in the production of a range of different social meanings, not only those proposed by the products' original marketing, what remains unchanging is their core function—the transfer of value. The optic of natural history makes it possible to disaggregate consumption further into an assembly of objects that act as charged particles transmitting and conducting value between people and between nations in the global distribution of inequality.

Africa in the Anthropocene

The totality proposed by the term *Anthropocene* operates at a level of abstraction that allows the generalization of responsibility through producing a new form of the collective universal—humanity. In the statistical rendering of the relation between this collective and "earth systems," the particularity of the postcolony becomes invisible. The differential nature of human impact continues to register empirically, but the term redirects attention. In the shift of the temporal and spatial scale from national and historical to global and geological, detail is obscured.

The "optics of natural history" (Pensky 2004, 235) offers a way of conceptualizing the relationship between nature and history not as a simple alignment of historical time and geological time but as a disturbance. Adorno's phrase *natural history* was intended not as an abbreviation for a complex idea or a defining marker for an intellectual territory but as an invitation to expand thinking out of its established routines. In a dialectical move, each concept disturbs the other. In this context, *natural*, for Adorno, signifies a particular relation to time, not the long history of geologic time, itself already an abstraction derived from a certain kind of disciplinary knowledge, but time that cannot be held on to—the transient. It is through the concept of the transient that materiality enters history—specifically, the materiality of suffering bodies who are required to fall out of memory in order for history to hold its form as the domain of progress. The optics of natural history thus provide a way of thinking the particularity of the postcolony in history, of contingent empirical facts and bodies, which exceed the schematics of the graphs.

To do this, it is necessary to disaggregate the Great Acceleration graphs of "human activity" and to look at them instead in terms of what they actually, in most cases, represent—the circulation of commodities. The number of new mobile phone contracts worldwide represents a "human activity," but it also represents a circulation of value. There are many different trajectories a mobile phone might follow. It might be designed in Scandinavia, made in China from raw materials mined in Africa, sold in the United States, and recycled in Africa. What this insistence on the materiality of these categories allows is a disaggregation of the world into distinct economies that produce and use up goods at different rates. It also reintroduces into the abstract category of mobile phone contracts worldwide different human activities, each of which impacts human bodies in different ways.

Holding the Anthropocene between rhetoric and science becomes a means of recognizing the validity of the scientific evidence of climate change without accepting the form of the totality that such research produces. While the "Anthropocene" enables one kind of politics, an argument against climate denialism, it disables another, the recognition of an ecological debt owed by the developed countries to postcolonial countries, which might include the wealth extracted in the form of mineral resources as well as the carbon emitted in the process of development—their contribution to global warming. In the name of the Anthropocene, the new collective humanity becomes the joint bearer of responsibility. In naming the urgent realism of the current condition, the Anthropocene erases history as a relevant category.

Following climate science out of nature into the particular details of everyday life involves trying to engage with the ephemeral and contingent categories of "life as we know it" and "standard of living" in order to understand how experience is structured by practices of consumption and valuation. The narrative of climate change seems to require the return of totality, a single system in which the act of an individual—the discarding of a mobile phone for a newer model, the Sunday-afternoon drive—impacts upon the experience of society as a whole. Yet as Foster and Clarke point out, to turn the critique on the consumer misses the fact that the consumer is part of an economic system that depends on a constant expansion of production. Climate change resurrects the autonomous individual so that he or she can take responsibility for global warming. The problem becomes displaced onto the individual (with disposable income) who can choose between refusing to consume or "shopping better." By refusing to consume and saving income, they point out, individuals indirectly support consumption, since the money in the bank will be used for investment, usually in companies that produce goods. "Shopping better" by buying organic, supporting fair trade, or championing conservation by visiting high-end game reserves simply creates a new enclaved market for high-ends goods.[17] Reading the remainder produced by the Great Acceleration graphs makes visible the blurred penumbra that surrounds the apparent clarity of concepts that elucidate the dimensions of the current crisis. What emerges is an accumulation of small details that give weight to the animate and inanimate bodies that suffer the damage of being merely side effects.

Hesitation

Living in the subjunctive offers a way of responding to the condition of uncertainty generated by climate change that hesitates even at the point of crisis. This hesitation enables the kind of diffuse gaze I mentioned at the start of this chapter in which background and foreground are held together in the field of vision and in which those burdensome aspects of an object that exceed classification are given due attention. Instead of acceding to the mythic inevitability of the Anthropocene in which the actual illogicality of consumer society can never be addressed, living in the subjunctive finds, in the estrangement of the everyday, the possibility for new techniques of living—new technologies but also new ways of imagining social collectives.

In the contemporary world in which individuals or even the collectivities of nation and community are no longer the most significant agents, Serres suggests that the pronoun *we* takes on a new meaning. He posits that human assemblages (he talks about the dense megalopolises from Milan to Dublin that can be seen from space) have taken on the power of a tectonic plate. In contrast to the peasant who is almost invisible to the world, a "fragile reed," human assemblages have a physical existence, an impact similar to that of an ocean or desert. Yet these megalopolises register not simply because of population density but because of the technique of life that gives form to these vast new urban conurbations. The infrastructure of modern life—road networks, petrol stations, electricity substations, piped water—means that these cities are preeminently spaces of consumption, hubs that draw into their orbit goods produced all over the world.

Serres's writing, aphoristic and poetic in style, refuses a disciplinary order and works according to a logic of juxtaposition and discontinuity. It provides less a sustained argument than a series of interventions or engagements with different kinds of knowledge—literary, philosophical, scientific, and experiential. Modernity, he argues, can be understood as a process of loosening the bonds that connect people to the earth. "Through exclusively social contracts," Serres suggests, "we have abandoned the bond that connects us to the world, the one that binds the time passing and flowing to the weather outside, the bond that relates the social sciences to the sciences of the universe, history to geography, law to nature, politics to physics, the bond that allows our language to communicate with mute, passive, obscure things—things that, because of our excess, are recovering voice, presence, activity, light. We can no longer neglect this bond" (1995, 48). The final section describes a series of events or experiences that signal a loosening of the bonds or chords that link us to the world. Serres ends his text with a description of his experience of an earthquake in Palo Alto in 1989:

> All of a sudden the ground shakes off its gear: walls tremble, ready to collapse, roofs buckle, people fall, communications are interrupted, noise keeps you from hearing each other, the thin technological film tears, squealing and snapping like metal or crystal; the world finally comes to me, resembles me, all in distress. A thousand useless ties come undone, liquidated, while out of the shadows beneath unbalanced feet rises essential being, background noise, the rumbling world: the hull, the beam, the keel, the powerful skeleton, the pure quickwork, that which I have always clung to. I return to my familiar universe, my trembling space, the ordinary nudities, my essence, precisely to ecstasy. (124)

The moment of the earthquake provides Serres with a pleasurable reminder of the materiality of the earth and its ability to assert itself in ways that disrupt the "thin technological film" that insulate humans from experience. The earthquake is shocking but also in some way freeing despite or perhaps because of the danger it poses to human life. For Serres, the quake is one of the voices in which the earth speaks, and he takes it as a form of invitation to negotiate a new contract between the earth and its inhabitants.

Serres's ecstatic recognition is in part because what the earthquake does is confront him with his own vulnerability, the thinness of the technological film that anchors him in the world of everyday. Yet it is satisfying precisely because it is a moment, a temporary interruption not part of everyday experience. It makes visible second nature, the myriad habitual actions of a body surrounded by objects. In Africa, the thinness of this film is in many places the condition of the everyday. In Lagos, breaks in electricity supply are part of the rhythm of the everyday. Even in South Africa, Africa's biggest emitter, the production of sufficient electricity for industrial processes and a lifestyle of consumption is uncertain.

Reflecting on the way global nature has entered history through the narrative of the Anthropocene and placing this alongside the particularity of certain instances from the postcolony, what emerges is that it is still possible to talk of the whole world and not to talk about Africa. Refusing the Anthropocene as rhetoric means refusing this universalizing gesture. The Anthropocene as a totality continues a tradition of thinking in which Africa is constituted as having too much nature and no place for philosophy. Instead, I argue that the current environmental crisis requires a new orientation toward the subject, one that can emerge most effectively from conditions of scarcity. The subjunctive mood is frequently introduced by the conjunction *if*. One thing depends on another. Neither can be predicted with certainty. Options and adaptions proliferate. If there is electricity today, one set of activities might be followed. If not, an alternative path must be charted. These are not the conditions conducive to efficient production. They are not ideal for capitalist growth. It is a condition that is unsettling, frustrating, even painful. Yet it does invite a certain familiarity with transience and unpredictability. As an ethical response to environmental crisis, to live in the subjunctive might mean to hesitate on the brink of this unknown.

4

The Primitive Accumulation of Nature

The warfare among men in war and in peace is the key to the insatiability of the species and to its ensuing practical attitudes, as well as to the categories and methods of scientific intelligence in which nature appears increasingly under the aspect of its most effective exploitation.

—Horkheimer

Distinction

On March 12, 2015, a fourth-year political science student, Chumani Maxwele, threw a bucket of human waste over a statue of Cecil John Rhodes situated at the foot of the central flight of stairs at the University of Cape Town, looking out over the Cape Flats toward the east, although presumably symbolically oriented toward Cairo. This gesture, part of the wider "poo protests" about inadequate sanitation in Cape Town's townships, was designed to bring into public visibility the vast discrepancy between the standard of living of most white students attending the university and those of most black students. Rhodes, businessman, mining magnate, and politician, had amassed his vast fortune through the exploitation of mineral resources in southern Africa in the late nineteenth century—first diamonds and then gold.

The statue of Rhodes offered a material manifestation of something that is far more ineffable—a particular vision of value, status, and distinction. Veblen's distinction between "exploit" and "drudgery" provides a useful way of parsing the terms of this colonial ideology (1943, 15–18). From the late nineteenth century, the period of colonial expansion, Africa becomes the domain of the "exploit," a space in which a certain set of predatory activities could acquire honorific status. One way in which this status was achieved was through the acquisition of wealth through seizure or primitive accumulation.

The objects and texts in this chapter's constellation are assembled to disarrange existing narratives about diamonds in South Africa. In their polished form, diamonds' ability to reflect and refract light generates a sparkle that distracts the eye's ability to focus. This constellation presents diamonds rather as rough surfaces that can be used to exert an abrasive force on narratives of justification, explanation, and glorification. Many such narratives exist, among them *The Diamond Mines of South Africa: Some Account of Their Rise and Development* (1902) by Gardner F. Williams, general manager of De Beers consolidated mines, and *The Story of De Beers* (1939) by Hedley Chilvers, a copy of which (leather bound in burgundy morocco) was presented to Queen Mary by the chairman and directors of De Beers in December 1939.[1] These narratives work to incorporate and smooth the new wealth generated by the primitive accumulation of colonial nature into the existing structures of elite British society. Placing these texts alongside exposés such as Edward Jay Epstein's *The Rise and Fall of Diamonds: The Shattering of Brilliant Illusion* (1982) and Lebanese security operative Fred Kamil's account of his interventions in illicit diamond buying, *The Diamond Underworld* (1979), provides material for a set of claims about the particular mode in which nature is appropriated as wealth in the colony. In addition to these books, the constellation includes four photographs of Kimberley in the late nineteenth century. Somewhat faded and curled at the edges, the images are part of an immense archive of photographs of Kimberley held by the Africana Library. Records show that a number of photographic studios operated in Kimberley during the years of the diamond rush. Open-cast mining, alluvial diggings, new technologies, diamond sorting, the development of the town, and portraits of diggers and dignitaries were all meticulously recorded. In 2007, the Africana Library published a small collection of its photographs titled *50 Years on the Diamond Fields, 1870–1920*. Three of the photographs I discuss are included in this book. The fourth I chose from the many other prints held by the archive. Employing the optic of natural history reveals these photographs as signs of transience as well as enduring if somewhat worn records.

These images provide visual fragments dense with background. Although photography was celebrated in the nineteenth century for its objective representation of reality, the photographs included in this chapter clearly participate in the work of composing visual displays of status and of documenting the exploit. Yet these images, despite their careful composition and framing, also include "unintentional reality," a kind of density of surface detail. Placed in relation to the previously mentioned texts, these photographs can be called upon as testimonies to the everyday fictions that arrange Africa in relation to its natural resources. The aim of this chapter is to dislodge diamonds from their safe position as ornaments and to make them do the work of anchoring these fictions in a chain of social transactions.

Raw Material

In chemical composition, diamonds are composed of the element carbon. In one of its other allotropes, carbon is central to narratives about climate change. The rapid release of carbon dioxide into the atmosphere as a result of the burning of fossil fuels is generally considered to be the central cause of global warming. In his article "Carbon Democracies," Timothy Mitchell describes how the material differences between coal and oil mean that their extractive processes produce very different kinds of social interactions and political configurations. Coal is heavy and inert; oil flows along pipelines. Coal extraction requires a large labor force and produces the forms of sociality associated with shared work (2011, 403–4). Oil rises to the surface driven by underground pressure and so permits the kind of enclaved extractive industries that characterize regions like the Niger Delta (407). Coal and oil, both natural substances, create different terrains both at points of extraction and at points of consumption. They also create different social configurations.

The choice to focus on diamonds rather than oil or coal might seem somewhat contrary. Unlike coal and oil, diamonds do not make a major contribution to global emissions. Diamond mining is a relatively peripheral extractive industry. Diamonds constitute a luxury market; they are not necessary for "capitalist life as we know it." Yet it is precisely this superfluous quality that makes the diamond a useful focus for a reading of the terrain of the colony not as a rational space but as a fantastic scheme of value extraction.

In South Africa, the discovery of diamonds initiates a new phase in the development of the colony. Their discovery in the 1860s rearranges the geographical distribution of value in the colonies, precipitating a new interest in the interior. The hot, semidesert region of the Northern Cape, previously dismissed at least by the dominant colonial power in the area (Britain) as a wasteland, became the focus for an intense new interest.[2] Diamonds are imbued with a concentrated, even magical value, and their existence in the colonial interior stimulates the development of secondary industries. Drawing diggers from all over the world, they give rise to a whole economy directed toward facilitating extraction. South Africa's status as Africa's largest emitter of greenhouse gases derives from these mineral discoveries and the shift they initiate in the trajectory of economic development. They also lay the groundwork for a particular mode of understanding raw material in Africa not as belonging to the ground from which they are extracted but rather as being unequivocally available for appropriation. Outside the specific regime of private property recognizable within English law, all land in the colony appears as an unfenced commons awaiting seizure.

The history of diamonds in South Africa has already been written as a history of capitalist accumulation, one that tracks the process from individual diggers at the start of the diamond rush to the formation of companies and finally to the establishment of a monopoly by the De Beers company, which persists, although in an altered form, to this day. It has also been written as a history of labor, describing the emergence of a racial hierarchy among workers and the development of the compound system. In this chapter, I do something different. Through an act of assembly and juxtaposition of different kinds of texts about diamonds in South Africa, I track how in this particular context, primitive accumulation finds its story. In the chapter on primitive accumulation in *Capital*, Marx explains the prehistory of capitalist production. "Primitive accumulation," he suggests, "plays approximately the same role in political ecology as original sin does in theology" (1976, 873). It is an anecdote from the distant past that is used to explain and justify the current situation. He writes, "The legend of theological original sin tells us certainly how man came to be condemned to eat his bread by the sweat of his brow; but the history of economic sin reveals to us that there are people to whom this is by no means essential. Never mind! Thus it came to pass that the former accumulated wealth, and the latter sort finally had nothing to sell except their own skins.... Such insipid childishness is every day preached to us in the defense of property" (873). *Capital*, a montage that includes extracts from reports, court proceedings, anecdotes, and theorization, offers this justificatory fragment in order to hold it up for ridicule. Marx presents what he sees as the founding narrative of political economy—the location of the origins of inequality in personal responsibility (or irresponsibility, as the case may be) in the historical past—and suggests that for political economists, this narrative holds a theological force. To counteract this "insipid childishness," Marx suggests the concept of "primitive accumulation" to describe the moment before capitalism has been fully established, when there is a violent seizure of the means of production. The example he provides is of the enclosure of the commons that took place in England and Scotland in the seventeenth century. He notes, "The expropriation of the agricultural producer, of the peasant, from the soil is the basis of the whole process" (876).[3] Later in *Capital*, he notes the critical role the colonies played in this process, mentioning the discovery of gold and silver in America, the conquest and plunder of India, and the trade of enslaved African populations. "Liverpool," he writes, "grew fat on the basis of the slave trade. This was its method of primitive accumulation" (924).

Primitive accumulation offers a useful way of thinking about natural resources in the colonies as elements of accumulation that begin with violent seizure, both physical and symbolic.[4] In South Africa in the nineteenth century, the invention of the diamond industry seems to reiterate this process, whereby the natural commons are seized by violence and coercive legislation, and this violence is then forgotten so as to naturalize a particular distribution of wealth and resources. In the friction created by different regimes of value existing in southern Africa in the nineteenth century, the violence of dispossession is dissipated into a difference of values. The wealth they generate on the world market becomes the legitimate reward of the thrifty and practical colonial elite.

Honorific Work

The first photograph of this constellation is of the Kimberley Club from the 1880s. Currently trying to invent itself as a "boutique hotel," the Kimberley Club represents a particular moment in the production of a colonial elite, a dusty anachronism that signals a particular arrangement of the everyday at a historical moment when nature as raw material first makes its appearance in South Africa. During the latter part of the nineteenth century, the gentlemen's club was an important part of elite masculine culture in London. For its members, a club provided a semipublic space of luxury and domesticity. Membership, by invitation only, ensured that although public, the club gave the impression of a

Fig. 4 The Kimberley Club. Photo © Africana Library, Kimberley.

private space.[5] Yet it was a space excellently suited to the display of leisure and consumption both to other members and to those excluded from membership. In the colonies, the gentleman's club was an institution for asserting the specific character of the colonial elite, at once determinedly British and assertively colonial insofar as it was uniquely placed to define itself through the means of the exploit. The word *exploit* holds a number of meanings within its ambit. As a noun, it refers to a "brilliant feat," but behind this meaning is an earlier one—the idea of an endeavor to gain mastery or advantage. In its verb form, it signifies "to utilize for selfish purposes; to make capital out of"—alongside the more neutral "to work (a mine, etc.) or turn to account" (Oxford English Dictionary).

The establishment of the Kimberley Club in 1881 registers a shift in the historical trajectory of diamond mining in Kimberley. Legislation in 1876 made a provision for the consolidation of a number of claims within the ownership of a single individual or company. This facilitated the emergence of an elite among diamond diggers formed by those able to raise capital to acquire multiple claims. The photograph shows a wide street, Dutoitspan Road, in 1884, with the club on the right and St. Mary's Cathedral beyond it. The caption explains that this is the first Kimberley Club building: "The prestigious Kimberley Club was destroyed by fire twice: in 1886 and 1895" (Sabatini and Duminy 2013, 71).

The Primitive Accumulation of Nature

In the photograph, the street is largely empty except for a horse tied to a post outside the club and several small carriages. The club is protected from the street by a fence and a small garden. The fence surrounding the club seems to protect it from the blankness and emptiness of its environment. The vegetation in the garden provides a striking contrast to the completely bare earth of what is outside the fence. Although not obvious from the faded black-and-white print, the extent of the sky and the intensity of the light convey something of the immense heat of the climate in summer. The garden itself is a luxury, an oasis in the heat and dust of the landscape of the Nama-Karoo, a biome that is semidesert. The absence of vegetation, a striking feature in many of the images, is also a sign of the impact of the diggers. The unexpected town that developed around the diggings consumed vast quantities of natural resources in the form of wood and, as we will see in the last photograph, wildlife.

Above the fence, the second story of the club can be seen, with wooden latticework protecting the outside balcony. A line of men in hats can be seen standing on the balcony, leaning against the railings and looking out over the town. In angling the shot to include a broad foreground of the baked-earth street, the photographer represents the ornate Kimberley Club building as the dominant structure in the frame, along with the cathedral visible beyond it. What this angle reveals inadvertently is the strange emptiness of the town. The club's elaborate wall topped with a wrought iron fence sets it apart not from a crowd of unworthy diggers but from an (almost) bare street. It appears, at least in this image, as a superfluous or symbolic boundary.

A Brief History of the Kimberley Club, a stapled set of photocopied pages provided for visitors to the club, explains that "Cecil John Rhodes was the prime mover in the founding of the Club. Some of the original members were Cecil Rhodes and his partner, Charles D. Rudd and Dr Leander Starr Jameson, as well as mining magnate Lionel Phillips and JB Robinson. Needless to say it was the men of the diamond industry who predominated." The number of members was initially limited to 250. Although in 1881, Rhodes was still living in a two-roomed corrugated iron house, the club provided him with the space in which to assert his membership in an imperial elite.[6] It provided the physical structure and accessories for a genteel standard of living. It provided the surrounding for negotiating business deals while maintaining the illusion of aristocratic leisure.

Diamonds are key to the invention of a tradition around nature that participates in the work of producing a colonial elite. In "Mass-Producing Traditions,"

Eric Hobsbawm suggests that the period from 1870 to 1914 was one of peculiar profligacy in the invention of traditions in Europe as diverse communities were reorganized into nations and new forms of social stratification emerged. He describes how this took place both at the level of the nation—through the production of statuary, monuments, and public rituals—and at the level of class as new middle-class elites sought to establish their legitimacy through marks of distinction. In Europe, states and classes make selective reference to history in order to legitimate rituals and monuments; in the colony, where the history of those wishing to establish themselves is thinner and shorter, nature comes to play an important role in the invention of an elite tradition. Especially for English settlers, a mythology of nature rather than actual historical events comes to stand in for an absent history.

In 1893, Rhodes purchased the Groote Schuur estate on the lower slopes of Table Mountain and, within the next few years, fifteen hundred acres of the adjoining land (Rotberg 1988, 380), which included a large portion of the mountainside up to the old blockhouse and a strip of mountainside from the house to Constantia Nek (Le Sueur 1913, 245). In his 1927 biography *Rhodes: A Life*, J. G. McDonald includes a brief description of an interaction between Rhodes and Australian painter Mortimer Menpes:

> "Why do I love my garden?" he [Rhodes] replied to a visitor one day. "Because I love to dream there. Why not come with me and dream also to-morrow morning?" "I went with him next morning to his garden," said the visitor (Mr. Mortimer Menpes), "and we spent several hours there. They were happy hours to me and I hope to Rhodes too. There was not a trace of the dominant imperial Rhodes, but only of the sympathetic and human fellow-being. . . . He caressed this plant and the other, drew my attention to the sky-blue hydrangeas against a background of pine-trees, and talked of opening a vista here and another there; of creating an avenue of camphor trees, another of pines, and a third of oaks." (332)

McDonald's description of this interaction is clearly designed to offer a redemptive vision of Rhodes as both a "great imperialist" and a "sympathetic" human being. What interests me is the particular arrangement of time and space suggested by this brief description. The garden for Rhodes offers both a time outside history—a dream time—and a space for the rearrangement of nature according to an existing template of English landscaping. He imagines imposing formal avenues typical of English country estates on the mountainside, defined by lines of trees. The hydrangeas are also a frequently mentioned feature of the Groote Schuur estate, particularly their color viewed in contrast to the dark pines. None of these plants are indigenous to the Western Cape.[7] Rhodes's vision is of a parkland complete with the "exotics" that were a fashionable part of English practices of landscaping. Oaks and pines were, of course, already part of Cape Town's landscape, having been introduced by early Dutch settlers. Rhodes did, however, introduce the North American gray squirrels, which had become a fashionable addition to English estates at the end of the nineteenth century.[8] Dividing absolutely the place of work from the place of leisure, the estate becomes yet another terrain for asserting mastery over nature. In the excessive gesture, disastrous for the fruit industry, of importing a new species purely to conform to a fashion in landscaping, Rhodes displays his ability to engage in conspicuous consumption and at the same time creates a frame for his conspicuous (although always only temporary) leisure or "dreaming."

Menpes, the "visitor," had come to South Africa to work as a war artist for the London weekly *Black and White*. Menpes includes a painting of the Groote Schuur estate with Rhodes sitting on a horse in the published collection of his painting titled *War Impressions*. In the foreground and to the right, Rhodes sits heavily on a chestnut horse, his hat creating a shadow over his face. Behind him, a path leads away and upward to a stand of stone pines behind which can be seen the outline of the mountain and the sky. On either side of the path, there are low indistinct bushes with yellow and orange flowers. While the composition of the painting resembles the conventional image of the lord of the manor occupying his park, in medium and style, it appears closer to a newspaper illustration. In the composition, Rhodes's careful invention of himself is lent the weight of tradition, but the style suggests instead the newness of Rhodes's position, dependent as it is on his recent acquisition of wealth. In this redistribution of the valuable, "nature" is always employed as an intimate partner that confirms the legitimacy of domination. This is not only, as many theorists have shown, through the employment of a general evolutionary narrative but also, in more intimate ways, through the evocation of nature as confirming the gesture of ownership.

Rhodes's vision is feudal, but he is a strange sort of aristocrat, utterly unconcerned with lineage in the narrow sense but obsessed with what he imagines to be something larger, the continuation of a civilization. In *The Decline of the West* published in 1916, Oswald Spengler registers Rhodes as a new type, one who is of profound significance for the destiny of the West:

> But even for Rhodes political success means territorial and financial success, and only that. Of this Roman-ness within himself he was fully aware. But Western Civilization has not yet taken shape in such strength and purity as this. It was only before his maps that he could fall into a sort of poetic trance, this son of the parsonage who, sent out to South Africa without means, made a gigantic fortune and employed it as the engine of political aims. His idea of a trans-African railway from the Cape to Cairo, his project of a South African empire, his intellectual hold on the hard metal souls of the mining magnates whose wealth he forced into the service of his schemes, his capital Bulawayo, royally planned as a future Residence by a statesman who was all-powerful yet stood in no definite relation to the State, his wars, his diplomatic deals, his road-systems, his syndicates, his armies, his conception of the "great duty to civilization" of the man of brain—all this, broad and imposing, is the prelude of a future which is still in store for us and with which the history of West-European mankind will be definitely closed. (38)

Spengler's tone is puzzling, at once celebratory and resigned. This desire for empire, for expansion, for Spengler marks the decline of a culture, its ending. Rhodes, with personally commissioned translations of Greek classics in his library and a copy of Marcus Aurelius in his pocket, imagines himself on a world historical stage, imperial in the Roman sense. His imperial vision provides him with a justification for violent seizure, for a certain ruthless determination that befits a man who acts on a world historical stage.

Rhodes invests in a form of distinction based on wealth but underwritten by racial discrimination. His endeavor to gain advantage or mastery is no simple capitalist desire for profit but rather is the desire to control the distribution of value—not only monetary value but also the more intangible measurement of social value. His aim was not merely "pecuniary emulation" but more ambitiously to define the ground on which such emulation might take place. Sitting on his horse in the Groote Schuur estate, his restrained yet authoritative gesture indicates what is to be considered the grounds for this new social order he imagines founding. If at one level, these grounds are ludicrous, made up of a strange and incoherent set of ideological fragments, at another level, they are profoundly disturbing, defining as they do not only what but also who is to be counted valuable in this new dispensation. Carefully planned to exclude unintentional reality, the flourishing garden at Groote Schuur creates a background that reflects the achievement of exploit while hiding the violence of seizure and exploitation.

The club, like the Groote Schuur estate, provides a physical structure that does symbolic work in cementing social ties among the small elite involved in the primitive accumulation of natural resources. The culture of the colonial elite produces nature as a source of wealth, the legitimate spoils of anyone canny enough to grab hold of it. This invention of tradition involves not only a set of practices that make nature available, through political influence, force, social networks, and access to capital but also a set of gestures and poses that arrange the body in an attitude of power. Through the aesthetic of the club, the business of diamond mining becomes the honorific work of exploit, not the drudgery of labor. The club provides a context for a social network of white men with political influence in the colonial office to transform diamonds from objects of nature into private property, separating them from other kinds of objects in the natural world that might be collected and making them a special class. It also involves a carving out from the undifferentiated class of diggers who might constitute the proper owners of diamonds.

Despite its current desire to function as a boutique hotel, the decor of the Kimberley Club remains largely unchanged—heavy carved wood furniture, Persian carpets, and worn armchairs. The walls are covered in memorabilia of the elite membership, signed photographs, portraits, and framed documents. The *Brief History* describes some of its rituals and prohibitions that assert the space as a preeminently male domain. No women were permitted until 1937, after which they were still required to use only the back entry until 1980, and they are still not permitted in the bar or the bar lounge. In the current restoration of the club, everyone uses the back entrance "for security reasons," and the main entrance from Dutoitspan Road is permanently closed.

Regimes of Value

The second photograph shows the De Beers mine itself, a landscape in the process of being turned inside out for the purposes of extracting value, a fine dividing up of the dirt so as to separate out what is valuable from debris. This image invites a reflection on the circulation of diamonds and the complex strategies of the diamond industry to control the movement and distribution of these stones.

The photograph represents in a very literal way the dismantling of a landscape. An open-cast mine of bare earth and rock is anchored to the surface by

Fig. 5 De Beers mine. Photo © Africana Library, Kimberley.

fine lines, or "whims," that were used to haul earth out of the mine. In the right foreground, a digger sits looking out over the mine. All around the edge of the mine are small figures, mostly black, although one white figure stands out clearly on a spur of land looking toward the camera. Beyond the mine, the land itself is only visible on the right. In most of the photograph, the horizon is hidden by the piled-up dirt. Where it is visible, it is very flat, with a few small trees and the corner of a tent appearing beyond the road entering the mine. Far in the distance, there is a faint outline of small mountains, or kopjes. Stenciled on the photograph itself are the words "De Beers Mine, 1872–." A further caption has been added by the author of *50 Years on the Diamond Fields, 1870–1920*, Dr. Sabatini: "The overburden or reef is piled dangerously high on the peripherals of the De Beers mine, 1872, and a gap for a roadway to enter and serve the mining area is visible on the extreme right of the photograph" (Sabatini and Duminy 2013, 25).

The mine represents the second stage of the diamond rush in South Africa. The first diamonds discovered in South Africa were alluvial diamonds picked up along the banks of the Orange River. There is a story told about the first diamond discovered in the Cape. In the tale told by Gardner F. Williams in *Diamond Mines of South Africa*, the stone is picked up as a plaything by the son of a poor farmer, Daniel Jacobs. His wife shows it to the neighbor, Schalk van Niekerk, who offers to buy it, though without any fixed sense of its worth. The thought of selling a stone is so absurd to the farmer's wife that she gives it to him for nothing. The stone is passed from hand to hand—an ambiguous object—considered probably worthless until it is sent to Dr. W. Guyborn Atherstone (in an unsealed envelope) in Grahamstown, who determines that it is a diamond of twenty-one and a quarter carats worth five hundred pounds (Williams 1902, 117–20). Williams presents this anecdote as part of the prehistory of diamond mining, the moment when a diamond is first recognized and makes its way hesitantly into the global circulation of value. It is first a worthless stone, then an object with potential, and finally named and identified and fixed with a price.

It is the discovery of a second stone, however, the one that comes to be called the "Star of South Africa," that begins the diamond rush and draws diggers from all over the world. This diamond too accumulates value as it travels away from its point of origin. Williams explains, "In March 1869, a superb white diamond, weighing 83.5 carats, was picked up by a Griqua shepherd boy on the farm Zendfontein, near the Orange River. Schalk van Niekerk bought this stone for a monstrous price in the eyes of the poor shepherd,—500 sheep, 10 oxen, and a horse,—but the lucky purchaser sold it easily for £11,200 to the Lilienfeld Brothers of Hope Town, and it was subsequently purchased by Earl Dudley for £25,000" (1902, 123).

Williams's comment shows how the diamond accumulates value as it moves through social and geographical space. Although Williams claims that "in the eyes" of the shepherd, five hundred sheep, ten oxen, and a horse represent a "monstrous price," he clearly recognizes the trajectory the stone follows, gathering value as it moves. The price is "monstrous," he implies, in the regime of value inhabited by the poor shepherd. The implication is that he is richly and fairly rewarded for his find, even though, in fact, the price he is given is far less than the exchange value of the diamond once it reaches the metropole.

Although initially, claims might be laid by anyone, and the newly discovered diamond mines attracted diggers from all over the world as well as from many parts of South Africa, by 1872, the white diggers had organized to exclude black diggers from holding claims. They did this because they could not compete with black diggers, the requirements of their everyday life—their technique of life—being such that their expenses were greater, eroding the profitability of their endeavors. By a political act, blacks on the diamond fields were thus excluded from the ownership of products of nature that whites could acquire by staking a claim. Initially, there were a number of different arrangements by which diggers might acquire claims. Arrangements could be made with farmers, usually involving a percentage of the diggers' finds, but gradually the land was bought up by mining companies with close links to the colonial government.[9]

In 1872, De Beers was one of five mines operating in the Kimberley area. The story of Rhodes gaining control of the diamond industry has been told many times, usually as a set of complex yet genteel negotiations, threats, and deals among competing interests. Chilvers explains how Rhodes "made a habit of entertaining Barnato [owner of the Kimberley mine], who was not a member, at the Kimberley Club, exploiting its atmosphere to cajole, argue and threaten" (1939, 64). By 1889, through persuading the London Bank of Rothschild to invest, Rhodes was able to buy controlling interests in all existing diamond mines, including the Kimberley mine:

> The Trust Deed created a Company in a remote part of South Africa with powers such as no business concern possessed since the days of the East India Company. The power knew no limits. The capital of the Company could be increased to any extent. It could acquire any asset. The head-quarters might be moved to any part of the world. It could deal in any minerals, machinery or patents. It could operate tramways and electric works, waterworks and railways. It would establish other companies of whatever kind it chose. Further, it was authorized to acquire "tracts of country" in Africa or elsewhere with any rights the rulers might grant, and to spend whatever money was required for its "development and maintenance of order and good governance." (Chilvers 1939, 65–66)

Against the wishes of certain board members, most notably Barnato, the company was created in the image of a state. It is, as Chilvers proudly notes, a successor to the East India Company. Following the long tradition of colonial charter companies, governance emerges as a subsidiary operation to the extraction of profit. Diamonds, as commodities, become the pretext and ground for the extension of corporate power into public space. The enclosed world of the mine and its compound rearrange the world outside the mine.

This company that imagines itself to be a state provides the basis for a cartel that gradually asserts its control over the entire diamond industry. In

1982, investigative journalist and former professor of political science Edward Jay Epstein published *The Rise and Fall of Diamonds*. The book, an exposé of the mythology that constitutes the value of diamonds, investigated the way in which a diamond cartel established by De Beers controls both the material flow of these commodities and their symbolic value. It describes how De Beers and Anglo-American, which acquired a controlling interest in De Beers in 1926, through a combination of negotiation, violence, and leverage, took possession of the diamond industry by creating a structure for maintaining the illusion of diamond scarcity.

Maintaining this illusion involves controlling production worldwide through direct ownership of mines or through agreements that require independent mines to sell their diamonds to De Beers. It also involves the development of highly policed forbidden zones surrounded by barbed-wire fences to prevent diamonds from exiting the closed system of De Beers control as well as the invention of a highly ritualized private market through the Central Selling Organization (established in 1930), in which only certain buyers are allowed to participate and under highly regulated conditions.[10] It also involves the development of a multinational company that resembles a state, with the resources to build infrastructure, private towns, dams, railways, and runways; to employ an intelligence service; and to wage small wars.

The material form of diamonds produces a particular orientation toward nature. Although diamonds, like coal, are formed deep beneath the earth's surface, volcanic eruptions drive diamond-bearing rocks upward toward the surface. At least until 1955, when the first diamonds were synthesized by General Electric, they are artifacts of nature that are dangerously available to anyone who might wish to pick them up. The practices of De Beers are part of an invented set of traditions around nature and ownership and illusion, a complex set of negotiations and violence by which diamonds from all over Africa (and other places in the world) end up stockpiled in the De Beers vault in London.

The contrast between the piled overburden and debris of the De Beers mines and the Kimberley Club and the Groote Schuur estate offers a way of assembling a historical image of nature circa 1890, one that does not remain in the past but repeats itself with difference at other sites of mineral extraction. It provides a form, a pattern of regard and disregard, of civilization and barbarism that makes visible the sly passing of value from hand to hand and the sleight of hand through which value always accumulates elsewhere than in the postcolony.

"The Necessities of Life Are Supplied"

The image of the compound shows the invention of a tradition that becomes a core part of South African extractive industries. Developed as a response to diamond smuggling and the panic about illicit diamond buying, the compound is a material structure that can be read as a condensation of anxieties about ownership. The ownership of diamonds, like the ownership of other minerals, is always a strange negotiation, since these sources of potential wealth exist in nature. They are not manufactured, even if in many cases their extraction requires industrial processes.

The photograph is taken from a high elevation and looks down at an elevated surveillance tower and on the corrugated iron roofs of the compound surrounding a wide courtyard. There are a few small trees with wooden pallets underneath. Beyond the compound, the town of Kimberley is laid out with neat, orderly lines of trees marking streets and property boundaries. Inside the compound, many small figures can be seen engaged in a range of activities: walking, sitting, or standing in groups. On the right of the picture, a rectangular

Fig. 6 De Beers compound. Photo © Africana Library, Kimberley.

pool surrounded by a rectangular roofed walkway is visible, perhaps a communal washing area. The picture (perhaps a postcard) reveals Kimberley as an orderly space. In contrast with the almost empty street outside the Kimberley Club, the desire of the picture speaks to a particular construction of work but also of containment.

In 1905, British chemist and authority on precious stones Sir William Crookes visited Kimberley and made the following comment about the compound system to the British Association:

> One great safeguard against robbery is the "compound system" of looking after the natives. A "compound" is a large square, about 20 acres, surrounded by rows of one-story buildings of corrugated iron. These buildings are divided into rooms each holding about twenty natives. Within the enclosure is a Store where the necessities of life are supplied at a reduced price, and wood and water free of charge. In the middle is a large swimming-bath with fresh water running through it. The rest of the space is devoted to games, dances, concerts, and any other amusement the native mind can desire. (1905, 16)

The compound system was developed in response to conflict over the removal of diamonds by mine workers and their sale to illicit diamond buyers. The system was introduced in the 1880s after a series of strikes, particularly by white workers, over the implementation of the Searching Ordinance, which made provisions for all workers, including overseers, to be searched on leaving the mine property. What is interesting about the narrative through which the white workers' grievances are articulated is the urgent desire for legislation to protect their status.

Earlier, white claim holders had agitated for the prevention of black ownership of claims. This was, they claimed, because denying blacks the possibility of legitimate ownership of the resource made illicit diamond buying easier to police. Black diggers had to be entirely alienated from nature as a means of accumulating wealth so that no ambiguity might exist as to who constituted the proper owner of diamonds or, to phrase this another way, who might be permitted to engage in the primitive accumulation made possible by natural resources. But it was also explained as a fear of competition. In a letter to *Diamond News* in 1872, A. F. Lindley states, "It would be almost impossible for white men to compete with natives as diggers; the mere difference between their living expenses, the cost of passage from abroad, the rates at which natives would sell their diamonds and, in fact, not to argue further on a truism the difference between their general wants, necessities, character, and position of the two races utterly forbid it" (quoted in Smalberger 1976, 423).

In this act of what Veblen would describe as "invidious comparison," Lindley moves smoothly from "general wants" and "necessities" to "character and position" in order to assert the value of a particular technique of life. Character and position appear dependent on a certain level of consumption. Brought into contact with a different technique of life, the need to perform a certain standard of living becomes an obstacle to a profitable extraction of resources. Yet Lindley's point is a different one. His statement invites agreement—he presents it as a "truism"—about the terms in which such comparisons should be made. Status, character, and position are dependent on consumption, and those inhabiting a different "regime of value," one that depends on a different distribution of value, constitute "unfair" competition. Excluding black diggers becomes an assertion of the value of a particular technique of life, one that must be defended through coercive and political intervention.

Securing these rights of exclusion involved both violence—in the form of torture and beatings that sometimes resulted in death—and political pressure.[11] Proclamation no. 49 of 1872 suspending native digging licenses and prohibiting the issuing of new licenses was a response to this pressure, and although Sir Henry Barkly, then governor of the Cape, refused to confirm this proclamation, it was replaced by another that achieved the same effect while avoiding direct reference to race. In the new proclamation, all claim holders were required to acquire a certificate of good character from a magistrate or justice of the peace.[12]

The compound system was the culmination of a series of maneuvers through which legitimate ownership of diamonds as a natural resource was established and policed. The panic and moral outrage around illicit diamond buying can be read as a displacement activity in which the latent or concealed actual uncertainty over ownership is given definite form as "illegitimate owners," usually black, are identified and reviled.

Despite the compound system, the unofficial traffic in diamonds continued. In the 1960s, Fred Kamil, a Lebanese trader who for quixotic reasons intervened (successfully) in illicit diamond smuggling between Liberia and Sierra Leone, was invited by Anglo-American chairman Harry Oppenheimer to conduct an independent investigation into diamond smuggling in South Africa.[13] The long history of Kamil's increasingly dark relationship with Anglo-American remains obscure despite his life story recounted in *The Diamond Underworld*, but what is of interest here is what his story reveals about the ongoing conflict over the legitimacy of the ownership of diamonds. What emerges is the curious contradiction between diamonds as natural and cultural artifacts. Describing an interview with one of the smugglers he has arrested, Kamil recounts the following conversation: "He [the smuggler] went on to explain that because he believed that diamonds, unlike drugs, were harmless and the industry was a monopoly, he saw little harm in taking his 'share.' 'No one knows how many diamonds there are on that coast, but I've seen. In some places, there are as many diamonds as there is gravel. When they discover these places, they immediately cover them with cement to keep the diamonds rare and prices high. For Christ's sake, why shouldn't a poor man's wife own a diamond?'" (1979, 144).

The smuggler's question addresses the contradiction that lies at the heart of a diamond's value. The symbolic value of diamonds depends on their continuing association with an elite, yet their natural abundance makes them potentially available to everyone. In each case Kamil investigates, the members of the apparently hand-picked and carefully vetted security team turn out to be part of the chain of social transaction through which diamonds leave the control of De Beers (later Anglo-American) and end up finding their way onto the market. The natural abundance of diamonds drives the ever-greater need for security while at the same time undermines the logical need for restraint for those in close contact with diamonds at points of extraction. As he describes it, Kamil's relationship with Anglo-American ultimately breaks down when, in the final case he investigates, evidence seems to implicate a member of Anglo-American management as part of a smuggling chain, something that the company refuses to consider.

What the anecdotes from Kamil's memoir suggest is an ongoing conflict over who constitutes the proper owner of diamonds, both at the point of extraction and at the point of consumption. The compound system and intensive security procedures limit but never actually stop the flow of illicit diamonds. At the same time, diamonds' symbolic value requires that "a poor man's wife" never own a diamond, as this would detract from its ability to signal elite status. Instead, an elaborate mythology must be maintained in which diamonds form part of a greater framework for conferring and denying status.

"Diamonds Are Forever"

As an ornament, the diamond does a particular kind of work; its display on the body signals the value and status of the wearer. Veblen publishes *Theory of the Leisure Class* only thirty years after the discovery of the diamond the "Star of Africa" initiates the diamond rush that transforms the landscape of the Cape Colony. Historically, the rarity of diamonds had made them excellent markers of status. Almost all histories of the diamond industry in South Africa begin with a chapter on the prehistory of the diamond that outlines its association with royalty. For Veblen, precious stones and metals form a particular category of objects of adornment that "owe their utility as items of conspicuous waste to an antecedent utility as objects of beauty" (1943, 129). In contemporary society, this "antecedent utility" is, however, overwhelmed by their more important role as "marks of honorific costliness" (131).

There is a small diamond museum attached to the Shimansky shop at the Cape Town's V&A Waterfront. Yair Shimansky is one of the few jewellers in South Africa whose company is licensed to buy and cut diamonds from De Beers. The museum contains a very brief history of diamond mining, some gumboots, and a display of replicas of famous diamonds, including the Cullinan Diamond. It also contains a replica of the diamond South African film star Charlize Theron wore at a party after she received an Oscar in 2004. Charlize donated the dress she wore on that occasion to the museum. Each visitor is given an individual guide to the museum that opens out into the display room. Theron's diamond, the guide tells me, is worth approximately twenty million rand. A little website dedicated to the promotion of diamonds includes the following entry: "After winning the Oscar for best actress in 2004, Charlize Theron came home to South Africa for a long-awaited homecoming. During her time here, Theron selected a 47ct D Flawless Emerald Cut Diamond necklace by Shimansky to wear at the bash celebrating her Oscar win for *Monster*. Coupling the exquisite piece with a shadowy, beaded Ralph Lauren dress, Charlize looked every inch the Hollywood icon."[14]

Shimansky's employment of Charlize Theron as part of their advertising campaign is in keeping with a long-standing tradition developed by De Beers of promoting the value of diamonds through their association with celebrity figures. In a typical example of Veblenian spleen, he notes, "We often declare that an article of apparel, for instance, is 'perfectly lovely,' when pretty much all an analysis of the aesthetic value of the article would leave ground for is the declaration that it is pecuniarily honorific" (Veblen 1943, 131). The beauty of a diamond translates into honor by signifying nothing more than that the wearer has the money to pay for it. The diamond as an ornament becomes, in the twentieth century, an integral part of the signifying code of increasingly global practices of consumption.

In the late 1930s, De Beers retained New York–based advertising agency N. W. Ayer & Son to undertake a campaign to promote the purchase of diamonds.[15] Since De Beers controlled the world's diamonds, the project was to promote not the company but rather the commodity in general. N. W. Ayer, in reporting the success of the campaign (the sale of diamonds in the United States had increased by 55 percent between 1938 and 1941), noted that it had developed a "new form of advertising which has been widely imitated ever since.... There was no brand name to be impressed on the public mind. There was simply an idea—the eternal emotional value surrounding the diamond" (N. W. Ayer report quoted in Epstein 2011, 726).[16] The advertising campaign, with its groundbreaking deployment of the new medium of film to create a desiring public, invented the tradition of the diamond engagement ring. Like all effective inventions, it built on something that already existed: the historical association of the diamond with rare value and its occasional use in rings marking the engagements of royal couples.

N. W. Ayer's program involved not only print advertisements but also lectures given at schools and product placement in Hollywood films. N. W. Ayer's intervention was designed to alter the conduct of Americans in their articulation of love, desire, and commitment. The Diamond Development Corporation, established in Hollywood in the 1930s and backed by De Beers, provided film producers with diamonds if they agreed to place them in scenes in such a way as to emphasize the association between diamonds and romance.[17] Celebrities were given diamonds and asked to wear them on public occasions and when making appearances on television. Portraits of "engaged socialites" were commissioned to provide role models for the buying public. N. W. Ayer noted that what was needed was "constant publicity to show that only a diamond is everywhere accepted and recognized as the symbol of betrothal" (quoted in Epstein 2011, 746). They also generated "news" stories about diamonds and paid fashion designers to talk about the new trend toward diamonds. Epstein quotes an N. W. Ayers memo that reportedly states, "Since Great Britain has such an important interest in the diamond industry, the royal couple could be of tremendous assistance to this British Industry by wearing diamonds rather than other jewels" (2011, 716).

In a recent article, Margaret Brinig suggests that the increase in the sale of diamond engagement rings corresponded not only to the N. W. Ayer advertising campaign but also to a change in law—the abolition in a number of states of the cause of action for a breach of marriage promise, which gave a woman legal recourse if an engagement was broken after sexual intercourse, as this lessened her chances of attracting another marriage partner. The advertising campaign found a receptive audience as the diamond ring came to represent a "bonding device" to replace the legally binding nature of an engagement (Brinig 1990). Yet this investment in the ritual of engagement, based as it is on the value of the diamond as a token of love, is undermined by the difficulty of selling a diamond for its "worth." The phrase "Diamonds are forever," coined by one of N. W. Ayer's copywriters, was designed specifically to discourage the resale of diamonds. Diamonds could only retain the impression of scarcity if they were not permitted to circulate through resale.

Writers in the genre of the exposé such as Epstein present the documentation from the N. W. Ayer archive as a sign of the outrageous duplicity of De Beers and the diamond industry.[18] What is of interest to me is rather the intensive work of mythification necessary to stabilize the value of natural resources whose relative scarcity and abundance depend on a careful management of the sites of extraction. In an ideological sleight of hand, natural resources are only valuable if they are in the hands of an elite, extracted from their point of origin cheaply, and sold elsewhere at a high price. The monopoly first established by De Beers becomes the mechanism for both materially marshaling the stones and concealing their abundance and mobilizing diamonds as a social token, a fetish in its barest form. The success of the N. W. Ayer marketing campaign was precisely its ability to manage the patent contradictions of the idea of an enclaved object that everyone should desire and could acquire (for two or three months of their salary—a sum worked out not with any reference to the cost of extraction but based simply as what sort of symbolic investment a man might be expected to make, what sort of sacrifice would demonstrate true commitment).[19]

In 1947, Jan Smuts, then prime minister of the Union of South Africa, invited the British royal family to visit South Africa. Their trip, which included a stopover in Kimberley and a tour of the diamond mines, is described in the *Brief History of the Kimberley Club*: "In 1947, King George VI and Queen Elizabeth and the two princesses Elizabeth and Margaret, used the Club during their one day visit to Kimberley. The Queen left a diamond ring in the bathroom which was found after their departure. It was sent on and the Club received a letter of thanks from the King's aide-de-camp."

There is a way in which this visit of the queen to the Kimberley Club, on the eve of the Nationalist Party victory, seems to provide a strange postscript to the invention of the diamond elite. The forgotten ring in some way reiterates the ambiguous status of the diamond, acutely valuable to the poor and middle class, free to those whose status makes them desirable ambassadors for the stone's worth. In one of the curious ceremonial performances required of royalty, this brief visit brings the royal bodies into close proximity with the extraction of diamonds. It is in some ways a dangerous move, since an investment in the fantastic value of diamonds, as a worth beyond money, involves a forgetting of the point of extraction. The Kimberley Club is called upon to perform the task of mediating the experience. Diamonds and royalty are brought together in a performance of associations, while at the same time the royal bodies are shielded from the reality of extraction through being provided with refuge at the club.

Debris

In 1998, the U.K.-based nonprofit organization (NGO) Global Witness released a report of their investigation into the role of diamonds in conflicts across Africa. The report, "The Rough Trade," indicted the diamond industry for its complicity in the trade in "conflict diamonds." In 1999, this was followed up with the Fatal Transaction Campaign. The emphasis was on the way in which diamonds, particularly from informal alluvial diggings, became both the cause and the means of sustaining violent conflict in Africa and elsewhere.

Although initially denying any responsibility for the origins of the diamonds they acquired, in 2000, De Beers responded to the campaign by declaring a change in their policy. Matthew Hart, author of *Diamonds: The History of a Cold-Blooded Love Affair*, notes that "in March 2000, De Beers began inserting into sight boxes notices guaranteeing that none of the goods had been purchased in contravention of the UN resolution against the war trade. It was a seminal event, serving notice that the leading diamond house was setting itself against the bloodied goods and aligning itself, in effect, with some of the harshest critics of the trade" (2002, 199).

In 2005, De Beers, Global Witness, Partnership Africa Canada, Rapaport, and the World Bank founded the Diamond Development Initiative, seeking to "optimize the beneficial development impact of artisanal diamond mining to miners, their communities and their governments" (quoted in Le Billon 2006, 787). Yet what this emphasis on "blood diamonds" or "conflict diamonds" has done is to conceal the long history of violence associated with diamond extraction. Although currently in a position to present itself as the moral form of capitalism, De Beers has been implicated in diamond wars in the 1950s and 1960s in both Sierra Leone and Angola. As Philippe Le Billon notes, "Ironically, the lasting effects of linking diamonds with violence may not be ethical consumption, but rather a stronger dystopian vision of Africa and legitimated position for large 'reputable' (western) companies over smaller local and regional operators" (2006, 794).

This dystopian view of Africa once again confirms the instrumental logic of De Beers, whose careful management of the industry preserves the diamonds' value. A particular sleight of hand makes any interference with the ownership of the industry self-defeating because of the precarious nature of the product's value. If the particular social life of diamonds is unique, it also has many things in common with the extraction of other raw materials. All involve enclaved spaces with high security, the violent seizure of natural commons, and a set of invented traditions and shadowy transactions between local and global elites that serve to define the proper ownership of these raw materials. All gain value as they move away from their point of origin into the global marketplace. In the long history of climate change, colonial expansion not only provided the raw materials that fueled the manufactories of the Industrial Revolution and enabled a technique of life based on the consumption of fossil fuels—Timothy Mitchell's "carbon democracies" of the metropolitan centers. It also provided a new stage for the display of wealth and leisure as part of a new and expanded form of invidious comparison in which all social forms were measured against the technique of life produced by industrial capitalism.

What emerges from these fragments of the history of diamonds in South Africa is the way the culture of consumption is developed in response to a fear of natural abundance. In *Carbon Democracies*, Mitchell describes how a way of life based on the car was not the logical outcome of technological developments but rather a strategic response to the abundance of oil that resulted from the discovery of the oil reserves in the Middle East. He describes how in the 1940s and 1950s, automobile and oil companies, through advertising and through the production of cars with bigger engines, "manufactured the carbon-heavy forms of middle-class American life that, combined with new political arrangements in the Middle East, would help the oil companies keep oil scarce enough to allow their profits to thrive" (2011, 42). The natural abundance of diamonds on the South African diamond fields was a risk not to the diamond's aesthetic value that presumably is immutable but to its ability to act as a marker of status and therefore its ability to be exploited for profit. Why should a poor man's wife not have a diamond? Abundance could hold the promise of a more egalitarian distribution of goods. However, the response of the diamond industry was similar to the response of the oil industry in the 1950s—control over the market and the deliberate invention of a technique of life through the intervention of government and the deployment of the advertising industry. Although as a form of carbon that is displayed, not burned, diamonds do not make an ongoing contribution to carbon emissions, their story illuminates the ways in which the technique of life of modern capitalism emerges—not as a result of "progress" but as a side effect of the drive for individual profit.

In 1867, the same year that the first diamond was discovered near Kimberley, Marx published the first volume of *Capital*, which includes both his theory of primitive accumulation and his theory of exploitation. For Marx, exploitation is linked to the production of surplus value. His use of the term *exploitation* refers to the gap between what the worker is paid (which is linked to his or her standard of living, what is required in order to sustain the work force) and the value he or she produces in the form of a commodity. It is the profit generated by this excess that drives capitalist production. In the diamond mines, this form of exploitation existed alongside the other more fantastic source of profit—primitive accumulation, or the seizure of the commons. For Kapp, the damage inflicted on people and nature constitutes the unacknowledged costs of production. In placing the texts and images together, I have tried to reveal this background. Each image contains some moment of unintentional reality that refers us to these hidden costs.

What is left over when value is extracted from diamondiferous ground is known as "debris." The landscape after diamonds, like the landscape after oil, offers an example of leftover reality, a space not subject to invention and artifice and tradition. Unlike the carefully managed gardens of Groote Schuur (now the residence of the South African president), these leftover spaces register nature not as an aesthetic object but as violently contested ground.

"Hunting with Mr Rhodes"

The final photograph, "Hunting with Mr Rhodes," shows another form of exploitation. In his description of early societies, Veblen suggests that hunting is an honorific activity because it is "not to be accounted productive labor but rather an acquisition of substance by seizure" (1943, 14). An employment undertaken by men, it confers status because it allows for the display of prowess and skill. In modern society, Veblen notes, a distinction emerges between hunting as sport and hunting as trade, in which the former retains its character as an exploit while the latter becomes merely an industry (40–41). This photograph shows a strange combination of aristocratic ritual and practicality as scores of animals are hung up in a formation that resembles the modern mass production of animal carcasses for the meat industry.

The photograph shows a tableau of hunters with the carcasses of the animals they have killed hanging from a set of pegs against the side of a building.

Fig. 7 "Hunting with Mr Rhodes." Photo © Africana Library, Kimberley.

The display is symmetrically arranged with springbok or impala on either side, with their telltale side strip of dark and light fur making a repeating pattern. The central section is slightly more complex, with a range of different kinds of buck, including some larger ones, perhaps eland. Beneath the springbok on either side are smaller game animals—on one side smaller buck and some cape hares and birds, perhaps francolin, on the other side what looks like guinea fowl. In front of these hanging carcasses stand seven white men wearing hats, and in front of them are two white men seated, three reclining on the ground, and seven hunting dogs. In the right corner in the shadow cast by the building are two black men. The one, wearing a hat, stands looking at the camera; the other is visible only as folded hands and crossed legs.

In the age of extinctions, this excess of animal death appears shocking. In *50 Years on the Diamond Field*, the image appears with the following caption:

> This photograph is entitled "Hunting with Mr Rhodes," although it appears to reflect a massacre! At a time when fresh meat was not that readily available, the use of game and venison was a practical alternative, and the guinea fowl, springbok and other game served this need admirably. The numerous De Beers farms were well stocked with game, and this De Beers "tradition" has continued to the present day. This photograph was probably taken in the late 1890's, before the outbreak of the Anglo-Boer War, as thereafter game would have become scarce due to large scale hunting on both sides. (Sabatini and Duminy 2013, 74)

The image describes a complex dynamic of scarcity and abundance. The caption reveals a tension between different conceptions of nature. The first statement in the caption, drawing attention to the massacre, reflects a consciousness of the finitude of nature. Such excess raises the specter of animal extinctions. The second comment returns the picture to its context, obliquely providing a justification for the excess—the animals are shot to provide meat for the town that had developed so quickly that there was no infrastructure to support its expanding population.

The photograph wants to keep score, to display the dead, but it also seems to lack ideological certainty. The title "Hunting with Mr Rhodes" attempts to fix the polyphony of the visual image. The inclusion of the title "Mr" performs a gesture of deference and at the same time singles Rhodes out as the organizing or motivating force of this exploit, something that is reiterated by his central position in the composition of the image. He is in a typical pose, one bent arm crossing his body to hold on to his lapel, the other leaning on an invisible support provided by the building. There is a curious blankness about Rhodes in this image and in many other images included in the archive. He is posed expressionless and often holding on to something or leaning against something but always central to the composition to indicate his status as the moving force of the exploit. Yet the hunt represented here is not, or not only, an exploit. It is also the practical response to a need—not a personal need, but the need to sustain the working of the diamond industry. The white hunters seem themselves to lack the vitality necessary to maintain the heroic posture necessary to fix this as a tableau of exploit.

Considering the unintentional reality in this image, its background makes visible some of the unpaid costs of the industry. The animal deaths are side effects, elements of the natural commons whose violent seizure supports the diamond industry not only by providing meat for the town but also by forcing those dependent on game for their livelihood off the land and into wage labor on the mines. These figures, the black participants, are ambiguously present, marginal, in the shadow, and in one case partly cut off. The black hands visible are calmly folded. Looking on obliquely, they are not part of the symmetry of the image. These partially visible figures, probably trackers and guides, gesture beyond the frame to what it excludes—the possibility of a different technique of life that this practice of industrial-scale hunting is in the process of destroying.

The photograph represents a moment in the history of the production of nature in the colony when overcoming the wilderness was seen as the heroic work of the civilized man. Yet it appears weighted by the dead animals that this civilizing mission requires. The men in their suits seem almost overwhelmed by the carcasses, which seem to prefigure the disassembly lines of the modern meat-packing industry that emerges in the first decades of the twentieth century. The reduction of animals to raw materials signified in this sad lineup of dead herbivores is the logical conclusion of positivist science and industrial capitalism.

By the early part of the twentieth century, however, wild game was already entering a narrative of loss. This abundance was, as Carl Akeley notes, part of an "Africa that is fast disappearing" (quoted in Haraway 1989, 48). Akeley's project of preserving specimens of African wildlife through taxidermy and display represents one response to this threatening loss. In the African hall in the American Museum of Natural History, these stuffed animals, products of Akeley's collecting expeditions, bear within them the trace of the hunt as a form of exploit that was increasingly no longer possible.[20] As the technique of life of capitalist modernity came to dominate everyday experience in the industrialized north, another role emerges for wild animals. No longer present as physical threats, they enter the imagination as exemplary figures for measuring and judging human societies and social behavior.[21] In particular, the predator, as I will discuss in the next chapter, imagined as the source of natural vitality and virile assertion, enters the realm of politics as a desired figure of power.

5

The Cult of the Wild

Depending on which aspect happens to be paramount at the time, Ideology stresses plan or chance, technology or life, civilization or nature.

—Horkheimer and Adorno

Wolves as a Remainder

On the stretch of the N2 highway between Plettenberg Bay and Knysna, part of the popular tourist itinerary in South Africa known as the Garden Route, signs direct visitors to the Tsitsikamma Wolf Sanctuary. The Lupus Foundation, which runs the Tsitsikamma Wolf Sanctuary, describes it on the website as the "only Registered Non-Profit Wolf Sanctuary in Southern Africa" and details its mission as supporting "the survival of the wolf around the world." It claims to do this both by preserving a healthy genetic strain of animal outside the wolf's natural habitat and by educating people about the behavior and the importance of all wildlife. It does not breed wolves but provides a "sanctuary and ultimately a 'natural habitat' for captive wolves" and stresses the importance of ending hybridization, or the crossbreeding of wolves with dogs. The website provides photographs and names for the approximately forty-four wolves that inhabit the sanctuary divided up according to six "dens," with a few words of description for each wolf. "Ultimately," it claims, "the rehabilitated packs will be moved to their natural habitat, as and when funds allow, but the sanctuary will remain open as a rehabilitation centre and a home for unwanted 'pets.'"[1]

Wolves in South Africa bring to the foreground nature as a product of history and provide the reference point for the assembling of a set of texts that enable a reading of nature under apartheid. Apart from the Ethiopian wolf, wolves are not endemic to Africa.[2] The wolves I discuss in this chapter constitute a curiously persistent remnant of a military experiment undertaken by the apartheid government. Unlike the conspicuous display of the late nineteenth-century primitive accumulators, the wolf dog breeding project was a covert operation, part of the apartheid government's experimentation with nature as an ally in the work of war. It took place behind the closed doors of the government breeding facility, and even now, information about these projects remains vague and incomplete.

In her book *Adorno on Nature*, Deborah Cook explains Adorno's insistence on the importance of dwelling on the particular. She writes that "although a particular thing is not 'definable without the universal that identifies it,' it cannot be subsumed without remainder under the universal" (2011, 13). These wolves, who are the side effects of history, allow us to consider nature as a complex object, one whose deployment always creates a remainder. It is not easy to categorize these wolves neatly, or perhaps what is most interesting about them is the way they lurk on the fringes of discourse, partly in the shadows, and in a typically sly wolfish way observe, challenge, and threaten the clear lines of established categories. Within the logic of synecdoche, they are a part that does not easily signify the whole. They are not exemplary; they do not offer a case history that might illuminate other alien species. Instead, they trouble the concepts of nature and naturalness. Placed in relation to other wild animals in South Africa, they bring something new to the picture. In crossing certain boundaries, they make new conceptual and actual territories.

The caption included beneath the photograph "Hunting with Mr Rhodes" in *50 Years on the Diamond Fields*, discussed in the previous chapter, expresses first shock at the represented "massacre" and then a recognition of the hunt in its context as practical response to need. It contains two moments in the natural history of the postcolony: the earlier moment of appropriation, when nature appears to the colonial elite as an unfenced commons, an abundance of unaccountably neglected wealth, and the more recent age of extinctions, when the painful scarcity of wild animals signifies wild nature's imminent disappearance.[3] The current chapter reflects on a set of events that lies in between these two moments, where animal wildness is evoked as the source of power and predatory violence in the field of combat. Although in some ways this moment seems superseded by the contemporary attitude to the wild as ephemeral and fleeting value, to be lovingly fostered, the earlier belief continues, I argue, to exert pressure on the present.

For the discourse of environmentalism, the wolf sanctuary in South Africa is an anomaly. Yet it is also, for this reason, a provocation to thought. For an environmentalism that conceives of nature as a totality that can be understood and regulated, the wolf sanctuary is something that can be easily dismissed as irrational. Yet to dismiss the sanctuary is to assume there is a rational logic to the distribution and redistribution of animals that is not bound up with human desires and sentiment. The existence of a wolf sanctuary in South Africa presents an interesting "knot," to use Donna Haraway's term, a point of resistance that makes visible in new and interesting ways the shifting coordinates of a key set of terms used to mark relations of belonging and strangeness—natural and unnatural, indigenous and alien, domestic and wild, territory and border.

The South African wolves are very clearly products of history, imported from North America to satisfy a particular political purpose—the breeding of wolf dogs for use by the South African military and police during the 1970s and 1980s.[4] Their breeding was part of an extended program for applying the scientific method to the problem of security that was indirectly the problem of maintaining the status of the white population and their "standard of living." However, this ostensibly practical purpose is shadowed by a wider investment by those involved in the project in a particular idea of violence, wildness, and ferocity. The texts assembled in this constellation include the wolf sanctuary and its website, transcripts from the Truth and Reconciliation Commission's hearings on chemical and biological warfare, two self-published border war memoirs, newspaper reports, and Boria Sax's reflection on the Nazi cult of the wolf in his book *Animals of the Third Reich*. The wolf in this constellation acts as a point of friction, a mobile, dangerous, but also vulnerable living symbol that invites curious transactions between material and metaphorical life. Tracing these local and global investments in "wildness" brings into focus the wolf as alibi for human desire.

The wolves in the sanctuary can be read as remainders both because they are left over after the apartheid military experiment is abandoned and because their history means they do not go into the concept of nature without leaving something behind.[5] Finally, as material animals, they leave their own traces on the actual and conceptual landscape surrounding wild predators and their place in South Africa.[6]

Animals are ambiguous, since their meaning is dependent on an enigmatic and only partly knowable material life. Animals in contact with human culture always have two lives: a figural life and a material life. The wolves in this chapter circulate both as metaphorical or mythic characters and as embodied creatures. A look at the dictionary suggests some of the ways in which wolves have symbolic currency in human language. What is the quality of wolfishness? The dictionary includes the following: "fierceness and rapacity" and also, interestingly, "a ravenous appetite or craving for food" (Oxford English Dictionary). The phrase "to keep the wolf from the door" is used in situations where someone is given food to prevent hunger, to prevent the emergence of the rapacious inner wolf.

The mid-twentieth century witnessed a reevaluation of the relative merits of wild animals and modern humanity. In his book *What Animals Mean in the Fiction of Modernity*, Philip Armstrong describes the way in which a celebration of wildness and animal vitality emerged as a response to the mechanistic lifelessness of modern society, the result of industrialization, and the expansion of a technique of life based on the increasing commodification of nature. "During the nineteenth and twentieth centuries," Armstrong notes, "as wild animals were hunted, eradicated, displaced or deprived of their habitat on an unprecedented scale, they reappeared . . . in horror stories, wish fulfillment, fantasies, jokes and art" (2008, 142). Africa played a particular role in this conception of nature as a regenerative force and source of authentic experience. African wildlife offered writers such as Ernest Hemingway a form of contact with wildness that was perceived to be lost to European culture. Like Akeley, whose preserved specimens populate the American Museum of Natural History's Hall of African Mammals, Hemingway believed in the practice of the hunt as an essentially redemptive form of contact with animal vitality and an assertion of masculine virility.

Simultaneously, the emergence of the modern discipline of ethology, the study of animal behavior, provided an apparently scientific basis for the evaluation of the characters and attributes of particular species of wild animals. The work of Konrad Lorenz, considered one of the founders of ethology, is interesting because of the way in which animals, in at least some of his work, come to act as cyphers in the distribution of social values. Although not central to Lorenz's scientific research, the wolf is an important reference point in his popular and highly anecdotal representation of animal behavior, *King Solomon's Ring*, a book aimed at conveying "the infinite beauty of our fellow creatures and their life" to the general reader while maintaining a "strict adherence to scientific fact" (1961, xxxv). For Lorenz, the wolf offered a model for a form of behavior uncorrupted by the weakening effects of domestication. In *King Solomon's Ring*, Lorenz puts forward the theory that dogs are divided between those descended from the Northern Hemisphere wolf and those descended from the Mesopotamian jackal. Although according to Lorenz, most dogs, apart from a few breeds such as huskies and chows, are what he called Aureus dogs, mostly descended from jackals, the introduction of some Lupus or wolf blood adds an important element to a dog's character. Lorenz writes that "in the life of a wolf, the community of the pack plays a vastly more important role than in that of a jackal. While the latter is essentially a solitary hunter and confined himself to a limited territory, the wolf pack roams far and wide through the forests of the North as a sworn and very exclusive band which sticks together through thick and thin and whose members will defend each other to the death" (119).

When in the 1990s it emerged that Lorenz had close ties with National Socialism and had written two articles supporting Nazi projects of population extermination, his apparently scientific observations of animal behavior appeared not simply inaccurate but ideologically motivated. Research has shown that Lorenz's comments about the two lineages for the domestic dog were inaccurate. All dogs, even the most obedient breeds, are descended from the wolf. Characteristics Lorenz described as attributes, it turned out, were not inherent qualities but rather projections based on the symbolic meaning and associations that surround animals in human culture. In these descriptions of the traits and characteristics of animals, a careful mapping of value is taking place.

Intellectual historian Boria Sax notes, "Anyone familiar with the Nazi period will recognize in Lorenz description of the dog breeds a canine equivalent of the idealized description of primeval Aryan tribes, whose putative qualities the Nazis and other nationalists endeavored to emulate" (2013, 14). Dogs descended from jackals were considered to be "capable of absolute obedience" but lacking in the "deeper traits of loyalty and affection" (14). Although Lorenz's descriptions of dogs do not seem to map as neatly onto Nazi ideology as Sax suggests, Lorenz is clearly engaged in an act of "invidious comparison." Different dog breeds are evaluated in order to assess their relative worth by measuring them against the ideal of the wolf. The qualities of the wolf are then used as a material measure to reflect on the value of different types of men. Behind the act of assigning qualities to animals lies a different form of figuration, an implied moral comparison between animals and between animals and humans. Lorenz's scientific observations, employed analogically, were used to make judgments about the relative worth of different groups of humans.

In crossing into Afrikaans, the word *wolf* extended its reference, yet the association with hunger remained. It is defined as "Enigeen van n vraatsugtige roofdiere van die Hondegeslag, Canis, wat groot skade onder vee, wild, beeste aanrig, en in n groep, die mens aanval veral die sort C. Lupus.... In sommige dele, benaming vir die hiena" (Any of a number of insatiable animals of prey of the the dog family, Canis, that cause great damage to stock, game, and oxen and in a group may attack humans, especially those of the C. Lupus family.... In some regions, the name for the hyena; Odendaal and Gouws 2000).

In a curious act of translation, some qualities associated with the Northern Hemisphere wolf are transferred to the wild animals of the dog family in South Africa, while at the same time the indigenous animals are assigned a lesser value. In describing the hyena, for instance, the first *Encyclopaedia of Southern Africa*, published in 1961, notes that it is "a coward and a scavenger" (Rosenthal 1964, 240). The Northern Hemisphere wolves, in contrast to their colonial relatives, remain the reference point for signifying a mythological aura of fierceness and independence. In South Africa, the wolves are ambiguous not only because of the complex of fantasies and desires they embody but also because they are imported along with their cultural associations from elsewhere.

Animals Out of Place

While the wolves are introduced into South Africa during apartheid precisely because of their wildness, their continuing existence places them in a category with other "alien" species introduced during the colonial and apartheid period. In a recent article on trout, Duncan Brown comments that he is "interested in the social and cultural issues around a species like trout in South Africa, and more broadly the place of that which is termed 'alien' in the postcolony" (2011, 15). In their careful reading of the news coverage of the intense wildfires in the Cape region in 2000, Jean and John Comaroff make the argument that public concern with the eradication of alien species, held to be responsible for the intensity of the burn, can be read, at least in part, as the work of displacement. The discourse of alien eradication, they argue, can be read as an articulation of the anxiety of the new South African nation about modes of defining belonging. They argue that "the unfolding controversy about indigenous plants and alien-nature became the vehicle for a public debate, as yet unfinished, over the proper constitution of the polity, over the limits of belonging, over the terms in which the nation, the commonweal, and the stakeholding subject are to be constituted in the age of global capitalism and universal human rights. In so doing, it permitted a vocalisation of anxieties and conundrums not easily addressed by politics-as-usual" (2001, 651).

Although Simon Pooley has shown through a careful tracking of the history of the changing definition of what constitutes an "alien" that "debates in South Africa over invasive introduced and indigenous plants" have always "been conducted alongside (and imbricated with) debates about autochthony and national identity" (2010, 613), what emerges in the current moment is the difficulty of thinking ecology and politics together rather than making one an allegory of the other. Trout, like (but also unlike) wolves, pose interesting questions about what constitutes the natural environment. Brown concludes his paper by asking, "How and where do we factor in the complexities of the cultural-social-symbolic, which are integral to human understanding of their interactions with all forms of life, in many cases to their very sense of being and belonging?" (2011, 17). Trout feature as part of Brown's own experience of inhabiting South Africa. They have become part of a cultural practice that in some ways defines his experience of belonging to South Africa as a place rather than a nation. It is an experience associated with a historically white tradition of fishing, a predominantly male activity in which knowledge, practice, and equipment form a particular mode of sociality. Historically, wildlife has played a key role in the production of white South African identities. Before discussing the particular history of the wolves, I want to discuss how the concept of wildness functioned as part of a discourse of nationalism in South Africa in the early to mid-twentieth century. Considerable research has been done in the field of environmental history investigating the ways in which science and ideology intertwined in the production of knowledge about the environment and in the development of practices of conservation in South Africa (see Beinart 2008; Bunn 1996; Carruthers 1995). This scholarship reveals how practices of conservation were intimately linked to the fantasy of belonging to the land. Jane Carruthers's history of the Kruger National Park traces the way in which the development of the park coincides with and is, in part, a result of transformations in the manner in which wild animals were conceptualized in the public imagination in relation to the nation. She notes,

> Its foundation [in 1926] took place at the same time as clear demonstrations of an aggressive, though perhaps still nascent, Afrikaaner nationalism, and a search for a white South African national identity. Among others, these manifestations included a new South African flag, the adoption of Afrikaans as a national language, the revival of interest in Voortrekker traditions, the resurgence of republican sentiment, and the loosening of ties with imperial Britain. . . . These outbursts of political and economic nationalism coincided with the end of the attitude that wildlife was a utilitarian commodity—at least for whites—and with the entrenching of a growing sentimental, romantic and aesthetic view of nature. (1995, 48)

The national park was seen as an important way of fostering national unity between English- and Afrikaans-speaking South Africans. Comments in the press, she notes, stressed wildlife as a common heritage and "how the South African 'character' had to some extent been moulded by the wildlife of the region, while the protection of a 'fairyland' in which 'spiritual regeneration' could take place was important" (Carruthers 1995, 62).

What distinguished white South Africans from other white Europeans was a character that had in some way been forged through contact with wildlife. They had escaped the weakening effects of domestication. This is illustrated by an anecdote about a lion included by soldier Paul J. Els in his memoir, *We Fear Naught but God*. Els relates a story about the training camp Fort Doppies, which he proudly asserts no woman was ever permitted to enter. The story tells of a lion cub, Terry, who was adopted by the Recces (Reconnaissance Commandos) after it could no longer be accommodated at the zoo where it was born. Els notes that "Terry's presence in the area gave a unique atmosphere to the orientation courses where young soldiers raised in the city were given their first taste of life in the bush among some of Africa's most dangerous animals—lions, buffalo, elephants as well as crocodiles, hippos and poisonous snakes. As a sociable young lion, Terry adopted the humans as his family and loved nothing better than a wrestle, a rough and tumble or a swim with the young men in the camp" (2009, 176).

Key to this reconstruction of an idyllic "fairyland" in which wild animals become playmates is the presence of the "Bushman" soldiers. Els writes, "The Bushmen never got over their amazement at seeing South Africa's own 'young lions' befriending and romping with an animal their culture and instincts told them to fear" (117). The friendly recognition by Terry allows Els to assert a connection with wild life both symbolic and real. The young white men are confirmed as belonging in the bush to such an extent that they can be described as "South Africa's own 'young lions,'" and this belonging is confirmed by the "amazed" witnessing by the "Bushmen" soldiers. The lion thus acts as a mediator who through a challenging kind of play, "romping" and "wrestling," produces a particular South African masculinity while at the same time affirming these young white men's place in the bush and their character as "South African." The lion can effect this symbolic transformation in part because of its own status as indigenous and wild. Although born in a zoo in what was then South West Africa, Els comments that "the call of the wild remained strong and Terry would sometimes disappear for days, wandering up to 50 or 60 kilometers from the base" (176). The quality of wildness that makes Terry dangerous is also what makes him fascinating. In withholding violence, he seems to offer a recognition and confirmation of the wildness of these young white soldiers. Although the wolves are not indigenous and so cannot play a role in confirming white belonging, they too are predators drawn into the South African military for reasons that appear more closely allied with fantasy than with military strategy.

Apartheid's Wolves

The material lives of wolves in South Africa are intimately linked to the apartheid government.[7] In an interview with journalist Robyn Dixon in 2004, the founder of the wolf sanctuary, Colleen O' Carroll, explains that she opened the sanctuary to accommodate wolves "left over" from a South African National Defence Force breeding program that aimed to develop wolf dogs for use in various military operations. Dixon comments, "It's not clear how many wolves remain in South Africa, or how the original wolves survived after the projects were abandoned. But the Tsitsikamma sanctuary cares for 35 wolves, has 23 on its waiting list—and is expecting soon to take in a new litter of pure wolf pups from someone connected with one of the original breeding programs. The sanctuary estimates that there are 200 pure wolves in South Africa and tens of thousands of hybrids" (2004). Information about the South African Defense Force wolf dog breeding program is difficult to trace. This is partly because it is, in many ways, a minor event in the history of the apartheid military's many horrifying experiments into "counterinsurgency" strategies. The project was one of many undertaken at the Roodeplaat Breeding Enterprises, a subsidiary of Roodeplaat Research Laboratories (RRL), a front company for what was essentially a military facility that experimented in the development of biological and chemical warfare and methods of social control for the apartheid government. In her doctoral dissertation, Chandre Gould traces the history of the South African biological and chemical warfare program, Project Coast. She notes,

> Some military officials have argued that the primary reason behind the development of the biological warfare facility at the Roodeplaat Research Laboratories (RRL), was to provide an animal testing facility for chemical agents developed at the sister company, Delta G Scientific. Both RRL and Delta G Scientific were military front companies, established to conduct research, and to both develop and produce products for Project Coast. In the event of detection the front companies were meant to shield the CBW programme and disguise its military connections. They also made it easier to import dual-use equipment and other items which may have raised alarms had it been known that they were destined for a military organisation. (2006, 61–62)

The Roodeplaat facility was set up in 1983, when veterinarian Daan Goosen was asked by notorious apartheid doctor and head of the biological weapons program Wouter Basson to set up an animal testing facility for chemical substances. Gould describes that in 1986, due to internal politics, Goosen lost his job at RRL but took up the position as head of Roodeplaat Breeding Enterprises, a facility established on the same property as RRL, which bred dogs for the security forces (Gould 2006, 126–27). In the transcripts of the Truth and Reconciliation Commission's hearings on chemical and biological warfare, the questioner, Hanif Vally, specifically recalls one of the witnesses, General Neethling, from his tendency to dwell on what was occurring at Roodeplaat Breeding Enterprises (Roodepoort Teel Ondernemings) and insists that the focus remain on the experiments in biological warfare being undertaken at RRL.

> GEN NEETHLING: Yes, let's start with RRL. RRL, I heard Dr Goosen. I visited them twice, I visited them three times, and it was about the fact that I was the Head of the South African Police Dog School. This Police Dog School had a very big problem and they had one big problem that was to trace explosives.

MR VALLY: Gen Neethling, I don't want to know about RTO, Roodepoort Teel Ondernemings, I want to know specifically about the biological facility RRL. (Neethling 1998, 778)

Compared with the more macabre work of RRL, which included the manufacture of ecstasy;[8] the development of strains of anthrax, enterobacteria, and botulinum; experiments into ways to cause sterility; and research into novel and effective ways of distributing more conventional toxins (Koekemoer 1998; Van Rensburg 1998), the wolf dog breeding program seems relatively innocuous. Yet in some ways, all these projects can be seen to participate in a similar logic—the chemical or genetic manipulation of nature in order to direct its deadly potential against specified targets. In her article, Dixon explains the rationale for the wolf dog breeding program as the creation of a security dog able to match the perceived threat of the armed struggle against apartheid. She writes that "in the apartheid era, scientists at Roodeplaat Breeding Enterprises imported the animals from North America in an attempt to create an attack dog that would have a wolf's stamina and sense of smell to track down black insurgents in the harsh border regions" (2004).

Various sources identify Peter Geerthsen, "a German-born former professor of genetics" (at the University of Pretoria), as the man in charge of the breeding program. Geerthsen is mentioned in an article published in October 1989 in the *Sunday Times* (London, England) titled "Wolf-Dog Joins Pretoria Forces; South Africa." In this curiously upbeat report, Geerthsen is reported to have explained the breeding program in the following terms: "We're looking for a dog with one or two of the outstanding characteristics of the wolf: its stamina, power, very resistant paw pads, superior coarse hair coat, stronger teeth, better heat resistance and its immunity to hip dysplasia" (Godwin 1989).[9]

Peet Coetzee, in his self-published (and poorly edited) book titled *Dogs of War: Memoirs of the South African Defence Force for Dog Units* (2011), tells a slightly different story. He describes the SADF wolf dog breeding program as starting with the donation of a young male Siberian wolf by the owner of the High Noon game farm, Kevin Wilson, near Villiersdorp to the Defence Force Horse and Dog Centre at Voortrekkerhoogde in 1971. The idea of breeding dogs with wolves, therefore, seems to predate the more formal and scientific breeding project established in the 1980s at Roodeplaat Breeding Enterprises. Coetzee notes, "The immediate dream of deploying Red on the border was immediately smothered by Dr Larendler[10] explaining that the modern dog contained components that the wolf did not have. He explained that the wolf is by nature a shy creature, adding that any wild animal contained the so-called 'wild syndrome.' Through this the fear and hate appears, especially when cornered. . . . By implementing a proper breeding programme a possibly superior and first-rate type of dog could be bred containing genes required and ideal for future needs" (2011, 145). There is evidence to suggest both that wolf dogs moved between the two facilities and that there was a certain amount of rivalry between the SADF dog unit and the ostensibly private company at Roodeplaat. One of Big Red's offspring, a wolf dog named Jungle,[11] reappears at the Roodeplaat facility in Godwin's newspaper report from 1989. "Jungle," Godwin writes, "one of the first generation of wolf dogs, who served with distinction as a tracker dog in the army and is now retired at Roodeplaat, typifies the breed's drawbacks: it takes three strong handlers with chains to put him inside his cage because, according to Geerthsen, 'he still has the wild in him'" (1989).

In the 1980s, the wolf was valued precisely for its suggestive and enigmatic rapacity. Coetzee's book includes several photographs of young white soldiers with their wolf dogs. Like the naming of its armored vehicles "hippo" and "buffel," the military apparatus of apartheid government seemed to value the association with the violence, power, and ruthlessness of wild animals.[12]

The Wit Wolwe was a notorious ultra-right-wing terrorist group that operated in South Africa in the 1980s and 1990s.[13] In the *Dictionary of South African English, wolf* is defined as "any of several mammals bearing some resemblance to the wolf of the Northern Hemisphere, particularly the southern African hyenas (but in some contexts, probably the aardvark or the wild dog)." However, in the memoir of the leader of the group, Barend Strydom, it is made clear by the inclusion of an illustration, "Die embleem van die Wit Wolwe teen die Vierkleur," that the "wolf" that symbolizes the group is not a South African animal but rather the Northern Hemisphere wolf. The image is of the head of the wolf—long muzzle, small pointed ears, and pale eyes—superimposed on the flag of the Transvaal Republic.

In *Die Wit Wolf: 'n Byleidenis* (The white wolf: A testimony), Strydom describes the goals of the Wit Wolwe:

1. Die bevordering van die Protestante Christendom (The development of Protestant Christianity)
2. Die uitkening, openbaarmaking, bestryding van veral die ANC/SAKP-alliansie, Satanisme, Kommunisme, Marxisme, Humanisme, Liberalisme,

Vrymesselary, die Broederbond. Die international Eenwereld-geldmag, met hulle bondgenote en frontorganisasies, met alle middele tot ons beskikking (The discovery, exposure, combating of especially the ANC/SACP-alliance, Satanism, Communism, Marxism, Humanism, Liberalism, Free Masonry, the Broederbond, with all means at our disposal; 1997, 57)

The use of the name "white wolves" utilizes whiteness as the apparently concrete quality that links dissatisfied white South Africans to the Northern Hemisphere wolf to create a metaphorical figure for solidarity and vengeance against this proliferating list of abstract dangers. Although Strydom represents an extreme case, Gould suggests that in the 1980s, the South African government also subscribed to a crudely polarized conceptualization of the world and saw black aspirations to political equality as part of the "total onslaught." She quotes General Magnus Malan, who articulates this extreme sense of ideological and physical threat: "As a point of departure we have to accept that the onslaught here in Southern Africa is communist-inspired, communist-planned and communist-supported. . . . Stalin said it for the first time in 1923 and Brezhnev subsequently reiterated quite a number of times what communism was striving for, was world domination. The onslaught is aimed at the prevailing State structure i.e. the present South African democratic (*sic*) way of life as represented and symbolized by Parliament. . . . The security of the Republic of South Africa must be maintained by every possible means at our disposal" (Malan quoted in Gould 2006, 51).

This intense anxiety about security extended to the white population, more generally creating an atmosphere in which extreme measures appeared necessary and justified. Gould suggests that "fear was instilled in ordinary white South Africans, reinforced by reports of ANC [African National Congress] speeches in which members were called upon to arm themselves. Racism and appeals to whites' fear of Africans became the basis of the total strategy mentality. This created an environment in which it was possible for the scientists who were to drive the chemical and biological warfare programme to justify their actions to themselves as being patriotic" (2006, 51). An intriguing report in a *Farmer's Weekly* issue from 1987 suggests that it was not only the state that saw wolf dogs as the answer to South African security problems. In an article titled "The Wolf Factor," Roy Billet reports on the use of wolves: "Far from keeping the wolves from his door, Ron Selley, who owns a security dog service, welcomes them and is using them to help produce a 'super guard-dog'. The dogs he breeds are crossbreds that are part wolf. They are used to guard orchards in the north-eastern and eastern Transvaal, and sheep at Humansdorp in the eastern Cape" (1987, 29).

In the context of the 1980s, the capacity of the wolf to inspire terror beyond its physical ability to do damage spoke directly to the profound anxiety of white South Africa. The wolf at the door facing outward to defend private property was required to confront the wolf at the door facing inward—the intense hunger of those excluded from property ownership, wealth, and political power. I have not been able to find any further information on Ron Selley's work with wolf dog hybrids, but it does seem that the Roodeplaat Breeding Enterprises project was not a success. In a chapter titled "Operational Border Deployment," Coetzee comments that "where the deployment of wolves are concerned, Johan Roux remembers this encounter with the crossbred wolves which at the time were deployed at Okatopi in Ovamboland. Things that he could remember were those unfriendly yellow eyes that seemed to follow one everywhere. They never barked, and he remembers them not being obedient at all. They only allowed their handler near their kennels. Even the other handlers were rather cat-foot around those yellow-eyed devils" (2011, 214).

The wolf dogs enhance the masculinity of these soldiers by acting as ferocious living weapons but also undermine it, since they are always on the edge of refusing these young men's authority. With their unfriendly yellow eyes and hostile attitude, they are uncanny reminders of the fact that weapons have no loyalty to the person who wields them.

There is an interesting way in which appeals to the wild also seem to serve the purpose of disavowing violence—or, at least, naturalizing it. The wolf as a technology of violence is acting according to its "nature." In a telling incident described by Goosen in his testimony to the Truth and Reconciliation Commission (TRC), Basson requests snake venom in order to displace the military or state violence onto "nature": "Dr Basson would tell us: 'Look, we've got access to this guy, we've infiltrated somewhere, we can get access, close access, we can hold him down, we can inject him and then we can kill a snake next to him and it would make it look to everyone else he was bitten by a snake'" (Goosen 1998, 769). Like the wolf, the snake acts as an extension of the apartheid state's violence but remains outside the law. The fact that a snake must die in order to complete this staging of a "natural death" shows that wild animals were valued both for their metaphorical force and their capacity to cause death but also were entirely instrumentalized. The weaponized snake venom turns the snake into an entirely expendable technology of warfare.

The wolves, unlike the snake, were themselves weaponized. Yet their material life, their temperament, and their physical traits interfered with the working out of the fantasy of violence that they embodied. The lawlessness of the wolves as well as the fact that they were not adapted to the terrain meant that the experiment to deploy them in the border war was not an unqualified success. Coetzee notes, "The assertion that Dr Larendler made in 1982 that crossed wolves would never be successfully utilized on the South West border region was proven right after numerous problems... were experienced. Some of these problems were the thick coat of these animals, the heat and thorns making them suffer to a great extent and rendering them unsuitable for operational utilization and they were withdrawn. The temperament of some of the later litters was surprisingly... friendly and [they made] good trackers" (2011, 147). The fantasy to harness the wolves' wildness could not easily be mapped onto the practical work of security. The legacy of the breeding programs is, however, the existence in South Africa of this unnatural population—according to the founder of the wolf sanctuary, hundreds of wolves and tens of thousands of wolf dog hybrids.

In her book *When Species Meet*, Donna Haraway chooses to mention the apartheid wolf-breeding program as an example of the curious "knots of entangled companion species—wolves, dogs and human beings" (2007, 36) that exist in the contemporary world. Responding to the article by Robyn Dixon, she comments on the proliferation in the postapartheid period of wolf dog hybrids: "The predictable result has been thousands of animals unable to be 'repatriated' to their continent of origin. Both epidemiologically and genetically 'impure,' these canids enter the cultural category of the disposable 'homeless,' or in ecological terms 'nicheless'" (Haraway 2007, 37). The material lives of these apartheid wolves and their descendants are precarious because of the weight of symbolic value attached to the category of wolf within the circuits of meaning of mid-twentieth-century Europe.

In biology, the category species is used to describe a naturally occurring population in which individuals are interbreeding. The apartheid breeding project created an "unnatural population" in which dogs and wolves were brought together for the purpose of creating a new kind of animal—a hybrid in which wildness and domesticity combined in order to fulfill a very specific purpose.

Part eugenics and part fantasy, the project to create wolf dogs by the apartheid state introduces a new dimension to the way in which the wild in South Africa might be conceptualized.

Living with Predators

In some ways, the wolf sanctuary resembles the natural installations I discussed in chapter 2, although the way it has been set up is much more idiosyncratic. The Dzanga-Sangha Rain Forest in the American Museum of Natural History and the Rain Forest Biome at the Eden Project in Cornwall produce, in very different ways, nature as an affective marker, as a texture that supplements and disturbs the concept of nature. The wolf sanctuary, a private though open to the public site, promises to create "a sanctuary and ultimately a 'natural habitat' for the wolves." The word *sanctuary*, originally meaning a holy place, also contains within it the idea of refuge, protection, shelter, and immunity from punishment by the ordinary operations of the law (Oxford English Dictionary). Although by now a familiar term for naming places created to protect animals, reflecting on its etymology reminds us of the particular inflection of its utopian promise. It is a space within society but outside of it, set apart from its laws. The wolves that inhabit this space are, like fugitives, temporarily protected, but only while they remain in their assigned place. The sanctuary also promises, although perhaps with an awareness of the impossibility of this promise signaled by its use of scare quotes, to produce the wolves' "natural habitat." The wolves housed in social groups that in some way resemble the social practices of wolves in nature are also like the natural installations I described earlier, fragments of displaced nature.

In "Of Other Spaces," first published in 1967, Michel Foucault suggests the term *heterotopia* to describe certain spaces produced by cultures that are "a kind of effectively enacted utopia in which the real sites, all the other sites that can be found within the culture, are simultaneously represented, contested, and inverted. Places of this kind are outside of all places, even though it may be possible to indicate their location in reality" (Foucault and Miskoviec 1986, 3–4). Although Foucault was concerned with very different kinds of spaces—the cemetery, the prison, the cinema, the brothel, the colony—the wolf sanctuary fulfills a number of Foucault's criteria for a heterotopia: it is managed space, it is set apart from the surrounding space but is nevertheless accessible, and it attempts to reproduce a particular social arrangement and, in doing so, reflects on the space outside. What the wolf sanctuary offers to reproduce, though in a reduced form, is a part of what is outside—a utopian ideal for the wolves, "their natural habitat." But in doing this, it also reflects on the character of a global culture in which nature has come to stand for a perpetually vanishing ideal.

The tone with which Dixon describes the wolf sanctuary in her report is distinctly melancholy, stressing the difficulty of inserting these political animals into narratives of conservation. Speaking about the founder of the project, Colleen O'Carroll, Dixon writes, "She is the patron of a lost cause. Ask her or McDonald about the future of the wolves at Tsitsikamma, and both look sadly into the distance: 'No future,' they murmur. 'It's a very sad story,' O'Carroll said. 'There's nothing we can do with them. We can't send them back to North America. They're animals in exile'" (2004). Unlike other animal sanctuaries protecting indigenous animals that are threatened in various ways, the wolves can never be part of the mainstream discourse of environmental protection. Neither can they be seen as a national resource, part of what makes South Africa singular in the global popular imaginary.

Foucault notes that another characteristic of a heterotopia is that it might contain "slices of time" (Foucault and Miskoviec 1986, 6). Somewhat contradictorily, the wolf sanctuary is at once a site of nature and the repository of a particular slice of South Africa's past. Like (but also unlike) a museum, it contains artifacts of apartheid history, creatures that act as reminders of the particular way in which nature was conceived of as a resource of violence by members of the apartheid military. In Rose Jolly's discussion of how animals featured in the distribution of violence and guilt in the testimonies at the TRC, she notes that the designation of being "like an animal" shifts between the different positions of perpetrator and victim. The animal is an unstable signifier that produces strange tautologies. Jolly writes,

> What these tautologies betray is the way in which the cult of instrumentalism disguises the question of ethical responsibility. The basic logic of "getting the job done" is one in which perpetrators present themselves as agents in a larger discourse merely fulfilling the will of church, nation or state. Yet when the state . . . is called upon to account for the violence committed in its name by the "animals" it has, in some sense, created, it refuses to do so; suddenly the perpetrators can no longer be termed "animals," because the state needs to attribute agency to the individual as a responsible individual. (2010, 45)

In the case of the wolves, this metaphoric displacement is made actual. The wolves, who are by nature violent (at least in the popular imagination of the apartheid military), are perfect ciphers for enacting a fantasy of violence without responsibility. Like the snake venom and the other bacteriological agents developed in the weapons program, the wolves can be represented as natural-born killers whose acts cannot be called to account by human laws. The fact that the program was unsuccessful, that the violence of wolves could not be directed toward what the army considered the proper targets, simply suggests the recalcitrance of real animals as distinct from their malleability as metaphors.

The wolves represent a knot that cannot be disentangled or undone, a group of unnatural animals whose existence in the wolf sanctuary is seen as fragile and overshadowed by the sign of loss. About the sanctuary, Haraway notes that "this is not an honored truth and reconciliation process trying to meet a socially recognized obligation to those humans forced into a 'becoming with' a scientific racial state apparatus. The sanctuary practices a private charity directed to nonhumans whom many people would see as better killed... in a nation where unaddressed human economic misery remains immense" (2007, 37).

As always, Haraway does not offer an easy answer but instead enjoins us to stay with the trouble. The wolves raise questions about what our responsibility might be to living beings that have been engineered for specific purposes but have become redundant. Yet it is not, or not only, the material lives of these wolves—who are being cared for, if in a somewhat haphazard and precarious way—that is at stake here. Instead, I am interested in what they reveal about wild animals more generally as entering into or being excluded from the nature industry. They cannot fall into the category of "endangered species." They do not provide the satisfaction of, for instance, a sanctuary for wild dogs or even for baboons. "Nicheless," they suggest that part of the sentiment associated with animals has to do with their attachment to location: part of the attraction of animals lies in the fact of their belonging to a particular place.

The wolves are described as a "lost cause" and "animals in exile" who cannot be sent back to their home. They are uncomfortable reminders of the precariousness of white South African's claim to belong in the new polity. At the same time, the wolf sanctuary website indicates their identifications with an international initiative dedicated to the "survival of the wolf around the world," a different kind of belonging. Through aligning itself with recent projects to reintroduce wolves into various places in Europe and North America from which they were eradicated, the wolf sanctuary creates an enclave of the global within the ground of the national. Yet for both the sanctuary and the rewilding projects, the wild predator's potential for violence remains, a knot where the materiality of animals' lives comes against human fantasies and desires.

Throughout their history in South Africa, the wolves have been ambiguous figures, admired and desired for their strength but at the same time relentlessly unforgiving of human weakness. In Coetzee's account, the level yellow gaze of the wolf dogs unmans the soldiers, making them "cat-foot" around the cages, presumably a metaphoric adaptation of the English figure of speech *pussyfooted*, but one that in its awkwardness conveys precisely the way fear might act on the human body to make it animal. The soldiers can only imperfectly assert their authority over these creatures. They are ultimately remaindered because too much of the "wild" remains within them. At the sanctuary, they remain prone to hostility, even, as the article suggests, toward McDonald, who provides their food.

I want to end this chapter with two points of contact where material animals confront humans not as metaphors but as complex subjects. Toward the beginning of this chapter, I told the story of Terry the lion as a way of illustrating the way in which indigenous wildlife was deployed by white South Africans as a way of asserting their identification with the land. There is a certain sad familiarity to the development of the story that, needless to say, ends badly for Terry. By the age of two and a half, Terry's strength and "wildness" threatened to overwhelm his frail human companions. After an attempt to chase him from the camp into the bush fails, a task assigned to the "Bushmen soldiers," the lion is shot by the base commander, who Els describes as "one of Terry's best friends" (2009, 177). What Terry's story reveals is the way that, within the context of the instrumental logic of the military training camp, the lion could be both intensely valued and completely disposable, sentiment and violence existing in close proximity.

The second point of contact is between Michael McDonald and the wolves:

McDonald, 42, used to work "in security" but won't be more specific.

Now he cares for the wolves—with no salary or even a pension, often surviving on the same meat the wolves eat: unwanted cow and calf carcasses donated by dairy farmers. He has few belongings and no money for clothes. He once had to pawn a watch to pay for the sanctuary's gasoline, and other times walked to collect dead cows with a wheelbarrow.

"It's a seriously hard life," he said.

Ask him why he does it and he sidesteps the question with a flurry of self-deprecating banter: "There was no one else to do it."

But he feels the wolves are his destiny, even if they don't always appreciate him.

The wolves, always ready to challenge the alpha, sometimes bite McDonald. But the day a female named Cleo nipped him on the rump, he felt a strange elation. (Dixon 2004)

In his discussion of Gregory Bateson's essay on animal play, Brian Massumi notes, "The difference between biting and nipping is what opens the analogical gap between combat and play. It is the style of the gesture that opens the minimal difference between the play gesture and its analogue in the area of combat" (2014, 5). Bateson's essay was inspired by watching two monkeys playing in the San Francisco Zoo. A very different relation exists between McDonald and the wolf, yet to nip is an act of recognition. It is an invitation to play. McDonald, whose past is not revealed and whose existence seems as precarious as that of the wolves themselves, without the security of a salary or pension, is, in that moment, invited to engage in an act of animal metaphoricity, to recognize a bite that is not a bite. His elation can be understood as a response to this invitation to belong with the wolves.

A Slice of Time

In the twenty-first century, to belong with wild predators has become a peculiarly seductive fantasy. Werner Hertzog's documentary *Grizzly Man* records Timothy Treadwell's attempts to enact this fantasy with grizzly bears. The term *rewilding*—which describes the restoration of an area to a natural, uncultivated state and the reintroduction of species that have vanished—was first recorded in the dictionary in 2011. The term's inclusion in the dictionary registers a shift in attitudes toward nature. The predator no longer stands for the feared and celebrated amoral killer but is regarded instead as a necessary part of the ecosystem. In his book *Feral*, George Monbiot devotes one chapter to the reintroduction of predators. While providing a carefully reasoned scientific argument for the reintroduction of the wolf to Britain on ecological grounds (the reduction of red deer and foxes), he acknowledges that it would be deceptive to claim that his interest in rewilding is purely instrumental. He writes, "I want to see wolves introduced because wolves are fascinating, and because they help to reintroduce the complexity and trophic diversity in which our ecosystems are lacking. I want to reintroduce wolves because they feel to me like the shadow that fleets between the systole and diastole, because they are the necessary monsters of the mind, inhabitants of a more passionate world against which we have locked our doors" (2013, 117).

What is interesting about Monbiot's reasoning is that it moves between a scientific attachment to the ecosystem and the promotion of "trophic diversity" and the more ephemeral claim that wolves act on the human psychic life in a profound way. His wolves, exemplary of "a more passionate world" that has been excluded by modernity, are both material creatures and figural "monsters of the mind," the one providing the necessary substance for the other.

Treadwell, like Monbiot, desires proximity with the bears for emotional reasons. But he enters the domain of the bears as a visitor for a given space of time. Even if the bears provide the meaning for his life, what sustains his life in material terms is elsewhere. He has no need to share the resources of nature with the bears. His act of ceding control, of voluntarily putting his body at risk, is, despite the urgency of his emotion, an act that is superfluous, a display of leisure. Like Monbiot, who returns, after his own urgent and often risky encounters with nature, to his house, the wild is an addition to a life sustained and reproduced elsewhere. Both are engaged in the somewhat contradictory project—the voluntary enactment of necessity. This is not to discredit the efforts and desires of either but rather to draw attention to what is overlooked—those lives lived in actual proximity to wild animals. Treadwell and his girlfriend, Amie Huguenard, are eventually killed and eaten by a hungry grizzly bear at the end of the season, long after they would usually have returned to their lives in modern America. But for many people in the postcolony, living with wild predators remains not a privilege but a threat to both life and livelihood. For people such as those represented in Zimbabwean novelist and filmmaker Tsitsi Dangarembga's documentary on elephant conservation, *Elephant People*, battling with elephants or other wild animals over the resources to survive, the vulnerability is not a choice but a condition of life.

These fragments from the history of the wolf in South Africa disturb the way in which the twenty-first-century nature has become the new moral goal from which history can conveniently be exorcized. To think of the wolf sanctuary as a heterotopic space allows us to move beyond the simple question of whether it represents an effective deployment of resources. The sanctuary is a "slice of time" that provides an embodied reminder of a specifically South

African history of violence. But it also refers beyond this to a historical moment in the wider production of the wild, when the predator figured as a model of strength and masculine vitality. As the bearer of a liberating violence, the predator was celebrated in the middle of the twentieth century as a corrective to the limiting domesticity of a technique of life organized around commodities and managed consumption. This defiant response to the specific condition of capitalist estrangement slides easily into an essentialized form of fascist self-assertion, selectively referring to attributes of the wolf to make judgments about the relative worth of people.

Yet the sanctuary does not only refer to the past. It is also, like the Eden Project, a defense against future loss. As an enclaved space, it in some ways resembles or reflects a utopian ideal of contemporary global society—the preservation of nature and animals restored to their natural habitat, divided into packs so that they might enact the social order of the wild wolf. The place is a sanctuary, but it is also a prison. These wolves that in South Africa have no place outside of this enclaved and highly managed space are held as genetic repositories against a future catastrophic extinction—the end of the wolf as a species. Caught between a past history of violence and an imagined future of extinction, the wolves in their sanctuary, nipping and snarling their way into the twenty-first century, are a reminder that the time of nature is also historical time. These wolves are biological specimens, but as specific animals, they do not go into the concept of nature without leaving as a remainder this trace of history and violence and loss.

6

Privatizing Nature

The more purely nature is preserved and transplanted by civilization, the more implacably it is dominated. We can now afford to encompass ever larger natural units, and leave them apparently intact within our grasp, whereas previously the selecting and taming of particular items bore witness to the difficulty we still had in coping with nature.

—Adorno

Mutation

Golden wildebeest, white lions with blue eyes, black or white impalas, and white kudus are all mutant variations bred specifically for the trophy hunting industry. Barry York, who bought his farm in Limpopo Province in 2007, justifies his breeding of rare mutations with the claim that the farm, previously devoted to crop farming with the associated pesticides, has now become the home to returning wildlife of all kind—jackals, bat-eared foxes, and caracals as well as troops of monkeys. Journalist Kevin Crowley notes, "South Africa is one of only two countries on the continent to allow ownership of wild animals, giving farmers such as York an incentive to switch from raising cattle to breeding big game" (2015). Color variants are believed to be the result of a recessive gene and have to be artificially maintained through separating breeding populations. In the wild, they do not confer any advantage on the animals and are often associated with susceptibility to specific diseases. Yet their appearance confers on them the distinction of rarity, and this makes them uniquely valuable to certain hunters. Like the wolves discussed in the previous chapter, they are not exemplary representatives of their respective species. Instead, they can be read as parts that stand for a new whole—wild nature entirely administered and shaped by consumer desire.

In this chapter, I turn to the private game reserve as a third site of the production of nature and one that takes on particular significance in the era of environmental crisis. In the last years of the twentieth century, as the effect of human activity on the environment becomes widespread, private game reserves emerge as a commercial and ideological response to the idea of nature's fragility. The private nature reserve, like the diamond mine and the wolf sanctuary, can be read as a fragment of nature that acts as a form of intensified reality, an emphatic and condensed site of the nature industry. The proliferation of high-end private game reserves, particularly (though not exclusively) in Africa, testifies to this new symbolic and emotional investment in nature. Unlike national reserves, whose proclamation makes nature at least conceptually a public resource, the domain of the nation, these reserves privatize nature, withdrawing it from the public realm. Though they do this no more than any other private property, such as farms or industrial sites, they do so in a particular way. The fact that land is reserved not for "use" but specifically as "nature" opens up a puzzling new category in the history of the transformation of space into resource or commodity. In "The Idea of Nature," Raymond Williams suggests that in England during the nineteenth century, the commodification of nature as scenery emerges as a by-product of the transformation of nature into a resource by industry. Although similar in many ways, private game reserves appear to be commodifying nature not as scenery but as essence. While participating in the global tourist industry, these reserves frame their ownership of land in Africa in terms of a global duty to preserve "nature" and the environment.[1]

The conservation of nature in reserves has a long history. Increasing anxiety about the disappearance of game at the end of the nineteenth century led to the establishment of reserves in a number of colonies and former colonies around the world. Initially these took the form of private hunting clubs. Historians William Beinart and Peter Coates explain that "if the medieval hunting park and chase of royalty and nobility provided a cultural reference point, nevertheless the modern version was more likely to be an associative or company venture that made opportunities available to the wealthy" (1995, 29). In South Africa, one of the oldest game reserves is the Rooipoort private game reserve near Kimberley. Established by Rhodes in 1893, it remains owned by De Beers, which now also owns a number of other private reserves.[2]

Game reserves—and private game reserves in particular—have a long history of participating in the work of the ritual affirmation of worth. In Veblen's argument, the two marks of status he considers most significant are conspicuous consumption and conspicuous leisure. The private game reserve offers a stage for the expenditure of both. The chapter will discuss the way in which this expenditure takes place in two domains—first through the design, construction, and symbolic logic of the lodge as a specific form of domestic space, and second through the practice of the trophy hunt as a reinvention of the exploit. The lodge Rhodes had constructed at Rooipoort in 1899 to accommodate "hunters and personal friends" is named the "Shooting Box" and was imported from England in its entirety and assembled from a kit.[3] The name evokes the aristocratic privilege of owning good hunting land and the practice of assembling a shooting party during hunting season. Rhodes, whose family "land" in the East End of London had already been turned into row houses by his property-speculating grandfather and great-uncle,[4] translates what is a generic category into a proper name, accruing to himself the value that had become sedimented in the phrase through its long association with aristocratic leisure and honorific exploit.

The history of the national game reserve in Africa has already been written both as a project of settler conservation that, along with agriculture, displaced the indigenous population from the land and as performing a certain ideological work in the production of the white nation in South Africa after its union in 1910. In this chapter, I investigate instead the private game reserve as framing two modes of encountering nature. In the first, the private game reserve serves as a place of conspicuous leisure; in the second, the space of exploit. The lodges designed for these reserves are deliberately aligned with a new conception of nature. In fact, the game lodges represent an interesting development in the ongoing production of a specifically African nature. By this I mean the production of African nature through representation but also the production of African nature as a particular kind of destination. Game lodges are not only representations—they are material rearrangements of space.

Usually at the center of large open spaces, they become hubs for the accretion of objects of various kinds. They are dense sites of engagement between people, between people and objects, and between species of various kinds. The game lodge acts as a site that mediates a particular kind of relationship between people and nature. Around the game lodge, there emerges a new discursive mode for articulating Africa and South Africa's relationship with the world—a novel aesthetic known as the "new safari."[5] Yet this new conception of nature also permits space for the older form of the safari that persists in an abbreviated form in the practice of the trophy hunt. Although the trophy hunt represents a different form of engagement with nature than the one mediated by the elaborately designed lodge, the experience remains one located in the establishment and display of status.

I begin by investigating a constellation of elements that contribute to the formation of this category named the "new safari." It is a design category, but one that goes beyond design to construct a moral and experiential fantasy that centers on the game lodge. It draws its value from an array of sources: a moralizing discourse about the environment, a celebration of the premodern and the traditional, and a nostalgic fantasy about the modern. These are all offered as areas of culture that hold the potential for a rediscovery of authenticity in the flattened age of capitalist modernity. My discussion focuses on some of the ephemeral texts through which this fantasy is articulated—an advertisement, some publicity material, and a design monograph. These all participate in the fugitive language of leisure, where pleasure and indulgence are expected to dominate. They reframe a worn set of fantasies at once threadbare and yet remarkably persistent. Their very persistence suggests that such invocations still hold considerable auric power. My discussion will begin with a consideration of conservation not as a practice but rather as an imagined value that makes possible a rethinking of the relation between the national and the global. The universalizing discourse of moral authority is then placed in relation to some concrete texts, a controversial Land Rover advertisement, and an interior design monograph, *The New Safari: Design, Décor, Detail*, which features a selection of lodges from private game reserves in South Africa. In the final section on the trophy hunt, I discuss the extension of design into the genetic form of the animals themselves, shaping nature to consumer desire. Referring to two cases of startling or surprising spikes in value, I discuss wild animals in the era of the Anthropocene as focalizers who bring into striking proximity very different regimes of value.

The Alibi of the Environment

In his satirical piece "How to Write About Africa," Binyavanga Wainaina makes the following comment about one of the main genres within which Africa is represented—the conservation narrative. He observes, "Often a book cover with a heroic-looking conservationist on it works magic for sales. Anybody white, tanned and wearing khaki who once had a pet antelope or a farm is a conservationist, one who is preserving Africa's rich heritage. When interviewing him or her, do not ask how much funding they have; do not ask how much money they make off their game. Never ask how much they pay their employees" (2005, 94). Satire provides for the interesting possibility of condensation. Wainaina's brief comment contains reference to a huge disorganized archive of statements about Africa and nature that circulate within a number of different contexts. They are written and spoken. They appear in advertising copy, magazine articles, news articles, travel and wild life programs, and everyday conversation. They are the apparently innocuous, slightly worn currency of a particular form of exchange and range from pure cliché to a kind of received wisdom, a convention of thinking that is both familiar and easy.

The complexity of this discourse is that it works at the intersection of two widely divergent registers. If, on the one hand, it revels in clichés from the realm of commercial advertising, on the other, it adopts the profound seriousness of discourse about the environment. It demands to be taken seriously as an ethical project while at the same time requiring indulgence for its repetition of the generalizations and catch phrases of commercial advertising.

Wainaina's comment draws attention to some of these contradictions. Writing about Africa, his piece suggests, permits a certain imprecision, a blurring of categories. Conservation in Africa opens up a new space in which whites can reinvent themselves heroically without worrying too much about the effects of their intervention. He draws attention to the gap between the rhetoric of self-congratulation associated with conservation and the economic and social reality of such enterprises.

What emerges as new in this contradictory discursive formation is yet another strange juxtaposition, the inclusion of "style" and the arrangement of objects alongside the value associated with the project of global environmentalism. As sites of a set of global and local desires relating to nature, land, and identity, private game reserves are "dense assemblages." They invite study of the developments in what might be called the global commercial moral economy—the complex relationship between moral and commercial value. Before continuing with a discussion of the emergence of a particular kind of aesthetic associated with the game lodge, I will discuss the use within the rhetoric of the reserve of "the environment" and sometimes nature itself as a sign of unassailably positive value.

In a book called *The Myth of Wild Africa*, Jonathan Adams and Thomas McShane express their concern about the way in which the West approaches conservation in Africa. They suggest that "wildlife conservation has become one of the most visible and contentious areas of contact between Africa and the west. The efforts to save Africa's natural heritage has, justifiably, been seen as an unquestioned good, practically a moral duty for the developed world" (1992, xiv). The "environment" appears to evoke a kind of moral self-righteousness that permits and indeed justifies interventions of various kinds. It offers itself as an absolute value, and the claims of the environment are represented, in certain contexts, as superseding all others. This is evident in some of the publicity material associated with various game lodges operating out of South Africa. The publicity material of Wilderness Safaris, for instance, reveals a nuanced reading of the value associated with nature in the era of global modernity. Its home page begins with the following statement: "At Wilderness Safaris we believe that in the world's wilderness areas lies the preservation of humankind. We want to make a difference in people's lives by enabling them to find new paths, and by leaving a legacy of conservation for our children" (Wilderness Safaris n.d.).[6] The phrase "the world's wilderness areas," on the surface an innocuous reference to wilderness areas in different parts of the world, reinforced by the reference to "humankind," works to divorce the notion of wilderness from specific localities. This deterritorializing of wilderness performs a mediating function. It constructs the wilderness as both an abstraction and a concrete destination. It also separates the notion of wilderness from national borders. Wilderness appears to exist outside the boundaries of national states and their particular political and social complexities.

An advertising pamphlet produced for the tour company Wild Frontiers provides another example: "Wide open plains covered with game, proud tribal warriors, snow-capped mountains, white sandy beaches, dark forests and deep lakes—real Africa. With a large portion of its area dedicated to the conservation of flora and fauna, Tanzania is the place for true nature lovers and people who appreciate wild places" (*Wild Frontiers* n.d., inside cover). The list described in the Wild Frontiers pamphlet makes it clear that what constitutes the real of Africa is everything that escapes the real of modern consumer society. Everything mentioned carries with it the aura of an unalienated life. Everything is animate, flourishing in the absence of the political, the economic, and even the social. The "proud warriors" can be included here because they are situated in a mythical prehistorical "tribal" period. Their battles cannot touch the modern visitor who travels as an individual in a different order of time. Wild Frontiers is a tour operator rather than a landowner. Unlike Wilderness Safaris, whose publicity material performs a far more complex task of legitimation, Wild Frontiers only needs to align itself with an already existing ethic of conservation associated with Tanzania and to reassure potential customers that "all ... operations are run in an environmentally aware manner." What such a claim masks is the particularly controversial nature of conservation in Tanzania. For a poor rural population, conservation, or the deliberate setting aside of land that could otherwise be used for hunting or grazing as "nature," is not likely to constitute an unquestioned good.[7]

The publicity material of both Wilderness Safaris and Wild Frontiers, in common with almost all material in the genre, reiterates terms such as *untouched*, *pristine*, *unspoiled*, and *empty*. Yet on further investigation, it becomes apparent that the landscape of the private game reserve is always a landscape with things. Partially obscured by the narrative of emptiness, there emerges a proliferation of objects whose configuration is necessary to frame the experience of nature.

The 4×4

Private game reserves are what anthropologist James Ferguson (2006, 42) calls "guarded enclaves" linked into the global economy through technology but separate from the surrounding land and society. Despite a move toward a more "community-orientated" approach to conservation, the space of the reserve remains defended from the encroachment of those considered poachers or trespassers.[8] For visitors, charter flights and transfers by the reserve mean that their experience of "Africa" is highly managed. The experience of nature itself is also guided. In Wilderness Safaris' travel information document, the following description of the safari itself is included: "Our safari vehicles are open 4×4 vehicles and are designed for all guests to have all-round visibility. There are some exceptions to this in order to accommodate certain environmental conditions such as excessive dust and/or heat" (Wilderness Safaris n.d.). One of the significant objects associated with the reserve is the 4×4. In a comprehensive reflection on the history of the automobile in colonial Africa, Gordon Pirie (2008) observes that the car forms a significant part of the colonial fantasy of conquest despite the lack of reliably passable roads. The 4×4, whose commercial popularity in the developed world coincides with the gradual disappearance of the kinds of terrain that would make them useful, is redeemed in the game park from the realm of fantasy. In this context, it becomes a functional mode of transport. In a discussion about the authenticity of objects, Jean Baudrillard comments on an architect's restoration of an old farmhouse. He mentions in particular an antique warming pan, which is displayed as part of the interior decor of the restored house. The architect, however, emphasizes that this warming pan is not merely decorative: it is also functional and is used during winter. Despite the fact that the house also has a more modern heating system, the warming pan, Baudrillard suggests, must retain its functionality in order to confer on the house a sense of authenticity. He writes, "Yet if it is not used it will no longer be authentic, will become mere cultural sign: the cultural, purposeless warming pan will emerge as an all-too-faithful image of the vanity of the attempt to retrieve a natural state of affairs by rebuilding this house—and, indeed, an all-too-faithful image of the architect himself, who fundamentally has no part to play here, his entire social existence lies elsewhere; his very being is elsewhere, and for him nature is nothing more than a cultural luxury" (1996, 83). In a similar though not identical way, the 4×4 in Africa confers authenticity on the experience. Reunited with its use value, the 4×4 becomes a technology for switching between the fantasy of adventure and the real of Africa.

For the 4×4 to perform this role, the inherent contradictions between the fantasy and the real need to be carefully managed. An incident of mismanagement by Land Rover and the advertising agency they employed reveals the ideological work being done in holding the 4×4 as a consumer object in this complex position. Visual culture theorist Jeanne Van Eeden describes the advertisement, which was published in a number of glossy magazines aimed at the men's market, including *African Environment and Wildlife*, *Car*, and *Complete Fisherman*. The advertisement represents an almost empty landscape containing a Himba woman in traditional dress of animal skins and ornaments. (The Himba, Van Eeden explains, are nomadic herders who live in northern and western Namibia.) The advertisement shows the woman with breasts unnaturally distorted to mimic objects swayed by the passing air of the Land Rover, which appears on the following page (2006, 344). In a detailed analysis of the advertisement, Van Eeden argues that it participates in a number of imperial mythologies about Africa and about the relation between white male explorers and indigenous inhabitants. She suggests that "the Himba advertisement romanticizes the notion of colonial adventure as the triumph of European knowledge and imperialism" (353). While this is no doubt the case, the advertisement clearly does more.

The advertisement was met with considerable indignation and, after a judgment by the Advertising Standards Authority in South Africa, was later withdrawn.[9] What is interesting, however, is the response of the representative of the advertising company, Hunt Lascaris, to the judgment. They stated that "it had been conceived as a 'harmless parody and exaggeration designed to amuse the consumer' and explained that a multiracial pilot study had found it inoffensive" (Van Eeden 2006, 349, quoting Jacobs 2000, 3). In a statement included in an article in *Leadership* magazine, Moira-Ann Moses, managing director of Land Rover in South Africa, explains that "it was not our intention to offend people." She also comments elsewhere that "quite a lot of men phoned in to say they had enjoyed the ad and that people who were offended should not be so sensitive" (quoted in Van Eeden 2006, 350). Both the representative of the advertising company and the men who called in to praise the advertisement stress the nonseriousness of the representation, which is designed to be enjoyed and to amuse. They share an assumption about what should be included within the category of the humorous.

The contestation of the Land Rover advertisement brings to the surface the contradictions lurking beneath apparently innocuous modes of representation. It is hard to imagine an advertisement showing a seminaked white man, his penis swinging sideways to point longingly after a passing Land Rover, though this might more accurately reflect the structure of desire contained in the scene. Such a scene, though potentially humorous, did not present itself to the advertisers as containing the appropriate circulation of value. I introduce this not simply as a "harmless parody" but rather to draw attention to the way the limits of the discourse become evident at the point at which something no longer appears funny.

The advertisement through its representation pushed the limits of the discursive field in such a way as to make its underlying structure visible. The representation of the Himba woman, with digitally distorted breasts, foregrounds what the advertisement was supposed to hide—that the relation of ownership is never one simply between the object and its owner but always includes the wider social structure that, among other things, protects private property. The fantasy the advertisement spins around the Land Rover has to do with freedom and escape. The Land Rover, the advertisement suggests, makes possible the fulfillment of a masculine dream to exit the constraints of society and to assume the heroic role of an individual in an unmediated relation with nature. But the satisfaction of this return to nature is predicated on an audience. The rural black woman, whose social existence is in this case intimately bound up with the natural world and for whom the Land Rover might in fact prove a useful vehicle, disturbs the authenticity of this fantasy by threatening to reveal it as mere vanity. The distortion of her breasts considered from this perspective might be read as a childish act of violence designed to diffuse the threat she poses. It is humorous only to those who resent any disturbance to the fantasy in which they are prepared to make a substantial economic investment.

In a strange way, the Himba woman in the advertisement occupies precisely the position that the tourist investing in a safari wishes to regain. She occupies a central position in an empty yet beautiful landscape. Yet what she references is not what the tourist industry's publicity material might wish to communicate. Her race, her class, and her nationality all force upon her a relation with nature that is material, not spiritual. She is subjected to a different "nature," though it may literally occupy the same space. What constitutes this absolute difference? What makes one human's place in the wilderness so different from another's? In order to understand the tourist's return to nature as the return to a different nature from the one occupied by the Himba woman, it is necessary to consider how the tourist's experience is framed both literally and symbolically by the careful design of the lodge.

The Lodge

In a peculiarly sympathetic reading of tourism, cultural theorist Fred Inglis, in *The Delicious History of the Holiday*, suggests that we should take our desires for luxury seriously. He suggests that "luxury has migrated into that realm of the social imagination where our art, our politics, our ethics struggle together to replace the communality of shared religion, and where as a result, we do what we can to picture paradise" (2000, 7). Holiday destinations, he argues, represent "attempts to render that ideal home" (7). The holiday, he suggests, brings into question the mode in which we imagine well-being and involves the prefiguring of the good life; therefore, our conceptualization of the holiday cannot be entirely separated from concern with moral questions. Inglis's discussion focuses on the mass circulation of English and European tourists during the Northern Hemisphere summer. While the game lodge caters to an altogether different holidaying constituency, it is useful to consider in what way the lodge too can be read as the articulation of a particular notion of well-being. By their nature exclusive, game lodges enter the wider public domain through the medium of the popular interior design monographs. Occupying an intermediary space between advertisement and publication, these coffee-table books serve both as promotional material and as a visual source, indexing the latest trends in interior design.[10] They feature artistic, full-color photographs alongside brief narratives that are an uneasy mix of poetry, advertising copy, and spiritual celebration. *The New Safari* is a slight variation on this familiar genre. It is one of a number of books that attempt to reclaim the notion of *safari* from its past association with European imperial travel and colonialism and to reinsert it in a new rhetorical structure linked with the "moral value" of environmentalism and the glamour of globalization and cutting-edge style.[11] Yet the status of the colonial remains curiously ambiguous. It lurks on the edges of the concept, not wholly discarded but rather overlaid by a new set of associations.

The photographer of *The New Safari*, Craig Fraser,[12] introduces the book with a reflection on the particular and unique features it attempts to capture: "One of the most exciting evolutions in the industry has been the fresh definition of the term Safari Style. Gone are the conventional rustic and overly-colonial style offerings we've come to expect. Instead, material and objects (some traditional, some contemporary) are being rethought, reworked and reinterpreted, resulting in architecture and interiors that are both site-appropriate and exhilaratingly original" (Fraser and Allen 2007, 5). I was struck by the term "overly-colonial." *Colonial* here appears to refer not so much to a specific historical period as to a particular set of objects and aesthetic values. The colonial as style but also as a particular set of practices that included "going on safari" is the partially rejected starting point for the new safari. It is the ambiguity of the colonial that the endless definitions and redefinitions of the new safari have to negotiate. Because if as style, it can be regarded as simply one aesthetic among others, as a set of practices, it includes, like the old safari, institutionalized forms of racial discrimination.

To be "overly-colonial" might be to evoke too clearly the disturbing practices of colonialism, which the new safari wishes to supersede.

In order to achieve this shift away from the past, the reworking of all aspects of the physical surroundings must be complete. All aspects of the environment, the frame or stage for this new experience, must be controlled. Unlike the old safari, the new safari is a conceptual rather than a physical challenge. It relies on the innovative work of professional architects and designers to structure a space in which nature and Africa can be experienced without the interference of the past. The lodge must perform the difficult task of physically embodying a compromise. It must reference the past but at the same time be emptied of that past. Fraser goes on to describe the particular significance of the lodges included in the book: "The camps and lodges included here have been selected for their pioneering spirit and dedication to creating a safari experience beyond the ordinary—a shared passion that finds expression in innovative architecture, design, décor and detailing. Regardless of whether they display an organic base or possess ultramodern sensibilities, each of these lodges has been designed to offer a memorable, life-enriching adventure that touches the soul" (Fraser and Allen 2007, 5). The lodge, it appears, must be emptied of the past so that it can be freed to fulfill its role as the space for "life-enriching adventures that touch the soul." The notion that nature—"pristine nature," as it is often called—is the site for spiritual renewal is not the exclusive domain of the new safari. It is a romantic notion that formed a part of the motivation for the old nineteenth-century safaris as well as their twentieth-century reinventions. What is new about the spiritual experience in the twenty-first century is that it requires detailing. The word *detailing* is at once technical and also wonderfully suggestive. It implies the need for absolute attention to detail so that no area of the space—no visual, auditory, or olfactory sensation—might disturb the complete experience.

In the foreword to the book, Liz Morris, editor of the South African version of the glossy international interior and landscape design magazine *Condé Nast House and Garden*, explains that the new safari "is an inspired surge of design that will be seen as a turning point in South Africa's design identity, and may even come to define it. Apart from a slew of great and tuned-in architects, designers and product developers, the New Safari couldn't have happened without the liberation of the country in 1994. Nor could it have happened without the platform of sound conservation standards and principles which have allowed the flourishing development of safari lodges and consequently the safari design discipline" (Fraser and Allen 2007, 8). Morris here, in a delightfully throwaway phrase, attributes the emergence and success of the new safari evenhandedly to the liberation of the country in 1994, the presence of great architects and designers, and the existence of sound conservation practices. It is as if, on the one hand, the liberation of the country freed both architects and designers and, on the other, conservationists from the demands of both politics and history—freed the colonial to become style and Africa to become a new lifestyle aesthetic. She goes on to note that "African-inspired lifestyle products are now so firmly sewn into the fabric of our daily domestic existence that it is a wrench to recall a time when empty ostrich eggs were not used as light fittings and bowls" (8). The new safari is, importantly, not simply a development in the aesthetic design of game lodges. It can also be brought home as part of a lifestyle aesthetic and can be used to transform the design of our interior domestic spaces. This value associated with the reserve can accrue in particular objects or lifestyle products, which can then be used to add value to the domestic space.

I am interested in trying to understand this complex composite value, which is at once site specific and mobile. The new safari emphasizes the spiritual but also leisure and luxury. In this, it is not very different from the old safari. It also relies on the moral value associated with environmentalism. The experience of leisure and luxury can be justified because this is merely a side effect of the real work of the reserve, which is to preserve nature for the good of humankind. What is new, however, is this emphasis on aesthetic value. It is through design, through detailing, that the range of apparently contradictory elements—the contemporary and the traditional, the African, the organic, and the ultramodern—can be mediated. What emerges is the sheer extent of cultural work that has to be done in order for the space of the lodge to perform its function as the frame or stage for the experience of pristine nature.

Morris praises the Singita Lodge, the first one to be represented in the book, as one of the first articulations of the new safari. She explains its appeal in the following way: "It provided moody drama, antiques, mystery, nostalgia, style and dressiness, the glamour of a Hollywood set and grand wood, glass and grass architecture in a thicket of huge canopy trees" (Fraser and Allen 2007, 9). Later in the monograph, the dramatic nature of Singita's architecture is emphasized. It includes "large vertical planes of glass exploring the idea of boundaryless space and offering the privileged visitor a dramatic encounter with both heaven and earth" (11). Morris describes Singita Lodge explicitly as a stage or a Hollywood film set. It provides the extreme artifice necessary to frame and to mediate the encounter between the visitor and pristine nature. Through the lodge, a curious rhetorical structure is established at the intersection of science, modernity, excess, fantasy, and colonial nostalgia that facilitates a particular kind of control and exchange of nature as a high-end global commodity.

Although not one of the lodges featured in *The New Safari* design monograph, the Serra Cafema Lodge provides an interesting point of contact between my earlier discussion of the Land Rover advertisement and my discussion of the lodge. Located in northern Namibia, the lodge is run by Wilderness Safaris through Tshokwane Safaris (which also lists Singita as one of their "partners"). Unlike Singita, the architecture of Serra Cafema is not dramatic. On the website, it is described merely as a "small rustic and peaceful camp with all the comforts" (Tshokwane Safaris n.d.), yet the photographs that accompany the text reveal that this is also a place in which detailing has taken place. The open-plan layout; the wicker chairs; the neutral colors; the carefully positioned lamps; the uneven, unfinished wood of the railing; and the copper basins suggest that even if the structure itself is modest, the placement of objects is still critical to the project of the lodge. The detailing in this case, however, is less overtly concerned with dramatic staging. Instead, the lodge in both its design and its decor emphasizes continuity between indoors and outdoors within an overall aesthetic of modernist functionalism softened by an unmodernist attachment to natural fibers and materials. Though tented, it avoids overt references to the earlier colonial safari. It does not include the iconic mosquito net or other classic objects of the nineteenth-century safari: the wooden chest, the rifle, the animal skin.

On the Serra Cafema Camp website, what is emphasized about the lodge is its remoteness. It is described as one of the remotest of camps, "reachable only by light aircraft." At the same time, the essential singularity of the camp is that it "shares this region with wonderful Himba people who are some of the last true nomadic people in Africa" (Tshokwane Safaris n.d.). The Serra Cafema Camp thus occupies a populated wilderness, which makes the negotiations about its relation to the environment it occupies more complex. The Wilderness Safaris website describes the relationship between the lodge and the local inhabitants as follows:

> This lifestyle, so different from many others', is fascinating to visitors and it is important, when meeting the Himba, to maintain the delicate balance necessary to be able to share this insight without impacting negatively on the people and their customs. Wilderness Safaris' Serra Cafema and Skeleton Coast Camp are both situated within

> Himba territory, and have approached the Himba people with respect, creating a positive relationship between the camps and the community. Serra Cafema Camp has excellent relationships with the local Himba villages and the regular guest visits to these villages are good examples of mutually beneficial and sensitive cultural tourism. (Wilderness Safaris n.d.)

The phrasing of this paragraph suggests an awareness of some of the criticisms that have been leveled at the practice of cultural tourism. In an article discussing the position of the Maori within New Zealand's tourist industry, anthropologist John Taylor argues that following the critical work of cultural theorists such as Dean MacCannell, John Urry, and others, the tourist industry has recognized and worked to manage the contradiction contained in the act of viewing "culture" as artifact and spectacle within the context of an increasingly pervasive global modernity.[13] Within the tourist industry, he suggests, anxiety is expressed about the integrity of culture once it has been exposed to the demands of commerce. Culture, like nature, is seen to be "under attack from the evils of late-capitalism." From this perspective, Taylor explains, "the cultures of the world (and here 'culture,' like 'ethnic,' refers solely to non-Western Others) are seen to thrive within 'natural habitats.' In order to remain natural, such habitats should also remain 'untouched'" (2001, 13).

The Wilderness Safaris website reflects a similar understanding of culture. It carefully uses the word *lifestyle* to avoid staging the relationship between tourist and local as one between modernity and tradition. A far cry from the cruder description in the Wild Frontiers pamphlet quoted earlier, where local inhabitants were identified only as "proud tribal warriors," the more neutral though also somewhat awkward formulation "this lifestyle, so different from many others" attempts to reframe cultural difference in terms of lifestyle choices. It stresses the need for "delicate balance" in the meeting between tourist and "the Himba people" in order to avoid any impact on the integrity of Himba culture while at the same time emphasizing the ongoing relationship that the camp has with these villages.

Taylor, writing in the very different context of New Zealand, is somewhat impatient with the reification of culture that results from this rethinking of the value of culture as an endangered resource within the tourist industry. He suggests that MacCannell's extremely critical view of the performances of the "primitive" by the "ex-primitive" involves a too-sweeping dismissal of all practices of cultural tourism. Writing about Maori performances of Maori culture, he argues that, despite its obvious limitations, "tourism situates people within zones of contact" and that within these performances, identities important to the performers are articulated (Taylor 2001, 14).

In the far more rural context of northern Namibia, the precise nature of the "zone of contact" established between the game lodge and the Himba villages appears more ambiguous. This chapter makes no claim to empirical evidence about the actual nature of the relationship between the lodge and the local inhabitants. Instead, it suggests that the lodge's publicity material seems unable to free itself from a particular set of categories through which the encounter might be imagined. On both the Tshokwane Safaris and the Wilderness Safaris websites, the encounter is described using the term *visit*: there are "regular guest visits to the villages." The Serra Cafema website suggests also that the camp "is often visited by the native Ovahimba families who live in the nearby vicinity which gives the guests the chance to learn all about their lifestyles and traditions" (Tshokwane Safaris n.d.). Masking the commercial nature of these transactions, this terminology tries to reestablish a domain of sociality in which both guests and local inhabitants might participate. Yet what this misses is the fact that the tourist and the local inhabitant occupy the space differently. The "zone of contact" is not a homogenous space of nature. Earlier in the chapter, I argued that the Himba woman in the Land Rover advertisement and the tourist are subject to different natures even though they might literally occupy the same geographical location. The Serra Cafema Lodge, with its careful detailing, enables the modern global traveler to feel at home. The lodge constitutes "home" through strategic use of a set of familiar international interior design principles. In doing so, the illusion is created that the traveler inhabits the space socially, that he or she has "a part to play here" that is not merely the part of consumption.[14]

The Trophy Hunt

It is this same impulse that seems to motivate the recent increase in recreational hunting. Trophy hunting creates a different sort of background to the lodge but obeys some of the same logic. In Carruthers's detailed history of game ranching in South Africa, she describes a significant shift from agricultural land use to game ranching, noting the rise of the contribution of tourism to the gross domestic product (GDP; approximately 6 percent between 1998 and

2002) and the decline of the significance of agriculture (from 20 percent in the 1920s to 3.4 percent in 2004).[15] Although wild game is farmed for meat, 66 percent of the monetary value of game ranching is derived from recreational hunting. Hunting refers to a complex and diverse set of practices. In chapter 4, I discussed a photograph of a hunt that combined elements of industrial production with aspects of the elite practice of sport hunting. Although at the time of the diamond rush, food was scarce and hunting formed a necessary part of provisioning the town, Rhodes's presence invests this practical hunt with an element of the elite performance. His investment in sport hunting is evident in his establishment of Rooipoort as a private hunting reserve. If, in the late nineteenth century, hunting outside Kimberley could be regarded as both sport and necessity, at the turn of the twenty-first century, sport hunting has acquired a new justification. In the era of extinctions, sport hunting is presented as providing the commercial support for conservation. In a strange claim reminiscent of Akeley's project of killing in order to preserve, commercial hunting is proposed as the solution to extinctions. The profitability of commercial forms of hunting means that setting aside land for and protecting game obeys the logic of the market. Wild animal numbers in South Africa have certainly increased in the last forty years. Carruthers includes a pie graph comparing the numbers of game (in comparison to domestic animals) that shows an increase in game from 575,000 in 1964 to 18.6 million in 2007 (2008, 161).

The rise of hunting as a global recreational activity has generated a new kind of nature industry in which wild animals enter a new regime of value. No longer considered as competitors for scarce grazing land or marauding predators of livestock, wild animals have become themselves valuable investments. Referring to the game industry, then deputy president Cyril Ramaphosa, who also owns the Phala Phala game ranch, comments that "it's a beautiful industry to be in, not only for its investment potential, but because it also serves conservation. It is the aim of every top buffalo breeder to bring back into life bulls the size of the ones that were decimated by colonial hunters in the late 1800s" (Christie 2012). Game ranching thus appears as both a commercial activity and a project of restoration—an investment that pays out not only in cash but also in a sense of emotional well-being generated by healing past colonial violence against nature. As climate change increases the sense of the fragility of nature, wild animals become charged with a more intense value. Occupying a position at the intersection of commercial and moral value, they become bearers of a special kind of meaning. The result is a strange inflation of their monetary value.

In the spectral form of global capitalism, with its limitless desire for novelty, rare game has become, according to online journal *Moneyweb*, an investment that pays higher dividends than property (Slabbert 2013).[16]

When in 2012, a buffalo cow and her heifer calf sold for twenty million rand at an auction held by Vleissentraal Bosveld Auctioneers on behalf of Pieter Du Toit, one of South Africa's most successful breeders of buffalo, it became clear that the value of these animals was disturbing even to the market itself. A member of the game insurance industry commented about the craziness of insuring such animals: "One dead super-buffalo plus a few smaller losses could literally wipe that company out" (anonymous broker quoted in Christie 2012, 3). The tone of those responding to journalist Sean Christie's questions about the extraordinary prices paid at the auction seems at once awed and anxious. In response to the fantastic returns on investments signified by these prices, Gustav Collins, founder of Wildvest,[17] said that investment companies would not forecast returns "based on those prices," but he noted that for rare game, the average price had continued to rise over the previous fifteen years (Christie 2012, 2). In the face of what appears to some as the hypervaluation of game, Investec, a specialist banking and asset-management group, is reported to have offered to fund a research project into the economic sustainability of game ranching.

Yet as the president of Wildlife Ranching South Africa explains, buffalo breeding in South Africa is driven by trophy hunting. Given that there are thirty-five million trophy hunters worldwide and only twenty-two thousand disease-free buffalo in South Africa, supply was still "well below international demand" (Gert Dry quoted in Christie 2012, 3). The buffalo then occupies the strange position of being both fantastically valuable and entirely disposable. Or rather, the fantastic value of the buffalo lies precisely in its availability for a particular sort of death.

Trophy hunting also generates a particular form of natural background. As Cousins, Sadler, and Evans point out, conservation driven by the market favors certain species above others. Market demands shape nature according to the desires of the consuming public. One of the respondents included in the survey by Cousins, Sadler, and Evans draws attention to the differential value of animals on a game ranch. At the other end of the scale from the hugely valuable big five are the small predators, like black jackal, wild dogs, and caracal: "Farmers don't like them as they kill and eat young antelope. They may be moved to another farm or sometimes they are shot. But jackals won't go into traps, they are too cunning, so you have to hunt them with dogs or go shooting. Whereas cats, all you have to do is put a mirror or something or tie cans together (in the trap) . . . you don't even need meat because they are so curious" (director, Wildlife Ranching Industry, Game Capture Company, quoted in Cousins, Sadler, and Evans 2008, 43). The clever jackal, rightly suspicious of the motives of man, who finds itself hunted by dogs and shot, and the curious caracal, who investigates mirrors only to find itself trapped, are the small side effects of trophy hunting. A lesson in the relation between use value and exchange value suggests itself in the form of an (imaginary) cartoon in which a furious farmer demands a payment of two thousand rand from a black jackal who sits back on his haunches, a leg of impala in his mouth, a startled look on his face, and a big question mark above his head.

In this strange redistribution of the relative worth of animals, while the jackal and caracal become expendable, certain novel variations of species become more popular. The breeding of animals for rare genetic variation, such as golden wildebeest, white lions with blue eyes, black or white impalas, and white kudus, creates a natural landscape according to the fantasies of the consumer. Although breeding for particular qualities has long been the practice in domestic animals, what is distinctive in the case of these mutant variations is that these qualities are purely aesthetic. They are not advantageous to the animal's survival, nor do they enhance the quality of the meat; instead, they are marks of novelty and distinction valued only by the trophy hunter. These mutant variations represent an extreme case of detailing in which the genetic code of the animal is manipulated to generate an improved nature, designed to enhance the experience of the hunt.

The inflated value of the buffalo in the auction is matched by a very different kind of inflation in value that became attached to a lion killed by a trophy hunter in Zimbabwe. The fact that, in the era of fragile nature, wild animals act as focalizers of different kinds of value becomes evident in the case of Cecil, whose death gave rise to an unprecedented media response. The lion, who had been given the nickname Cecil by researchers, inhabited the Hwange National Park, but his range included privately owned land on which trophy hunts were conducted. On July 2, 2015, American dentist Walter Palmer shot the lion, who had crossed into the private game farm, with a bow and arrow. According to lion researcher Brent Stapelkamp, the lion hunt was illegal because, in various ways, it violated the regulations of lion hunting in the region.[18] Since the precise details of lion-hunting permit regulations are not widely known outside of Zimbabwe, it was not the illegality of the hunt that appeared to be the key factor generating media outrage. Instead, for reasons that remain puzzling, this death entered global consciousness as a limit case.

In an attempt to understand why this particular death, rather than the many other animal deaths, caused this reaction, David W. MacDonald, one of the researchers at the Oxford University Wildlife Conservation Research Unit (WildCRU), analyzed the media coverage of the event. The scale of the coverage was immense, "reaching 99,000 reports per day in the social and editorial media combined" at its peak at the end of July (MacDonald et al. 2016, 7). Protest also took place outside Palmer's dental surgery in Minneapolis. MacDonald was interested in whether "the global interest in the killing of this lion diagnoses a moment in history at which a wide citizenry revealed their disposition to value, and thus to conserve, wildlife more broadly" (3). He suggested a number of reasons this particular death might have triggered such a powerful response—the fact that he was a large, majestic lion; had an "English" nickname; was well studied; and had a distinctive black mane. There was also an easily identifiable villain—the wealthy white American who shot the lion with a bow and arrow, resulting in an apparently lingering death. MacDonald suggests that "it seems plausible then that it is their combination, certainly unusually and perhaps uniquely, that led to the viral explosion. It might also be the case that the episode was so remote from the daily experience of many people, that they felt able to make a straightforward condemnation of it, with no feeling of related guilt about their own behavior" (MacDonald et al. 2016, 8). MacDonald, a zoologist, analyzed the media coverage in terms of numbers—the extent of the coverage and its distribution. I am interested in the form of the lion that emerges from these reports. Like the buffalo that was sold for twenty million rand, this lion becomes, for a period of time, fantastically valuable, although within a different regime of value. The media coverage both testified to and generated a demand for a mode of evaluation that is not monetary.

Within the many narratives of the event, the lion appears in a number of guises. He is perhaps most prominently a distinctive character, Cecil, described often as "much loved." This lion, who is the lion of children's storybooks, coexists with the researchers' characterization of him as the representative of a type, the alpha male, the leader of the pride, who maintains the social order of the lions of the area. Stapelkamp explains, "He made a great spectacle, and was so confident that even if you were right next to him, he'd ignore you and just do what lions do. He wouldn't sit and watch you. He'd just carry on being a lion"

(Ramsay 2015). For the hunters, he was an older male and therefore was both valued for his size and disposable, since according to their logic, he was no longer in his prime. Like the wolves in the previous chapter, the lion bears the weight of human meanings, combining in his furry body storybook character, biological specimen, good leader, responsible patriarch, and the long heraldic tradition of majesty and power—the very qualities that make his killing such a valuable sign of prowess. Disaggregating these meanings allows a reading of the media phenomenon as both an investment in the utopian potential that wild animals present and the continuation of a long tradition of colonial misreading.

To describe the emotional attachment to Cecil as, in part, a result of his transformation into a storybook character is not to undermine the importance of this response. For Adorno, it is precisely the child's ability to recognize the value in what has no utility that makes children recognize the worth of wild animals. He writes, "The relation of children to animals depends entirely on the fact that Utopia goes disguised in the creatures whom Marx even begrudged the surplus value they contributed as workers. In existing without any purpose recognizable to men, animals hold out, as if for expression, their own names, utterly impossible to exchange" (1978, 228).

Yet despite the beneficial emotional charge that identified the lion as valuable beyond his utility, what the moral outrage overlooked was the fact that his global appeal was achieved in part by eliding his place in a specific social network. The fetishization of Cecil, like the fetishization of consumer goods, by foregrounding the immediacy of the connection between person and object or, in this case, person and animal, conceals the fact that what is in fact at stake in any exchange is the relationship between people. Cecil's life and death were the result of transactions between people. The most obvious of these and easiest to condemn is the commercial transaction between recreational hunter and guide, but as I hope has become evident in the course of this book, the recreational hunt in Africa participates in an ongoing colonial tradition of display. Hunting animals and conserving them participates in a logic that positions white visitors in a particular relation to local inhabitants. In both, Africa remains the domain of exploit.

When U.S. talk show host Jimmy Kimmel made an appeal to the public to prove that not all Americans were like the "jackhole" trophy hunter by supporting WildCRU, donations poured in (Kimmel quoted in MacDonald et al. 2016, 2). In fact, MacDonald and colleagues report that there were so many people trying to make donations that the websites of both WildCRU and Oxford

University crashed. Yet it is interesting to note that despite the fact that the immediate loss of Cecil was to Hwange National Park in Zimbabwe, the donations were being made to an Oxford University–based research unit. It is as if the postcolony once again is positioned outside the global circuit of value, unable to benefit (directly) even from this intense global investment in its lions.

Administered Nature

Among the assembled material in this final constellation, certain things are transient, like an advertisement already outdated by newer formulations of desire, and certain are enduring, like the seemingly endless discursive repetition of Africa's naturalness. An advertisement is a fleeting intervention that for a brief period strives to organize desire around a certain object. My reading of the Land Rover advertisement suggests that the human figure in the wilderness is an ambiguous image dependent on its decoding of the cultural objects that are present in the frame. If the image of the seminaked white man in nature seems too incongruous to inspire desire, this is perhaps because it draws attention to the vulnerability of the individual that the hard carapace of the Land Rover is designed to conceal. The same might be said of the trophy hunter carrying an array of weapons. Veblen classes hunting alongside angling and other sports as activities designed to show prowess. He presents the recreational hunter in industrial society as a caricatured figure: "It is noticeable, for instance, that even very mild-mannered and matter-of-fact men who go out shooting are apt to carry an excess of arms and accoutrements in order to impress upon their own imagination the seriousness of their undertaking. These huntsmen are also prone to a histrionic, prancing gait and to an elaborate exaggeration of the motions, whether of stealth or of onslaught, involved in their deeds of exploit" (1943, 256).

The problem confronting the recreational hunter, like the visitor to the private game lodge, is that his "entire social existence lies elsewhere" (Baudrillard 1996). The act of killing authenticates his presence in nature by re-creating briefly and with carefully managed risks the drama of survival. In the age of global warming and increasing levels of pollution, nature appears fragile and subjugated to an increasingly global industrial civilization. But as individuals, as "natural beings," we remain vulnerable not to nature in the abstract but to specific natural environments whose indifference to our particular life is absolute.

In the quotation with which I began this chapter, Adorno suggests that reserves indicate the loss of nature rather than its recovery. An increasing concern with the preservation of nature testifies, he argues, most tellingly to its complete subjugation. For Adorno, to have "difficulty" in "coping with nature" is a sign of the continuing life of nature as something outside the instrumental logic of consumer society. The proliferation of private game reserves seems to confirm Adorno's assertions. They literally open their doors to nature while at the same time controlling entirely the material and symbolic frame in which the encounter with nature can take place. This control is extended beyond simply the design and detailing of the lodge and the breeding of species for rare and aesthetically striking mutations.

Accessible only to the wealthy traveler, the game lodges and trophy hunting expeditions of private game reserves mimic, with significant differences, a feudal order of society. As in a feudal society, the visitors, surrounded by luxury, are the focus of sustained attention by those whose duty it is to serve them. Like the Kimberley Club, the lodge of the private game reserve offers a domestic space designed to confirm wealth and status. But visitors to the game reserve are also lost, superfluous in nature, which is alien territory to them. Their social existence lies elsewhere, and in this encounter with pristine nature and the "real" Africa, they require constant guidance. In the domain of the "new safari," their actions are elaborately circumscribed by the contradictory requirement that they inhabit this space without touching it, without leaving a trace. The lodge's excess; the piling up of authentic, traditional objects; and the elaborate staging all seem to work to conceal the simple fact of this alienation. The unsettling realization not only of natural indifference but also of the commercial nature of the social interactions taking place is concealed by the careful design of the lodges, which stages nature as a series of glamorous settings for eating and drinking. These enclaves are no longer racially exclusive, but in mobilizing the symbolism of the imperial and colonial past, they repeat with minimal difference the form of invidious comparison that historically judged black lives to be of less value than those of whites. The division between the usually black service staff and the usually white patrons reproduces in disturbing ways the social relations of the colonial era.

The trophy hunt, on the other hand, marks this temporary encounter with nature by an act of superfluous violence, which produces the trophy as its material marker. The carefully managed experience allows the hunter to mimic the moment of risk without risking anything. The choice to shoot with a superseded technology (the bow and arrow) reveals only the extent to which the lion no longer presents a threat—at least to those traveling with a well-armed guide. Unlike those who live in the region for whom an encounter with a lion represents a real danger, the trophy hunt stages vulnerability in order to overcome it.

The basic premise of conservation is that science can provide positive information about how best to manage the residual and threatened natural world. While scientific research does provide interesting and potentially useful information about aspects of the material world, it does so in a way that only partially intersects with the fantasy of nature that has become the object of such excruciating desire. In these private game reserves, conservation is a value that serves a desire to possess and assert control symbolically and practically over space that is no longer considered primarily in terms of national boundaries. In the era of the Anthropocene, the environment is, after all, the responsibility of humankind. The discourse of conservation acts as a guarantee confirming a particular construction of the self in relation to nature.

In Europe and the United Kingdom, a number of different projects exist to reintroduce wild game into the countryside. For Monbiot, rewilding in the United Kingdom offers the promise of a spiritual restoration, an escape from "ecological boredom" that characterizes life in industrial or postindustrial and thoroughly modernized countries. Monbiot's concept of ecological boredom describes a particularly twenty-first-century form of alienation, a condition in which everyday experience is entirely structured by commodities and limited encounters with the managed natural world of parks (2013, 7), or what Adorno might describe as "the administered life"—one in which all aspects of life are subject to professional management. Like York, who justifies his breeding of mutant variations in terms of conservation, Monbiot proposes commercial hunting as a profitable alternative to the traditional but marginally profitable sheep farming in the United Kingdom that might open up the land for the restoration of wild species of all kinds, both plant and animal. This utopian fantasy to create a new wild to replace the one that has been lost in the process of modernization echoes the hope of the Eden Project described in chapter 2. In some ways a practical response to the fact that the commodities that sustain the technique of life in advanced capitalist countries are now produced elsewhere, it repeats an investment in nature as an escape from the everyday. It relies for its realization on the vast network of shipping that will continue to deliver the commodities that give shape to everyday life to such postindustrial countries.

For the most part, this desire for wild nature is made possible by the existence of the house. It stands with a huge solidity, networked into the electrical grid, the municipal water and sewage system, and refuse removal, a center for all the everyday transactions of biological survival. The dwelling—house, flat, apartment, and all its multiple variations—is an integral part of the idea of an "acceptable standard of living." It defines as an object and an aspiration the understanding of habitation in the technique of life of capitalist modernity. It is the hard carapace, the form that makes possible the assembly of things. It is the protection of the house that makes it possible to step outside. This infrastructure produces the impression of freedom and autonomy, but it is in reality an infrastructure of dependency.

Nostalgia for the wild is an understandable emotional response to inhabiting the historical moment when the hidden costs of such a mode of living become evident. The lives of the jackals and the bat-eared foxes who magically return to reinhabit York's farm in Limpopo Province cannot be discounted even though their existence is dependent on the profitability of golden wildebeest and a fickle consumer desire for novelty. Yet what these fragments from the history of loss reveal is that public sentiment is itself always shaped by a global distribution of what is considered valuable. Nostalgia for wild nature comes uncomfortably close to nostalgia for "capitalist life as we know it," which includes wild nature as one of its most valued commodities. In the era of mass extinctions, selectively preserving wild nature through making it once again the privilege of the elite changes nothing. It merely repeats the long history of exploit and exploitation.

7
Living at the End of Nature

In the dark, I spill some of my spring water as I try to decant it from the ten-liter bottle to something smaller for everyday use. I misjudge the amount, and it wells up over the rim of the smaller container and splashes onto my bare feet. Since the beginning of March, there has been load shedding again. Unlike the first time ten years ago, this time the blackouts are carefully scheduled. Someone has developed an app that sends notifications, although often it apologetically announces that the traffic on the site is too high. "Please wait," it says, "we are firing up more servers." The South African energy generator Eskom has been the center of political scandal for many years, dogged by incompetence and corruption. For years a shadowy nuclear deal with Russia has meant that cheaper renewable energy generation projects have been blocked. The sudden increase in load shedding this week, though, the one that has left me in the dark, is apparently the result of a tropical cyclone hitting Mozambique. The storm and subsequent flooding killed hundreds of people and displaced many more. It also disrupted the Kabora Bassa hydroelectric plant that supplies South Africa with 900 MW of power, a small but crucial supplement to the country's aging electricity-generation infrastructure.

It is easy to become furious at load shedding, especially when it reaches stage 4 and cuts occur several times a day. For those linked to the grid who are accustomed to the technique of life of capitalist modernity, it interrupts the simplest everyday activity—making a cup of tea, charging a cell phone, sending an email. Actions that should be straightforward are suddenly complicated. It interferes with monetary transactions, temporarily bringing business to a standstill. Like the water crisis, it estranges the everyday. With each interrupted gesture, we are reminded of our dependency on others. The outages that are largely the result of poor-quality coal are a reminder of the fact that lives lived this way are using things up that are not inexhaustible. Quickly before the next power cut, I look on the internet. The dams supplying the city of Cape Town with water are at 52.1 percent of capacity. The Western Cape Provincial Minister of Local Government, Environmental Affairs and Development Planning is quoted in the newspaper as being "hopeful" about a good rainfall this winter.[1]

The form of the constellation does not comfortably accommodate a conclusion. In following the logic of juxtaposition, synecdoche, and parataxis, the book has sought a form adequate to the inconclusiveness of the current moment—an expressive mode for living in the subjunctive. The power of such a form lies in its ability to interrupt thought, not violently with emotion but slowly through an invitation to dwell on the perplexing nature of reality in the time of climate change. In the current era of accelerated perception, it slows the velocity of thought by presenting a puzzle, things that do not belong together, parts that refuse to add up to a whole, general concepts that fail to contain particular instances, abstractions that cannot account for material details, a whole seemingly oblivious to its parts. The puzzle, in refusing to give up its meaning immediately, reproduces the inexplicable nature of the current reality, in which a technique of life seems to have developed its own inexorable logic.

In this book, each strategic juxtaposition was designed to illuminate the inexplicable in a particular historical configuration, a moment when nature was produced and consumed in a distinct way. But these moments do not represent exemplary stages in an overall development. They cannot be linked together to form a continuous history. They are, instead, fragments in an incomplete picture that is momentarily brought into focus only to blur again as the discursive role of nature in the global political order changes. Yet what emerges from lingering with these constellations, feeling the rough edge of the everyday world, are certain repetitions, unsettling patterns, echoes, and reverberations.

Living in the subjunctive requires living with questions that cannot be answered, at least not easily, not immediately. Radical change is predicted, but as yet, only fragments of damage circulate in the news—the loss of the Cavendish banana,[2] the disappearance of an island,[3] extinctions, a tropical cyclone in Mozambique. In the face of this slow catastrophe, one response has been the production of nature in the form of a persistent nostalgia. The Biodiversity Hall of the American Museum of Natural History and the Eden Project provide exemplary instances of this education in loss. Yet as older exhibitions reveal, this is an education in loss repeated. From the dinosaurs to the Akeley dioramas, the story of the museum participates in a narrative arc of nostalgia and disappearance—the tragedy of nature in the age of modernity. Even though the dinosaurs in historical terms predate human intervention, the story they are deployed to tell—of their own rise and fall—gives great weight to the mythic inevitability of this narrative arc of loss. The ambitious Eden Project creates a defiant abundance but only as a consolation for and defense against this anticipated loss.

The two exhibitions, with good intentions, provide bad advice. In maintaining the illusion that the problem of climate change requires revising humanity's relation with nature, they redirect attention away from the real problem, which is not humans' relation with nature but people's relations with each other. The popularity of the term *Anthropocene* is both the indication of real public concern and a mode of framing the problem that misdirects attention. Positing an undifferentiated collective "humanity" against nature makes it impossible to see that finding the solution to human impact on the planet requires understanding what sort of activities are causing the damage. The name *Anthropocene* wins out over *Capitalocene*[4] in general circulation precisely because of its apparent neutrality, its geological pedigree, even as the Great Acceleration graphs hint at what is really going on, not human activity in general but specific activities—the production and consumption of goods. These activities so carefully documented by the Great Acceleration graphs are not the outcome of humanity's relations with nature.

Instead, as Veblen reminds us, consumption is driven not by the rational assessment of need, an interaction with nature based on its use value, but far more by the desire to communicate to others our self-worth through our power of display. Or to express his point in a way that more accurately reflects the conditions of the twenty-first century, the desire to communicate our self-worth through participating in a technique of life promoted as the only one of any value—the lifestyle of consumption. The science of the Great Acceleration graphs correctly measures not only ocean acidification but also the number of new cell phone contracts. Yet in this very act of measuring cell phone contracts alongside ocean acidification, human activities themselves seem to take on the status and form of natural processes, as if taking out a cell phone contract was an inevitable part of the life cycle of the species.

The domination of everyday life by technology and consumption has become a kind of second nature. The habits and conventions associated with this technique of life seem to resist the operations of critical thought in part because they seem so mundane. They form the "senseless necessities" of everyday life. From the late twentieth century, but with immeasurably greater intensity in the twenty-first century, invidious comparison has become globalized through the massive increase in technologies of communication and the work of a culture in which certain techniques of life are obsessively and repetitively represented. Throughout the world, a new category has emerged of "global consumers" whose transient desires are not only reconfiguring the physical substrate of the earth but also obliviously repeating earlier forms of exploitation.

More useful advice under the current circumstances might be the injunction to recognize in everything you own or consume the debt that you owe to others, a debt that is not canceled by the money you paid for it. In the exhibitions, Africa features wild animals, a rain forest, and the home of natural ecologists. The reality of contemporary landscapes of extraction like the Niger delta and of waste like the Agbogbloshie dump site—the devastating afterlife of consumed technology where old cell phones, refrigerators, and computers, exported from wealthy countries as "second-hand goods," leak toxicity into the ground—remains invisible. All of these are parts of the much larger whole, but in choosing one set rather than the other, the exhibitions direct attention away from the unequal costs of maintaining a particular technique of life and back to nature. These other sites, the beginning and end points of key commodities (gasoline and everyday technological items), would be a reminder of the fact that the Eden Project is implicated in a process of excessive consumption that requires the voracious using up of other parts of the world. Capitalist modernity is dependent on a surplus extracted from various sites in the postcolony.

Nature supplies the alibi. Drawing on the same global narrative of concern, the game reserves and tour companies justify their privatization of natural landscapes in terms of their contribution to practices of conservation. This exclusive tourist encounter with wild nature, whether at a luxury lodge or through trophy hunting, is presented as a form of giving without sacrifice. In paying, the visitor contributes to a just cause and at the same time enjoys the status conferred by conspicuous leisure. It permits the creation of the conditions of colonial-style privilege without the guilt or anxiety. Instead, this luxury is framed as the reward for contributing to the work of conservation.

Yet it is also unfair to burden the individual with the massive emotional debt of the society into which they are born without having much choice in the matter. This would only send them staggering to the museum coffee shop to comfort themselves with fair-trade coffee in a cornstarch to-go cup and cake made with locally sourced ingredients.[5] The desire to be considered valuable is not in itself an illegitimate desire. It could be the basis for political action. Advertising is powerful because it addresses a legitimate desire—the desire for the society in which we live to recognize our worth. By playing on structurally produced doubts, advertising offers each individual separately a way to confirm their worth through the seemingly private transaction of the purchase. Yet this purchase in reality involves many people. In the twentieth century, the diamond, as the physical token of a purely symbolic value, became a test case for the power of publicity to manufacture desire. Untroubled by use value, its value could rise exponentially as it was strategically introduced into the circuits of wealth and status associated with the new celebrity elites created by the movie industry. One of the successes of the Ayers publicity campaign was its ability to skillfully associate diamonds with inherited privilege while promoting them as an essential part of the emotional life of every individual.

Veblen's ire is directed at the deceived individual who does not recognize the motive force of their own desire to accumulate. He bitterly rejects the error of the modern world in which vestigial but powerful instincts for social aggrandizement bring humanity into conflict with the potentially rational world of industrial production. Adorno offers a corrective to what he calls Veblen's "splendid misanthropy." "Human beings," he writes, "are no worse than the society in which they live" (1981, 87). For Adorno, even people's mistaken attempt to establish self-worth through "invidious comparison" points beyond this to something else—the distortion of society. It is not that he denies the invidious nature of consumption; rather, he sees in the public character of consumption a recognition of the social nature of happiness. Pleasure is not and cannot be a private affair.

The Anthropocene admits only two categories: the individual who is addressed and humanity that is held responsible, with nothing in between. What should be in between is society. Perhaps more useful advice to individuals would be to suggest they address themselves to amending society's modes of recognizing worth. Would it be possible to imagine a society in which people would not require the mediation of commodities to establish a sense of worth? Could commodities instead be categorized, even regulated, according to the contribution they make to the life of society?[6]

At the beginning of the twenty-first century, it is easy to share Veblen's fury at the wastefulness of modern forms of consumption. His commentary on practices of consumption at the end of the nineteenth century seems an accurate assessment of the irrationalities of capitalist production in the twenty-first century designed for short-term profit, whose social and ecological costs, always devastating for the poor, now threaten to disrupt the possibility of life itself. The name *Anthropocene* registers the increasingly generalized nature of damage but not the long history of externalizing costs.

Insisting on the postcolony as a concept necessary for understanding climate change is a way of confronting the alibi of nature. Each of the constellations maps out the way in which nature in the postcolony is produced through a complex process of material and symbolic appropriation. The objects I have chosen to bring together are in part defined by their publicity. This is because what interests me is the way in which in each case, the materiality of diamonds, wolves, and landscapes is produced as nature only through the deliberate work of publicity and that these processes always leave a remainder. Around these points of intensity, where nature is turned into profit, there is an accretion of effects. In each case, the particular instance and the surrounding representations are offered as a disturbance of the general category of which they are a part. Employing the optics of natural history makes it possible to see this remainder, to find the suffering bodies that are required to fall out of memory in order for this production of nature as the source of authentic value to be complete.

If in the twenty-first century the value of nature becomes increasingly the realization of an abstract idea, sequestered from the everyday world of work and requiring an ever-increasing attention to detail, the constellations also reveal the persistence of the same—anxiety about loss, fantasies of luxury, the hunt and immediacy tempered by desire for the sense of power, and the control and ease provided by money. At the same time, what recurs is the need for violence to protect privilege and the work of an explanatory narrative, however threadbare, to justify the pleasure of exclusive access. Nature itself, like diamonds, has been marketed in the twentieth and early twenty-first centuries to emphasize its rarity value. Yet postcolonial countries, despite their richness in this particular scarce resource, seem unable to realize it as value. What emerges in these constellations is that the abstraction that characterizes the inflation of nature's value makes it a curiously mobile and immaterial commodity and that international circuits of value continue to produce deficits within the postcolony that are both material and symbolic.

The moments I have described all constitute instances of the reification of nature, when it is immobilized or arrested in a particular form. But this is not the only way in which nature can be grasped. As Adorno notes in "The Idea of Natural History," recognizing nature instead as transience confers on it a different role. As a reminder of transience, nature interrupts the narrative of progress and development. One of the utopian possibilities of nature is that it implies something that is beyond private property. Yet this quality is also what makes it vulnerable to appropriation. What emerges from the fragments I have discussed is the way in which nature continues to be seized in an ongoing process of primitive accumulation as the notion of nature as a common ground becomes increasingly besieged by private and corporate interests.

In the final part of this conclusion, I want to propose two acts of rereading that offer a different sort of conceptual disorientation of the hierarchical arrangement in the field of ecological knowledge production of Africa and the world. Neither of the two texts that I read is concerned with climate change, but they both do reflect, in very different ways, on techniques of life. The first, *The Gods Must Be Crazy*, is a South African film released in 1980. The film was an unexpected box office success not only in South Africa but also subsequently in the United States, France, Hong Kong, Taiwan, China, and Japan. The small town I grew up in on the west coast, now an outlying suburb of Cape Town, had no cinema, and only a very few people owned television sets. Once a year, the small primary school I attended organized a school outing to the city to go to the movies. There we would be given a Coke or a Fanta and a bag of chips and ushered into a huge, plush theater. While I took immense pleasure in the junk food and the luxury of the cinema, I regarded the films themselves with profound anxiety. The films we saw, always a double feature screened exclusively for the school, included the wildlife comedy *Beautiful People* (1974), the drama *e'Lollipop* (1976), and *The Gods Must Be Crazy*. A literal-minded child, unused to the logic of screen narratives, I could not take pleasure in the fiction. Every represented gesture seemed shockingly real.

The narrative of *The Gods Must Be Crazy* is initiated by the careless gesture of a pilot tossing an empty glass Coke bottle out of the window of a small plane over the Kalahari. It is found by a member of a hunter-gatherer society living in idyllic isolation from the rest of the world. This bottle, because of the hardness of the glass, becomes desired for its use value, but because it is unique, it quickly provokes jealousy and conflict. Realizing its capacity for disruption, the protagonist, Xi, played by G/au, sets off on a journey to throw it off the end of the world. Although the film begins in a pseudodocumentary style with a reflection on adaption—the Ju/'hoansi's perfect adaptation to their environment contrasted to the impossibility of adapting to the demands and changing environment of the city—the action takes place not in the city but in an unnamed small town in Botswana.

Following the logic of reversal, Xi's journey is treated with seriousness, carried by the charismatic quality of G/au, whose calm but determined demeanor gives weight to his simple refusal of the assumptions of modernity. Typical of the sly humor of the film, it is the empty Coke bottle, not the commodity itself, that proves to be useful. Remarkably, for a film made during apartheid, it is the white male character who carries the physical humor of the film. Incapacitated by shyness around women and thwarted by a refractory and uncooperative Land Rover, the character, biologist Andrew Steyn, played by Marius Weyers, shows a patient resignation at the recalcitrance of the physical world as he becomes incoherent, trips, falls, drops things, smashes things, knocks things over, gets covered in flour, and accidentally winches his Land Rover into a tree.

Watching the film as a child, I saw nothing funny in Xi's rational response to the absurdities of modernity, and I was terrified by the wayward behavior of the Land Rover. The pilot's careless gesture of throwing the bottle out of the window seemed shockingly irresponsible. In his fascinating study of the Ju/'hoansi of Namibia, *Affluence and Abundance*, James Suzman describes the history of the film and his meeting with actor G/au. At the time the film was first released, it was criticized for its numerous failures to adequately represent the real. At the height of apartheid, it simply ignored racial segregation, and it represented the idyllic world of the Bushman untouched by capitalist modernity when in reality, they had already experienced years of dispossession, recruitment by the South African National Defence Force, and enforced labor by colonial farmers expanding into the Kalahari. Yet the film offers, as Suzman notes, perhaps the only critique of capitalist modernity from a hunter-gatherer's perspective.

In his book, Suzman offers a fascinating account of a technique of life that is not driven by invidious comparison. His study of the Ju/'hoansi of Namibia is far from utopian. He unflinchingly describes the consequences of their long history of dispossession and marginalization both under colonialism and in postliberation Namibian society. Yet what the history of the Ju/'hoansi offers is an intriguing alternative model for the distribution of social value. Suzman explains how in the fiercely egalitarian society of the Ju/'hoansi, acquiring goods is not regarded in itself as a form of satisfaction. Instead, in a culture with minimal things, the display of goods appears not as an assertion of self-worth but rather as a sign of greed and antisocial behavior. The mechanism of social cohesion lies not in invidious comparison but in its obverse—the avoidance of jealousy. Jealousy is regarded not as a moral failing but rather as a legitimate response to inequality. To display goods works not as an assertion of self-worth but as a sign of moral and social failure.

Read not as realism but as allegory, a mode that the film self-consciously invites, the film presents an unusual critique of the technique of life of capitalist modernity. Deliberately lowbrow, the film makes no claim to a serious intellectual argument. In the mode of slapstick, it provokes humor through drawing attention to everyday absurdity and overturning accepted values. The film is, of course, not really from the perspective of a hunter-gatherer, but at least the filmmaker, Jamie Uys, can imagine such a perspective and gives G/au sufficient space to assert his presence.[7] It offers, although under the erasure of humor, an alternative model for organizing social desire.

From the perspective of the twenty-first century, it shows a remarkable irreverence toward the set pieces of the nature industry—wild animals, the white male hero, the Land Rover, the primitive, the exploit, and the hunt cycle through the film, but each takes on an altered form. Read seriously, against its own intentions, it presents the ridiculousness of modernity when considered from the perspective of a different technique of life.

The second act of rereading concerns the form of the aphorism, which also has a long history as part of an African tradition of moral instruction. As against the realism of information and instruction, which allows no space for interpretation, the aphorism provokes the same hesitation that the riddle does. It creates a structure of implication in which each element seems to gesture beyond the immediate context and to hold a wider significance. At the same time, its realist detail ties it to the particularities of time and place. The aphorism thus provides a form for presenting the relation between the particular and the universal, the individual and the collective, in a way that materializes and disorganizes simple hierarchies of concept and category.

The story is one discovered in the colonial archive and is from a collection by linguist and missionary H. W. Woodward, who gathered the tales from the Makua in southern Tanzania.[8] I offer this not as an example of traditional wisdom but as exemplary of a different mode of giving and receiving advice. Within the story itself, advice is given and then at a crucial moment discarded, resulting in the loss of the dogs who, as excellent hunters, figure as the providers of the pleasure and nourishment of meat. But the story itself also has the form of a parable offering a kind of advice that is far more enigmatic. My aim is not to try to reconstruct the original meaning of the story but rather to read it as an allegorical figure for developing a mode of dwelling with nature.

"Men, Women, and Dogs"

Once upon a time, men and women did not live together. There was a very big river called Chowo, and the men lived on their side of the river and the women on their side. But the women had dogs, and the dogs were great hunters, so the women every day had their relish of meat. But the men never tasted meat because they had no dogs. Now one day, the men said, "Let us go and borrow the dogs." So they crossed the river and came to the women, and after greeting them, the men said, "We have come to borrow the dogs." The women said, "Take them, but do not shout at them, 'Catch it, catch it, catch it,' but say when you see an animal, 'Kwi, kwi, kwi,' in a whisper." And the men said, "Very well." And they took leave and said, "We will bring them back after two days." As soon as they reached home, the men went hunting, and when the dogs found an animal, they said, "Kwi, kwi, kwi," and the dogs caught as many as four animals. And when they returned, they said, "Let us go again." And they went and caught more. But the next day, when they found game, they said, "Catch it, catch it, catch it, do not be beaten by your own kind! Aka, aka, ko, ko, koooo!" Thus they forgot "kwi, kwi," and when the dogs heard those words, they ran away and were not seen again. And the men said, "What shall we do now that we have lost the owners' dogs? Let us go and tell them." And the women said, "You are our debtors; you are trapped. Now you must build us houses." The men answered, "Very well." And they build their houses to this day. That is why, when men get things, it is for the women. They get them houses, clothes, plantations, and other things that women have, all because of the dogs.

In the story, the actions appear fraught with background.[9] It appears to begin in the middle, in a situation that is already strange. Many questions are raised in the course of the story that are not answered. Why is society organized in this way, with men living on one side of the river and women on the other? Why is it that only women possess dogs? These exist on the periphery of the story but are never directly addressed. Instead, the focus is on a crisis point that alters the shape of society. The crisis takes place in the context of the seemingly everyday act of hunting. The dogs in this story have a definite use value. They facilitate hunting and allow the women privileged access to meat. Yet they are not merely instruments, since there is a secret for gaining their cooperation, one that is related above all to the proper form of address. The dogs must be spoken to using particular apparently untranslatable words ("kwi, kwi, kwi") and in a particular way (a whisper, not a shout). No explanation is

Living at the End of Nature

given for why the men, on the second day, fail to follow the advice, except that in the moment of the hunt, they "forget" what they have been told. What they say to the dogs, what precipitates the crisis, is an act of classification. The dogs are identified as being of the same "kind" as those they are pursuing. At the moment in which they are addressed in these terms, the dogs run away, and the structure of society changes forever. Houses, clothes, plantations, and other things are all a compensation for the loss of the dogs, which is also the loss of a particular way of life based on the hunt. No regrets or emotions are expressed in the story, and there is very little that implies a narrative judgment on the events that have unfolded. The only judgment that occurs is in the women's reply that identifies the men as "debtors" and uses the word "trapped" to describe their situation as the consequences of their actions. The men, in their abbreviated acquiescence, seem to acknowledge the justice of the women's demands.

The story does not provide practical advice about how to inhabit the world. It is not possible to extrapolate from it the importance of recycling, saving electricity, and keeping savings under the mattress to prevent banks from investing them in projects of capitalist growth. Instead, it makes a philosophical intervention. Its allusive narrative form calls into being an unsuspected background, a forgotten prehistory of the present order, and the possibility of a different mode of dwelling. This book has tried to do something similar.

For critique to be possible, an opening must be found between the real as it presents itself relentlessly to experience and the forms of knowledge and interpretation that work to smooth the diverse and incommensurable elements into a recognizable surface. The work of this book has been to charge these surfaces with background and to find in the various awkward gatherings the roughness necessary for critical purchase. If "Men, Women, and Dogs" can be said to offer advice, it might be to pay attention to detail, to respect connections, and to understand the potential of intimate forms of communication. Like hands passed "over the landscape's hair" (Adorno 1978, 48), whispers are delicate connections. They presuppose an intimate proximity. The strange associations proposed in this book are about recognizing both the violence and coercion that structure the everyday distribution of value in the postcolony and elsewhere and those moments that seem, despite everything, charged with promise.

Notes

Chapter 1

The epigraphs for this chapter are drawn from Adorno (1978, 48), and Adorno (1998, 7).

1. The phrase comes from Georg Simmel in "The Metropolis and Mental Life" (1903). I explore the idea in the article "Modernity's Dirt: Carbon Emissions and the Technique of Life":

> Techniques of life, like techniques in art, impose certain limits on the expressive possibilities of a particular historical moment. The phrase offers a way of capturing the surface quality of the form of everyday life that characterizes a historical period [and geographical location]. It tries to identify what habits and gestures have become ingrained by the objects and technologies that surround and shape social interactions. It registers in the sorts of objects available on supermarket shelves, the gestures and postures of the body (such as the way a body might adapt to holding a mobile phone), the pace and flow of transactions, and the focus and direction of attention. (Green 2018, 240)

2. In his book *Carbon Democracy*, Timothy Mitchell notes, "The ecosystem appears to be approaching two limits simultaneously: an end to the easy availability of fossil fuel, whose abundance allowed the development of modern, mechanised life; and the loss of its ability to regulate global temperatures within the range that allowed human sociality itself to develop" (Mitchell 2011, 203).

3. See also Eric Jarosinski's discussion of this aspect of the constellation in his article "Of Stones and Glass Houses: *Minima Moralia* as a Critique of Transparency" (2010).

4. This notion is discussed in *Reflexive Modernization: Politics, Tradition and Aesthetics in the Modern Social Order* (Beck, Giddens, and Scott 1994).

5. For instance, phrases such as the "hospitality industry."

6. Describing conditions in England in the nineteenth century, Raymond Williams notes that industrialization reforms the category of nature to designate wild nature (Williams 1980, 77; Ferguson 2006). The new industrial processes generate wealth that enables the purchase of estates and country retreats and effectively splits nature into unrelated parts, raw materials to be extracted, and wild nature to be enjoyed. Williams comments that "the real split, perhaps, is in men themselves: men seen, seeing themselves as producers and consumers. The consumer wants only the intended product; all other products and by-products he must get away from, if he can. But get away from—it really can't be overlooked—to treat leftover nature in much the same spirit: to consume it as scenery, landscape, image, fresh air" (81).

7. For further discussion, see my entry on "Nature" in *Fueling Cultures: 101 Words for Energy and Environment* (Green 2017).

8. See Kate Soper's *What Is Nature?* for a discussion of the complex dimensions of nature as a cultural category. Recent ecocritical materialist theorists argue that nature is itself an agent in the process of meaning making: "There is, however, a

particularity in this 'nature.' 'Nature,' in the context of the new materialisms, has a much broader semantic spectrum; it has less to do with 'green ecology' than with a much more blurred and multihued dimension. It is something both physical and meta-physical. It is nature and its very condition: matter. Matter possesses an eloquent and signifying agency, which articulates itself in the differentiating of its forms" (Iovino 2015, 72).

9. This is particularly true of feminist theorists, who have good reason to be wary of it. See discussions in Soper (1995, 119–48), Haraway (1991), and Plumwood (1993).

10. Susan Buck-Morss comments that it represented "Adorno's contribution to the debate on historicism which had been going on at the university since Max Scheler and Karl Mannheim taught there in the twenties and worked to establish a sociology of knowledge" (Buck-Morss 1977, 53).

11. Max Pensky describes this process in the following way: "The idea entails the corrosion, the petrification, or the freezing-up of any large, harmonizing and ultimately delusive claims toward trends of totality and meaning in the historical process, and instead an insight of the historical process itself as generating only concrete, singular, and utterly empirical facts and bodies, each 'transient,' which is to say, incapable of being incorporated into a meaning-giving conception of historical continuity and historical experience" (Pensky 2004, 234).

12. The image of the charnel house appears in Lukács's discussion of first and second nature in *The Theory of the Novel*. He writes, "This second nature is not dumb sensuous and yet senseless like the first: it is a complex of senses—meanings—which has become rigid and strange, and which no longer awakens interiority; it is a charnel house of long dead interiorities" (Lukács 1978, 64).

13. Neil Smith (1984) uses the term *uneven development* to describe the geography of capitalism and the way in which it produces particular kinds of spaces through environmental transformation.

14. In *The Old Curiosity Shop*, Dickens describes such a landscape: "On every side, and as far as the eye could see into this heavy distance, tall chimneys, crowding on each other, and presenting that endless repetition of the same dull, ugly form, which is the horror of oppressive dreams, poured out their plague of smoke, obscured the light, and made foul the melancholy air" (2001, chap. 45).

15. The phrase "the end of nature" is the title of a book published in 1990 by environmentalist Bill McKibben. I discuss his work in some detail in chapter 3 of this book.

16. The IGBP's "Strategic Vision" begins with the following statement: "For over twenty years, the International Geosphere-Biosphere Programme has assembled overwhelming evidence of the unprecedented scale of changes to Earth's most important biological, chemical and physical processes. The pace of change has accelerated since the 1950s. A growing population, exponential resource use and rapid industrialization are responsible for most of these changes and strongly influence others" (http://www.igbp.net/download/18.2709bddb12c08a79de780001017/1376383018329/IGBPDraftvision 27September.pdf).

17. Both Rob Nixon and Naomi Klein warn against the production of doubt by right-wing climate denialists. See Nixon's *Slow Violence* (2011, 39–40); Klein's *This Changes Everything* (2014, 31–63).

18. This is something I begin to do in the article "Modernity's Dirt: Carbon Emissions and the Technique of Life" (Green 2018).

19. For Mbembe, reference to Africa is always fraught: "I refer to the impossibility of signification, not so much because the African sign resists every process of symbolization, but because Africa has been, for so long, the name of the irreducible outside, an impossible remainder whose meaning and identity cannot be spoken about except by way of an originary act of expropriation" (2001, 153).

20. Auty claims that "the roots of the mineral economies' underperformance *vis-à-vis* other developing countries lies in the mining sector's production function (i.e., ration

of capital to labor), domestic linkages and deployment of mineral rents. Unlike most (but not all) developing country primary exports, mineral production is strongly capital intensive and employs a small fraction of the total national workforce with large inputs of capital from foreign sources. This means the mining sector displays marked enclave tendencies" (1993, 3).

21. In their article "Colonizing Currencies," Jean and John Comaroff explain the close association among missionaries, commerce, and the introduction of money among the southern Tswana. They note that "storekeepers stocked all the quotidian objects deemed essential to a civil 'household economy': clothes, fabrics, furniture blankets, sewing implements, soap and candle moulds" (2005, 160).

22. See, for instance, the article in the *Guardian* by John Vidal, "Amnesty Accuses Shell of Failing to Clean Up Niger Delta Oil Spills" (2015).

23. James Ferguson discusses the notion of Africa as including enclaved spaces of resource extraction and conservation in his book *Global Shadows: Africa in the Neoliberal World Order* (2006, 13–15, 42–48).

Chapter 2

The epigraph for this chapter is drawn from Adorno (1978, 115–16).

1. An early version of this discussion of the Biodiversity Hall in the American Natural History Museum was included in the article "The Aphorism and the 'Historical Image': Adorno's Politics of Form" published in *Johannesburg Salon* (Green 2012).

2. It is not the only project of this kind. The Zurich Zoo opening of the biosphere housing a replica of the Masoala rain forest from Madagascar in 2003 is described as marking "a milestone on Zoo Zurich's journey to becoming a conservation centre" (Zurich Zoo n.d.). The Montreal biodome provides examples of four ecosystems found in the Americas in order to draw attention to major environmental issues such as water, climate change, and ecotechnologies.

3. Norberg writes, "The practice of dwelling or lingering turns out to be a key notion for Adorno, insofar as it suggests an enduring focus that alone can trace individual subjects' loss of their scripted roles in the social whole" (2011, 403).

4. In a letter to Adorno in July 1931, Benjamin comments on Adorno's description of the task of philosophy: "I subscribe to this position. Yet I could not have written it without referring to the introduction of my book on Baroque Drama, where this entirely unique and, in the relative and modest sense in which such a thing can be claimed, new idea was first expressed" (Adorno and Benjamin 1999, 9).

5. The Voluntary Human Extinction Movement suggests that "when every human chooses to stop breeding, Earth's biosphere will be allowed to return to its former glory, and all remaining creatures will be free to live, die, evolve (if they believe in evolution), and will perhaps pass away, as so many of Nature's 'experiments' have done throughout the eons" (http://www.vhemt.org/aboutvhemt.htm#vhemt).

6. See, for instance, the best-selling *The World Without Us* by Alan Weisman, which Chakrabarty discusses in his article "The Climate of History" (2009).

7. Carl Akeley (1864–1926) was a taxidermist, sculptor, photographer, and conservationist who specialized in African mammals. He worked at the American Museum of Natural History from 1909 to his death in 1926.

8. Tim Smit, cofounder and chief executive of the Eden Project, and John Willis were both involved with the Lost Gardens of Heligan in Cornwall, a project to restore the gardens of an estate that had fallen into neglect since the First World War.

9. There are a number of websites devoted to information about Panama disease. My

information is drawn from the following: http://panamadisease.org/en/theproblem; http://phys.org/news/2015-11-panama-disease-banana-clone-fusarium.html.

10. Dan Koeppel is a popular science writer whose book *Banana: The Fate of the Fruit That Changed the World* was published in 2008. The details about the banana industry are from the introductory chapter, "The World's Most Humble Fruit."

11. Bloomberg journalist Phoebe Sedgman quotes Gert Kema, researcher at the University of Wageningen (http://www.bloomberg.com/news/articles/2015-06-04/banana-killer-on-the-march-fuels-risk-of-fruit-s-next-extinction).

Chapter 3

The epigraphs for this chapter are drawn from Adorno (1973, 162), and Kracauer (1995, 5).

1. The by now notorious remark by president of the World Bank Lawrence Summers serves as the epigraph for the introduction to Nixon's book *Slow Violence*: "I've always thought that countries in Africa are vastly under polluted" (2011, i).

2. The English translation, *The Natural Contract*, was published in 1995.

3. See the IGBP website, http://www.igbp.net.

4. McKibben's definition of nature as that which excludes humans has attracted criticism from those pointing to its history as part of the romantic American tradition from which Native American engagement with the land has been erased.

5. Crutzen notes, "A daunting task lies ahead for scientists and engineers to guide society towards environmentally sustainable management during the era of the Anthropocene. This will require appropriate human behaviour at all scales, and may well involve internationally accepted, large-scale geo-engineering projects, for instance to 'optimize' climate. At this stage, however, we are still largely treading on *terra incognita*" (2002, 23).

6. The International Commission on Stratigraphy has appointed a working group on the Anthropocene to determine whether the name should be formally adopted:

> Broadly, to be accepted as a formal term the "Anthropocene" needs to be (a) scientifically justified (i.e., the "geological signal" currently being produced in strata now forming must be sufficiently large, clear and distinctive) and (b) useful as a formal term to the scientific community. In terms of (b), the currently informal term "Anthropocene" has already proven to be very useful to the global change research community and thus will continue to be used, but it remains to be determined whether formalization within the Geological Time Scale would make it more useful or broaden its usefulness to other scientific communities, such as the geological community. (Working Group on the "Anthropocene")

7. Timothy Mitchell makes the argument that the form of life of Western democracies is dependent on the exploitation of first coal and then oil. He refers not only to the forms of everyday life but also to the kinds of political life that become possible (2009).

8. The phrase the "human enterprise" is used by Steffen et al. (2015, 82); information about the data from the graphs comes from the same article.

9. In 2014, an updated series of graphs was published that extends the time frame to 2010 and differentiates between countries from the Organization for Economic Co-operation and Development (OECD), BRICS (Brazil, Russia, India, China [including Macau, Hong Kong, and Taiwan, where applicable], and South Africa), and the rest of world. This differentiation was done largely as a response to criticisms that the acceleration graphs did not take into account the

degree to which different countries contributed to the increase in human enterprises as well as the increase in pressure on earth systems (Steffen et al. 2015, 83). The CAIT Climate Data Explorer website now provides much more detailed information about the differential contribution of different countries and regions. See note 13 in this chapter.

10. See, for instance, *Colonizing Currencies* (Comaroff and Comaroff 2005), as well as a more general reflection on the use of the commodity as an agent of colonialism, *The Commodity Culture of Victorian England* (Richards 1990).

11. Satterthwaite explains that the global fair share has been identified as two tons per person per year. He comments that "it is not fair to equate increases in GHG emissions per person among low-income populations (say from 0.1 to 0.5 tonnes of CO_2e per person per year) with comparable GHG increases among high-income populations (for instance, from 7.1 to 7.5 tonnes per person per year)" (2009, 551).

12. The CAIT Climate Data Explorer now provides a tool for measuring and comparing greenhouse gas (GHG) emissions according to sector (energy, industrial processes, agriculture, waste, bunker fuels, and land-use change) and by energy subsector (heat, manufacturing, transport, other fuel combinations, and fugitive emissions) and across countries and regions (CAIT.wri.org). See also my discussion of these graphs in "Modernity's Dirt: Carbon Emissions and the Technique of Life" (Green 2018).

13. The article "Even Stunning Blue Water Is Infested with 'Plastic Smog'" in *Rodale's Organic Life* includes a sidebar titled "10 Ways to Kick Plastics" that mentions rejecting the ziplock bag as one way of reducing plastic waste (Johnson 2015, 84).

14. Durning is following in a tradition stretching back to the 1970s that criticizes consumption and recommends a different, simpler lifestyle. See, for example, Schumacher's *Small Is Beautiful* (2010), first published in 1973; Duane Elgin's *Voluntary Simplicity* (2010), first published in 1981.

15. For a detailed discussion of the role of advertising in the development of American capitalism, see "The Sales Effort and Monopoly Capitalism" (Holleman et al. 2009).

16. See, for instance, the Alan Curtis documentary *The Century of the Self* (2002), which explores the way Freud's theories have been used by the advertising industry.

17. See, for instance, the complex ideological contortions of the magazine *Monocle*, which promotes environmentalism and the values of an "artisanal" lifestyle for the super-rich. Thanks to Ute Kuhlmann for drawing my attention to this.

Chapter 4

The epigraph for this chapter is drawn from Horkheimer (2013, 76–77).

1. The copy of Chilvers's *The Story of De Beers* (1939) held by the Royal Collections Trust lists these details in the catalog as part of the book's provenance.

2. In Gardner Williams's description of the history of diamond mining, he notes, "The demand [for diamonds] was enough to stir the pulse of production in every part of South Africa, and the heartening impulse thus given was sustained and advanced far beyond the stretch of this novel requirement by the rising faith in the possibilities and future of South Africa as a field for investment, which now began to lift the drooping spirits of the colonists and to attract the cooperation of the home country and the leading nations of the world" (1902, 555).

3. See "Disaggregating Primitive Accumulation" (Nichols 2015).

4. Marx writes, "And this history, the history of expropriation, is written in the annals of mankind in letters of blood and fire" (1976, 875).

5. See Amy Milne-Smith's discussion of the gentleman's club in "A Flight to Domesticity? Making a Home in the Gentlemen's Clubs of London, 1880–1914" (2006, 796–818). In Kimberley, unlike in London, the club represented the only form of domesticity available, since many of the members still lived in temporary corrugated iron houses.

6. See *The Secret Society: Cecil John Rhodes's Plan for a New World Order* for a description of this vision of a world elite (Brown 2015).

7. Pines and oaks are both relatively widespread in the Northern Hemisphere, while the camphor and hydrangeas originate in China and various parts of East Asia.

8. "The squirrels, too, liberated at Groote Schuur have spread in vast numbers over the Cape peninsula, and levy a heavy toll upon all manner of nuts, and destroy thousands of peaches in getting at the kernels in the stones. Serious attempts are being made to exterminate them" (Le Sueur 1913, 246–47).

9. There were also differences in the laws of the Cape Colony and the Orange Free State about the ownership of mineral resources found on the land; see Lunderstedt (2008, 45).

10. Several writers describe this process: The participants are invited to London, where they are presented with a box of diamonds. The requirements are that the buyers cannot question which diamonds they get, they cannot haggle over price, they are required to take the whole box or none at all, and they are not permitted to resell the uncut diamonds (Epstein 1982; Kanfer 1993).

11. Smalberger describes a horrifying incident reported in the local paper, *Diamond News*, in which a digger pulls out all the teeth and lacerates the gums of a black worker he suspects of stealing diamonds (1974, 428).

12. Smalberger notes that "thus the racial implications of prohibiting the issue of licenses to black diggers was camouflaged by a clause requiring all claimholders to acquire a certificate of good character from a magistrate or a justice of the peace, who was likely to be sympathetic to white diggers' wishes" (1976, 430).

13. Anglo-American acquired De Beers in 1926.

14. The website Charlize Theron's Shimansky Moment is no longer available, but the content with slightly altered wording has been recycled in the online advertising newsletter *Cape Town Magazine* (Nevitt n.d.).

15. According to Epstein, De Beers undertook a similar advertising campaign in Japan with a similarly dramatic increase in diamond ring sales.

16. This was important also because De Beers could not operate in the United States because it violated U.S. antitrust laws (Kanfer 1993, 270).

17. See Epstein's *Have You Ever Tried to Sell a Diamond?* (2011, 631).

18. A recent article reveals a further aspect of N. W. Ayers's campaign: During World War II, advertisements implied that buying gem diamonds assisted the war effort by financing the mining of industrial-grade diamonds. In fact, mining ceased during the war, the stockpile in the London vault being sufficient to meet the needs of both gem sales and industrial uses of diamonds (Ghilani 2012).

19. Matthew Hart describes how a De Beers marketing campaign addressed to men specified not only the necessity of buying a diamond for the woman they love but also what they should pay: "In North America, an ad demanded 'Isn't she worth two months' salary?' This figure was adjusted according to market study of what men in the different parts of the world would pay. European men got off with one month's salary; the Japanese were asked for three" (2002, 147).

20. In the twentieth century, the hunt acquires a philosophical dimension as a pursuit in which man might test his mettle through an authentic encounter with nature. In *Meditation on Hunting*, written in 1942, philosopher José Ortega y Gasset writes, "Hunting submerges man deliberately in that formidable mystery and therefore contains something of the religious rite and emotion in which homage is paid to what is divine, transcendent, in the laws of Nature" (1972, 112).

21. Philip Armstrong notes that "where industrial modernity reduces animals to a collection of raw materials or a sequence of processes, modernist aesthetics sublimates them into essence" (2008, 149).

Chapter 5

The epigraph for this chapter is drawn from Horkheimer and Adorno (2002, 118).

1. The organization is no longer called the Lupus Foundation, and the website has since been updated. A copy of the original website is available at https://web.archive.org/web/20140723093739/http://www.wolfsa.org.za/content_mission.htm.

2. The Ethiopian wolf organization suggests, "Most likely, the Ethiopian wolf evolved from a grey wolf-like ancestor that crossed to northern Africa from Eurasia as recently as 100,000 years ago, when Afroalpine habitats in Ethiopia covered vast extensions." Only a small population exists in the Ethiopian highlands (http://ethiopianwolf.org/taxonomy-and-genetics).

3. Although it is only recently that extinctions have become part of the dominant narrative of nature, by the end of the nineteenth century, colonial administrators had reluctantly recognized the diminishing of wild animals and tried to exert a control (Beinart and Coates 1995).

4. Sandra Swart and Lance van Sittert mention these wolf dogs in the context of their fascinating history of the dog in South Africa. Their discussion follows a different line of inquiry, seeing these wolves as part of a particular set of associations with guard dogs, security, and violence that emerged in South Africa during the colonial and apartheid periods (2008).

5. In *Negative Dialectics*, Adorno writes, "The name dialectics says no more, to begin with, than that objects do not go into their concepts without leaving a remainder, that they come to contradict the traditional norm of adequacy" (1973, 5).

6. An early version of this research, titled "Apartheid Wolves: Political Animals and Animal Politics," was published in *Critical African Studies* (Green 2016).

7. The South African military was not the only one to experiment with breeding wolves with dogs. A paper given at a conference held on the European wolf in 2008 mentions the breeding of wolf dogs in the Czech Republic, although not much information is provided: "There is practically no literature about wolf hybrids in the Czech Republic. The first reliable documentation about crossing dogs and wolves is from the 1950s to 1980s. Biometrical data and photographic documentation from experimental crossbreeding of wolves with Border Guard dogs exist in military archives. The aim of crossing was to verify the possibility of crossing between different species and observe the endogeny of dogs, wolves and their hybrids. The hybrids were regularly measured and weighed and their character traits were observed. The project of experimental crossbreeding was led by col. Ing. Karel Hartl" (Šebkova et al. 2008, 42).

8. In the TRC chemical and biological warfare hearings report, Johan Koekemoer admits to producing 912 kg of ecstasy at the request of Wouter Basson in the early 1990s (Koekemoer 1998, 214–15).

9. Godwin begins the article with the following statement: "Padding along the streets of Johannesburg, yellow-eyed, snarling with a tendency to howl, is the city's latest crime-fighting weapon: Shep the wolf-dog" (1989).

10. Coetzee explains that Istwan Larendler was a friend and advisor of the dog unit who helped them with the breeding program. According to Coetzee, he had obtained a doctorate in zoology, majoring in the wolf, at the University of Budapest, Hungary (Coetzee 2011, 144).

11. Coetzee includes a photograph of a wolf dog named Jungle with the caption "Jungle as aggressive as can be" (2011, 148).

12. In another military memoir describing the establishment of the 32 Battalion, the author Piet Nortje explains, in a chapter on symbols and traditions, that "for 32, a buffalo was chosen, not only in honor of the vast herds of animals that roamed the Caprivi where the unit was formed, but in recognition of the fighting spirit the men of Buffalo Base shared with this fearless and most dangerous of wild animals" (2003, 79).

13. The South African Broadcasting Corporation Truth and Reconciliation Commission (SABCTRC) website contains a number of references to activities ascribed to the Wit Wolwe (sabctrc.saha.org.za). See also Janet Smith's article on Barend Strydom, the alleged leader of the group (2008).

Chapter 6

The epigraph for this chapter is drawn from Adorno (1978, 115–16).

1. An article in the journal *Conservation Biology* indicates that most reserve managers at least conceive of environmental protection as their primary role (Langholz 1996).

2. De Beers also owns Benfontein and Dronfield private game reserves in the Northern Cape and Venetia Limpopo Nature Reserve in Limpopo province. Information about its history available at http://www.kimberley.co.za/city/rooipoort-nature-reserve/.

3. This information is included at http://www.projectafrica.com/heritage-conservation/rooipoort-nature-reserve/.

4. Sean Gubbins describes the Rhodes family involvement in the development of Hackney in his M.A. thesis (2004).

5. An early version of this section of the chapter was published in *Social Dynamics* as "A Landscape with Objects: Private Game Reserves, Game Lodges and the 'New Safari'" (Green 2010).

6. All further references to Wilderness Safaris are to their website.

7. For a discussion of the complex nature of conservation in Tanzania, see Roderick Neumann's *Imposing Wilderness: Struggles over Livelihood and Nature Preservation in Africa* (1998).

8. Ferguson refers to Roderick Neumann's study of parks in Tanzania and notes that community participation has not replaced militarization; rather, it has supplemented it (Ferguson 2006, 43).

9. According to Van Eeden, complaints were lodged by members of the public, the Human Rights Commission, the Commission on Gender Equality, and the Namibian Ministry of Foreign Affairs, Information and Broadcasting (2006, 348).

10. Information about the interior design monograph from personal conversation with architect and cultural theorist Noëleen Murray.

11. Others would include books such as Bibi Jordan's *Safari Chic* (2000) and Sharna and Darryl Balfour's *Simply Safari* (2001).

12. Craig Fraser is described in an article in the online magazine *Just the Planet* as a "renowned lifestyle photographer." In an interview with Fraser published by the magazine, Fraser makes the following comment: "Game lodges allow one to travel back in time, 'before man.' They take you to a place so far removed from everyday urban life, providing a complete escape and a life-changing experience that puts life into perspective" (Fraser n.d.).

13. MacCannell suggests that "the touristic ideal of the 'primitive' is that of a magical resource that can be used without actually possessing or diminishing it" (1992, 28). This is a "utopian vision" of the relation between tourist and "other," which MacCannell argues is impossible.

14. In the comment quoted earlier in the chapter, Baudrillard emphasizes that the architect in his restored country cottage

"fundamentally has no part to play here, his entire social existence lies elsewhere" (1996, 83). In a similar way, the work of the lodge is to simulate such a "social existence."

15. These figures are included in Carruthers's discussion of the rise of the private game reserve (2008, 162). She suggests a number of reasons for this shift: "Specifically the loss of subsidy to commercial farming and the deregulation of the agricultural sector, the loss of political power of white farmers, the increase of livestock theft and the rising costs of labor, the cost impact of animal disease control, as well as HIV/AIDS and the re-emergence of malaria, land restitution claims and climate change" (176).

16. Journalist Antoinette Slabbert presents the opinion of game farmer Johan van der Merwe: "Taking into account the value of the offspring and production cost, Van der Merwe says the annual return on capital employed can be 84.86% per year on nyala, 130% on black impala, breeding with regular impala ewes. Sable is the most modest performer among the rare game with a 31.2% annual return on capital" (2013).

17. Wildvest is South Africa's first wildlife investment company.

18. Stapelkamp claims that there were no quotas issued for lion hunting in that area in 2015, that regulations require a game ranger to be present on a hunt, that a special permit is required to hunt with a bow, and that the existing permit was acquired through an illegal quota swap (Ramsay 2015).

Chapter 7

1. See https://www.iol.co.za/capetimes/news/cape-towns-dam-levels-decline-only-by-01-19953898.

2. See the article by Stuart Thompson in *The Conversation*, "The Quest to Save the Banana from Extinction" (2019).

3. East Island, a low-lying island of the Hawaiian archipelago that was being studied by researchers to note the effects of climate change, entirely disappeared after Hurricane Walaka. The researcher Chip Fletcher comments that while he knew East Island would be underwater eventually, he expected it to take several decades (Eagle 2018).

4. See the discussion in Jason Moore's introduction to *Anthropocene or Capitalocene: Nature, History and the Crisis of Capitalism* (2016).

5. See "We Won't Save the World with a Better Kind of Disposable Coffee Cup" (Monbiot 2018).

6. In David Pilling's book *The Growth Delusion*, he explains that, as it is currently calculated, any economic activity counts toward the gross domestic product, even those that have a seriously negative impact on society and the environment. At the same time, he notes that while "no serious advocate of GDP would claim it is a measure of well-being . . . few would deny that in public discourse it has morphed into a proxy for just that" (2018, 296).

7. According to Suzman, the film was popular among the Ju/'hoansi and for many years ran on a continuous loop at Tsumke general store (2017).

8. "Men, Women, and Dogs" is included under the heading "Makua Tales," contributed by the Ven. Archdeacon H. W. Woodward in *Bantu Studies* (1932).

9. The phrase "fraught with background" is borrowed from Erich Auerbach's discussion of the Bible in the first chapter of *Mimesis* (1986). He uses it to describe the narrative form of the Bible, in which much is implied but not explained. In comparing the narrative form of the Bible to Homer's *Odyssey*, where all events, fully and completely described, appear in the foreground, the Bible, he suggests, is "fraught with background" (10).

References

Adams, Jonathan, and Thomas McShane. 1992. *The Myth of Wild Africa: Conservation Without Illusion.* Berkeley: University of California Press.

Adorno, Theodor. 1973. *Negative Dialectics.* New York: Continuum.

———. 1978. *Minima Moralia: Reflections from Damaged Life.* Translated by E. F. N. Jephcott. London: Verso.

———. 1981. "Veblen's Attack on Culture." In *Prisms*, translated by Samuel and Sherry Weber, 75–94. Cambridge: MIT Press.

———. 1984. "The Idea of Natural History." *Telos* 60:111–24.

———. 1991. "The Essay as Form." In *Notes on Literature*, by Theodor Adorno, edited by Rolf Tiedermann, translated by Shierry Weber Nicholsen, 3–23. New York: Columbia University Press.

———. 1998. "Why Still Philosophy." In *Critical Models: Intervention and Catchwords*, by Theodor Adorno, translated by Henry W. Pickford, 5–17. New York: Columbia University Press.

Adorno, Theodor, and Walter Benjamin. 1999. *The Complete Correspondence, 1928–1940.* Cambridge: Harvard University Press.

Alao, Abiodun. 2007. *Natural Resources and Conflict in Africa: The Tragedy of Endowment.* Rochester: Rochester University Press.

Armstrong, Philip. 2008. *What Animals Mean in the Fictions of Modernity.* Abingdon, Va.: Routledge.

Auerbach, Erich. 1986. *Mimesis: The Representation of Reality in Western Literature.* Translated by William Trask. New York: Doubleday Anchor Books.

Auty, Richard. 1993. *Sustaining Development in Mineral Economies: The Resource Curse Thesis.* London: Routledge.

Balfour, Sharna, and Daryl Balfour. 2001. *Simply Safari.* Cape Town, South Africa: Struik.

Baudrillard, Jean. 1996. *The System of Objects.* London: Verso.

Beck, Ulrich, Anthony Giddens, and Scott Lash. 1994. *Reflexive Modernization: Politics, Tradition and Aesthetics in the Modern Social Order.* Stanford: Stanford University Press.

Beinart, William. 2008. *The Rise of Conservation in South Africa: Settlers, Livestock and the Environment, 1770–1950*. Oxford: Oxford University Press.

Beinart, William, and Peter Coates. 1995. *Environment and History: The Taming of Nature in the USA and South Africa*. London: Routledge.

Bernstein, Jay. 2001. *Disenchantment and Ethics*. New York: Cambridge University Press.

Billet, Roy. 1987. "The Wolf Factor." *Farmer's Weekly*, January 16.

Brinig, Margaret. 1990. "Rings and Promises." *Journal of Law, Economic and Organization* 6 (1): 203–15.

Brown, Duncan. 2011. "Are Trout South African? Or: A Postcolonial Fish." *Johannesburg Salon* 4:15–17.

Brown, Robin. 2015. *The Secret Society: Cecil John Rhodes's Plan for a New World Order*. Cape Town, South Africa: Penguin.

Buck-Morss, Susan. 1977. *The Origin of the Negative Dialectics*. New York: Free Press.

Bunn, David. 1996. "Comparative Barbarisms: Game Reserves, Sugar Plantations and the Modernization of the South African Landscape." In *Text, Theory, Space, Land Literature and History*, edited by Kate Darian-Smith, Liz Gunnar, and Sarah Nuttall, 37–52. London: Routledge.

Carmody, Padraig. 2011. *The New Scramble for Africa*. Cambridge: Polity.

Carruthers, Jane. 1995. *The Kruger National Park: A Social and Political History*. Pietermaritzburg, South Africa: University of Natal Press.

———. 2008. "'Wilding the Farm or Farming the Wild': Evolution of Scientific Game Ranching in South Africa from the 1960s to the Present." *Transactions of the Royal Society of South Africa* 62 (2): 160–81.

Chakrabarty, Dipesh. 2009. "The Climate of History." *Critical Inquiry* 35:197–222.

Chávez, Hugo. 2006. "Together We Can Change the World." *Mail and Guardian*, July 30.

Chilvers, Hedley. 1939. *The Story of De Beers*. London: Cassell.

Christie, Sean. 2012. "Wild Life Prices Too Big for Genes." *Mail and Guardian*, April 20. Accessed August 12, 2016. http://mg.co.za/article/2012-04-20-wildlife-prices-too-big-for-genes.

Cleveland, Todd. 2014. *Stones of Contention: A History of Africa's Diamonds*. Athens: Ohio University Press.

Coetzee, Peet. 2011. *Dogs of War: Memoirs of the South African Defence Force Dog Units*. Noorsekloof, South Africa: Self-published.

Comaroff, Jean, and John Comaroff. 2001. "Naturing the Nation: Aliens, Apocalypse and the Postcolonial State." *Journal of Southern African Studies* 27 (3): 627–51.

———. 2005. "Colonizing Currencies: Beasts, Banknotes, and the

Colour of Money in South Africa." In *Commodification: Things, Agency, and Identity*, edited by Wim Van Binsbergen and Peter Geschiere, 145–73. New Brunswick, Canada: Transaction.

Cook, Deborah. 2011. *Adorno on Nature*. Durham: Acumen.

Cooper, Frederick. 2002. *Africa Since 1940: The Past of the Present*. Cambridge: Cambridge University Press.

Cotroneo, Christian. 2014. "Woolly Mammoth Clone Now Possible, Say Scientists." *Huffington Post Canada*, March 14.

Cousins, Jenny A., Jon P. Sadler, and James Evans. 2008. "Exploring the Role of Private Wildlife Ranching as a Tool for Conservation in South Africa: Stakeholders Perspectives." *Ecology and Society* 13 (2): 43. http://www.ecologyandsociety.org/vol13/iss2/art43/.

———. 2010. "The Challenge of Regulating Private Wild Life Ranches for Conservation in South Africa." *Ecology and Society* 15 (2): 28. http://www.ecologyandsociety.org/vol15/iss2/art28.

Crookes, William. 1905. *Diamonds: A Lecture Delivered Before the British Association at Kimberley*. London: Chemical News Office.

Crowley, Kevin. 2015. "In South Africa, Ranchers Are Breeding Mutant Animals to Be Hunted." *Bloomberg*, March 11. Accessed January 16, 2019. https://www.bloomberg.com/graphics/2015-hunting-mutant-big-game-in-south-africa/.

Crutzen, Paul. 2002. "The Geology of Mankind." *Nature*, no. 415, 23.

Crutzen, Paul, and Eugene Stoermer. 2000. "The Anthropocene: A New Epoch of Geological Time." *International Geosphere-Biosphere Newsletter* 41. http://www.igbp.net/.

Curtis, Adam, dir. 2002. *The Century of the Self*. BBC documentary series. 235 min.

De Botton, Alan. 2004. *Status Anxiety*. London: Penguin.

Dickens, Charles. 2001. *The Old Curiosity Shop*. London: Penguin.

Dixon, Robyn. 2004. "Sanctuary for the Wolf Orphans of Apartheid." *Los Angeles Times*, October 17. Accessed September 27, 2010. https://www.latimes.com/archives/la-xpm-2004-oct-17-fg-wolf17-story.html.

Durning, Alan. 1992. *How Much Is Enough?* New York: W. W. Norton.

———. 1993. "How Much Is Enough?" *Social Contract*, Spring, 177–79.

Eagle, Nathan. 2018. "Just Vanished." *Honolulu Civil Beat*, October 23. Accessed May 23, 2019. https://www.civilbeat.org/2018/10/this-remote-hawaiian-island-just-vanished/.

Elgin, Duane. 2010. *Voluntary Simplicity*. New York: HarperCollins.

Els, Paul J. 2009. *We Fear Naught but God*. n.p.: PelsA Books (self-published).

Elsworthy, Jo. 2015. *Eden Project: The Guide*. London: Transworld.

Enzensberger, Hans Magnus. 1996. "A Critique of Political Ecology." In *The Greening of Marxism*, edited by Timothy Benton, 23–43. New York: Guilford.

Epstein, Edward Jay. 1982. *The Rise and Fall of Diamonds: The Shattering of a Brilliant Illusion*. New York: EJE.

———. 2011. *Have You Ever Tried to Sell a Diamond? And Other Investigations*. New York: EJE.

Escobar, Arturo. 1988. "Power and Visibility: Development and the Invention and Management of the Third World." *Cultural Anthropology* 3 (4): 428–43.

———. 1995. *Encountering Development: The Making and Unmaking of the Third World*. Princeton: Princeton University Press.

Esteva, Gustavo. 1992. "Development." In *The Development Dictionary: A Guide to Knowledge as Power*, edited by Wolfgang Sachs, 6–25. London: Zed Books.

Ferguson, James. 2006. *Global Shadows: Africa in the Neoliberal World Order*. Durham: Duke University Press.

Foster, John Bellamy, and Brett Clark. 2010. "The Ecology of Consumption." *Polygraph* 22:113–32.

Foucault, Michel, and Jay Miskoviec. 1986. "Of Other Spaces: Utopias and Heterotopias." *Diacritics* 16 (1): 22–27.

Franklin, Sarah. 2000. "Life Itself: Global Nature and the Genetic Imaginary." In *Global Nature, Global Culture*, edited by Sarah Franklin, Celia Lury, and Jackie Stacy, 188–227. London: Sage.

Fraser, Craig. n.d. "The Inside Story on The New Safari." *Just the Planet*. Accessed October 11, 2009. http://www.justtheplanet.com/safari/the-new-safari-craig-fraser.php.

Fraser, Craig, and Mandy Allen. 2007. *The New Safari: Design, Decor, Detail*. Cape Town, South Africa: Quivertree.

Ghilani, Jessica L. 2012. "De Beers' 'Fighting Diamonds': Recruiting American Consumer in American World War II Advertising." *Journal of Communication Inquiry* 36 (3): 222–45.

Godoy, Julio. 2009. "Development: The Second Scramble for Africa Starts." *Interpress Service News Agency*, April 20. Accessed June 29, 2015. http://www.ipsnews.net/2009/04/the-second-scramble-for-africa-starts/.

Godwin, Peter. 1989. "Wolf-Dog Joins Pretoria Police Forces; South Africa." *Sunday Times* (London, England), October 22. Accessed February 26, 2014. http://www.sunday-times.co.uk.

Goosen, Daan. 1998. *Testimony of Daan Goosen*. Western Cape, South Africa: TRC Chemical and Biological Warfare Hearings.

Gould, Chandre. 2006. "South Africa's Chemical and Biological Warfare Programme, 1981–1995." Ph.D. diss., Rhodes University.

Green, Lesley. 2013. "Contested Ecologies: Nature and Knowledge." In *Contested Ecologies: Dialogues in the South on Nature and Knowledge*, edited by Lesley Green, 1–9. Cape Town, South Africa: HSRC.

Green, Louise. 2010. "A Landscape with Objects: Private Game Reserves, Game Lodges and the 'New Safari.'" *Social Dynamics* 36 (2): 288–301.

———. 2012. "The Aphorism and the 'Historical Image': Adorno's Politics of Form." *Johannesburg Salon* 5:80–85.

———. 2016. "Apartheid's Wolves: Political Animals and Animal Politics." *Critical African Studies* 8 (2): 146–60. https://doi.org/10.1080/21681392.2016.1209873.

———. 2017. "Nature." In *Fueling Culture: 101 Words for Energy and Environment*, edited by Imre Szeman, Jennifer Wenzel, and Patricia Yaeger, 227–29. New York: Fordham University Press.

———. 2018. "Modernity's Dirt: Carbon Emissions and the Technique of Life." *Social Dynamics* 44 (2): 239–56. https://doi.org/10.1080/02533952.2018.1489582.

Gubbins, Sean. 2004. "Rhodes Town—How Lamb Farm Became Hackney Suburbia." M.A. diss., University College London.

Haraway, Donna. 1989. *Primate Visions: Gender, Race and Nature in the World of Modern Science*. New York: Routledge.

———. 1991. *Simians, Cyborgs and Women: The Reinvention of Nature*. London: Free Association Books.

———. 2007. *When Species Meet*. Minneapolis: University of Minnesota Press.

Hart, Matthew. 2002. *Diamonds: The History of a Cold-Blooded Love Affair*. London: Fourth Estate.

Hobsbawm, Eric. 1983. "Mass-Producing Traditions: Europe, 1870–1914." In *The Invention of Tradition*, edited by Eric Hobsbawm and Terence Ranger, 263–307. Cambridge: Cambridge University Press.

Holleman, Hannah, Inger L. Stole, John Belamy Foster, and Robert W. McChesney. 2009. "The Sales Effort and Monopoly Capitalism." *Monthly Review: An Independent Socialist Magazine*, April 1. Accessed December 2018. https://monthlyreview.org/2009/04/01/the-sales-effort-and-monopoly-capital/.

Horkheimer, Max. 2013. *The Eclipse of Reason*. London: Bloomsbury Academic.

Horkheimer, Max, and Theodor Adorno. 2002. *Dialectic of the Enlightenment: Philosophical Fragments*. Edited by Gunzelin Schmid Noerr. Translated by Edmund Jephcott. Stanford: Stanford University Press.

Hullot-Kentor, Robert. 2010. "The Exact Sense in Which the Culture Industry No Longer Exists." In *The Culture Industry Today*, edited by Fabio Akcelrud Durao,

5–22. Newcastle: Cambridge Scholars Publishing.

Independent Online. "Cape Town Dam Levels Decline Only by 0.1%." March 18, 2019. Accessed March 2019. https://www.iol.co.za/capetimes/news/cape-towns-dam-levels-decline-only-by-01-19953898.

Inglis, Fred. 2000. *The Delicious History of the Holiday*. London: Routledge.

Iovino, Serenella. 2015. "The Living Diffractions of Matter and Text: Narrative Agency, Strategic Anthropomorphism and How Interpretation Works." *Anglia* 133 (1): 69–86.

Jameson, Fredric. 1990. *Late Marxism: Adorno or the Persistence of the Dialectic*. London: Verso.

Jarosinski, Eric. 2010. "Of Stones and Glass Houses: *Minima Moralia* as a Critique of Transparency." In *Language Without Soil: Adorno and Late Philosophical Modernity*, edited by Gerhard Richter, 157–71. New York: Fordham University Press.

Johnson, Jack. 2015. "Even Stunning Blue Water Is Infested with 'Plastic Smog.'" *Rodale's Organic Life: Food Home Garden Well-Being*, August 22, 84–86.

Jolly, Rosemary. 2010. *Cultured Violence: Narrative, Social Suffering and Engendering Human Rights in Contemporary South Africa*. Scottsville: University of KwaZulu-Natal Press.

Jordan, Bibi. 2000. *Safari Chic*. London: Thames & Hudson.

Jourdan, Philip. 1910. *Cecil Rhodes: His Private Life by His Private Secretary*. London: John Lane.

Kamil, Fred. 1979. *The Diamond Underworld*. London: Allen Lane.

Kanfer, Stefan. 1993. *The Last Empire: De Beers, Diamonds, and the World*. London: Hodder & Stoughton.

Kapp, Karl William. 1971. *The Social Costs of Private Enterprise*. New York: Schocken Books.

Klein, Naomi. 2014. *This Changes Everything: Capitalism vs. the Climate*. London: Allen Lane.

Koekemoer, Johan. 1998. *Testimony of Johan Koekemoer*. Western Cape, South Africa: TRC Chemical and Biological Warfare Hearings.

Koeppel, Dan. 2008. *Banana: The Fate of a Fruit That Changed the World*. New York: Hudson Street.

Kracauer, Siegfried. 1995. *The Mass Ornament: Weimar Essays*. Edited by Thomas Levin. Cambridge: Harvard University Press.

Langholz, Jeff. 1996. "Economics, Objectives, and Success of Private Game Reserves in Sub-Saharan Africa and Latin America." *Conservation Biology* 10 (1): 271–80.

Latour, Bruno. 2009. "Will Non-humans Be Saved? An Argument in Ecotheology." *Journal of the Royal Anthropological Institute*, no. 15, 459–75.

Le Billon, Philippe. 2006. "Fatal Transactions: Conflict Diamonds and the (Anti)Terrorist

Consumer." *Antipode* 38 (4): 778–801.

Le Sueur, Gordon. 1913. *Cecil Rhodes: The Man and His Works*. London: John Murray.

Lindsey, Peter, Robert Alexander, Guy Balme, Neil Midlane, and J. Craig. 2012. "Possible Relationships Between Captive-Bred Lion Hunting Industry and the Hunting and Conservation of Lions Elsewhere." *South African Journal of Wildlife Research* 42 (1): 11–22.

Liverman, Diana M. 2009. "Conventions of Climate Change: Constructions of Danger and the Dispossession of the Atmosphere." *Journal of Historical Geography* 35 (2): 279–96.

Lorenz, Konrad. 1961. *King Solomon's Ring*. London: Methuen.

Lukács, Georg. 1978. *The Theory of the Novel*. Translated by A. Bostock. London: Merlin.

Lunderstedt, Steve. 2008. *The Big Five Mines of Kimberley*. Kimberley, South Africa: Kimberley Africana Library.

Luxemburg, Rosa. 1951. *The Accumulation of Capital*. Translated by Agnes Schwarzschild. London: Routledge and Kegan Paul.

Lyman, Francesca. 1998. *Inside the Dzanga-Sangha Rainforest*. New York: American Museum of Natural History.

MacCannell, Dean. 1992. *Empty Meeting Grounds*. London: Routledge.

MacDonald, David W., Kim J. Jacobsen, Dawn Burnham, Paul J. Johnson, and Andrew J. Loveridge. 2016. "Cecil: A Moment or a Movement? Analysis of Media Coverage of the Death of a Lion, *Panthera leo*." *Animals* 6 (26): 1–13.

Malm, Andreas, and Alf Hornborg. 2014. "The Geology of Mankind? A Critique of the Anthropocene Narrative." *Anthropocene Review* 1 (1): 62–69.

Marx, Karl. 1976. *Capital: A Critique of Political Economy*. Translated by Ben Fowkes. Vol. 1. Harmondsworth: Penguin.

Massumi, Brian. 2014. *What Animals Teach Us About Politics*. Durham: Duke University Press.

Mbembe, Achille. 2001. *On the Postcolony*. Berkeley: University of California Press.

McDonald, J. G. 1927. *Rhodes: A Life*. London: Geoffrey Bles.

McKibben, Bill. 1990. *The End of Nature*. New York: Random House.

Milne-Smith, Amy. 2006. "A Flight to Domesticity? Making a Home in the Gentleman's Clubs of London, 1880–1914." *Journal of British Studies* 45 (4): 796–818.

Mitchell, Timothy. 2011. *Carbon Democracy: Political Power in the Age of Oil*. London: Verso.

Mitchell, William John Thomas. 1998. *The Last Dinosaur Book*. Chicago: University of Chicago Press.

Monbiot, George. 2013. *Feral: Rewilding the Land, Sea and Human Life*. London: Penguin.

———. 2018. "We Won't Save the World with a Better Kind of Disposable

Coffee Cup." *Guardian*, September 6.

Moore, Jason. 2016. *Anthropocene or Capitalocene? Nature, History and the Crisis of Capital*. Oakland: PM Press.

Morson, Gary Saul. 2006. "Bakhtin, the Genre of Quotations, and the Aphoristic Consciousness." *Slavic and East European Journal* 50 (1): 213–27.

Neethling, Lothar. 1998. *Testimony of Lothar Neethling*. Western Cape, South Africa: TRC Chemical and Biological Warfare Hearings.

Neumann, Roderick. 1998. *Imposing Wilderness: Struggles over Livelihood and Nature Preservation in Africa*. Los Angeles: University of California Press.

Nevitt, Lisa. n.d. "Celebrities and South African Jewels." *Cape Town Magazine*. Accessed December 11, 2019. https://www.capetownmagazine.com/shimansky-celebrities.

Nichols, Robert. 2015. "Disaggregating Primitive Accumulation." *Radical Philosophy* 194:18–28.

Nixon, Rob. 2011. *Slow Violence and the Environmentalism of the Poor*. Cambridge: Harvard University Press.

Norberg, Jakob. 2011. "Adorno's Advice: *Minima Moralia* and the Critique of Liberalism." *Modern Language Association* 126 (2): 398–409.

Nortje, Piet. 2003. *32 Battalion: The Inside Story of South Africa's Elite Fighting Unit*. Cape Town, South Africa: Zebra.

O'Connor, Brian. 2000. *The Adorno Reader*. Oxford: Blackwell.

Odendaal, F. F., and R. H. Gouws, comps. 2000. *HAT (Verklarende Handwoordeboek van die Afrikaanse Taal)*. Johannesburg: Perskor.

Ortega y Gasset, José. 1972. *Meditation on Hunting*. New York: Charles Scribner's Sons.

Oxford University Press. 1944. *Oxford English Dictionary*. 3rd ed. Oxford: Oxford University Press.

Pensky, Max. 2004. "Natural History: The Life and Afterlife of a Concept in Adorno." *Critical Horizons* 5 (1): 227–58.

Pilling, David. 2018. *The Growth Delusion: The Wealth and Well-Being of Nations*. London: Bloomsbury.

Pirie, Gordon. 2008. "Automobility in Colonial Africa Before 1939: Uses, Constraints, Dependence." Unpublished paper presented at the South African and Contemporary History and Humanities Seminar, Centre for Humanities Research, University of the Western Cape.

Plumwood, Val. 1993. *Feminism and the Mastery of Nature*. London: Routledge.

Pooley, Simon. 2010. "Pressed Flowers: Notions of Indigenous and Alien Vegetation in South Africa's Western Cape, c. 1902–1945." *Journal of Southern African Studies* 36 (3): 599–618.

Ralph Appelbaum and Associates. n.d. "Hall of Biodiversity." Accessed August 25, 2015. http://www.raany.com/commission/hall-biodiversity.

Ramsay, Scott. 2015. "The Aftermath of Cecil—Interview with Lion Researcher, Brent Stapelkamp." October 27. Accessed December 11, 2016. http://www.lovewildafrica.com/stories/the-aftermath-of-cecil-interview-with-lion-researcher-brent-stapelkamp/.

Richards, Thomas. 1990. *The Commodity Culture of Victorian England*. London: Verso.

Rosenthal, Eric. 1964. *Encyclopaedia of Southern Africa*. London: Frederick Warne.

Rotberg, Robert. 1988. *The Founder: Cecil John Rhodes and the Pursuit of Power*. Johannesburg, South Africa: Southern.

Sabatini, R. J. L., and Kokkie Duminy. 2013. *50 Years on the Diamond Fields, 1870–1920*. Vol. 1. Kimberley, South Africa: Kimberley Africana Library.

———. 2014. *50 Years on the Diamond Fields, 1870–1920*. Vol. 2. Kimberley, South Africa: Kimberley African Library.

Satterthwaite, David. 2009. "The Implications of Urbanization and Population Growth for Climate Change." *Environment and Urbanization* 29 (2): 545–67.

Sax, Boria. 2013. *Animals in the Third Reich*. Providence: Yogh & Thorn.

Schumacher, Ernst F. (1973) 2010. *Small Is Beautiful: Economics as If People Mattered*. New York: HarperCollins.

Šebkova, Naděžda, Jindřich Jedlička, Karel Hartl, and František Hrach. 2008. "Is a Hybridization with Dogs a Threat to Free-Living Wolves in Czech Republic?" In *Perspectives of Wolves in Central Europe*, edited by Miroslav Kutal and Robin Rigg, 42–47. Olomouc, Czech Republic: Hnuti DUHA Olomouc.

Serres, Michel. 1995. *The Natural Contract*. Translated by Elizabeth MacArthur and William Paulson. Ann Arbor: University of Michigan Press.

Simmel, Georg. (1903) 1971. "The Metropolis and Mental Life." In *On Individuality and Social Forms*, edited by Donald L. Levine, 324–39. Chicago: University of Chicago Press.

Slabbert, Antoinette. 2013. "Why Does Johann Rupert Invest in Buffalo?" *Moneyweb*, September 9. Accessed March 2, 2016. http://www.moneyweb.co.za/archive/can-game-farming-outperform-the-jse/.

Smalberger, John. 1974. "I.D.B. and the Mining Compound System in the 1880s." *South African Journal of Economics* 24 (4): 247–58.

———. 1976. "The Role of the Diamond Mining Industry in the Development of the Pass-Law System in South Africa." *International Journal of African Historical Studies* 9 (3): 419–34.

Smit, Timothy. 2011. *Eden: The Whole Inspiring Story of the Eden Project*. St Austell, England: Eden Project Books.

Smith, Janet. 2008. "What Became of the Big Wit Wolf?" *IOL News*, November 15. Accessed January 11, 2013. http://www.iol.co.za/news/south-africa/what-became-of-the-big-wit-wolf-1.424408.

Smith, Neil. 1984. *Uneven Development: Nature, Capital, and the Production of Space*. Athens: University of Georgia Press.

Soper, Kate. 1995. *What Is Nature?* Oxford: Blackwell.

Spengler, Oswald. 1916. *The Decline of the West*. Translated by Charles Francis Atkinson. New York: Alfred A. Knopf.

Steffen, Will, Wendy Broadgate, Lisa Deutch, Will Gaffney, and Cornelia Ludwig. 2015. "The Trajectory of the Anthropocene: The Great Acceleration." *Anthropocene Review* 2 (1): 81–98.

Stepanak, Stephanie Loeb, and Frederick Ilchman. n.d. *Goya: Order and Disorder*. Boston: Museum of Fine Arts Publications.

Strydom, Barend. 1997. *Die Wit Wolf: 'n Belydenis*. Mosselbaai, South Africa: Vaandel-Uitgewers.

Sudjic, Deyan. 2009. *The Language of Things*. New York: W. W. Norton.

Suzman, James. 2017. *Affluence Without Abundance: The Disappearing World of the Bushmen*. London: Bloomsbury.

Swart, Sandra, and Lance Van Sittert. 2008. *Canis Africanis: A Dog History of Southern Africa*. Leiden: Brill.

Swyngedouw, Erik. 2010. "Apocalypse Forever: Post-political Populism and the Spectre of Climate Change." *Theory, Culture and Society* 27 (2–3): 213–32.

Taylor, John P. 2001. "Authenticity and Sincerity in Tourism." *Annals of Tourism Research* 28 (1): 7–26.

Thompson, Stuart. 2019. "The Quest to Save the Banana from Extinction." *The Conversation*, April 11. https://theconversation.com/the-quest-to-save-the-banana-from-extinction-112256.

Tshokwane Safaris. n.d. Accessed February 17, 2010. http://www.tshokwanesafaris.com/namibia/serra-cafema-camp.php.

Van Eeden, Jeanne. 2006. "Land Rover and Colonial-Style Adventure." *International Feminist Journal of Politics* 8 (3): 343–69.

Van Rensburg, Schalk. 1998. *Testimony of Schalk Van Rensburg*. Western Cape, South Africa: TRC Chemical and Biological Warfare Hearings.

Veblen, Thorstein. 1943. *Theory of the Leisure Class: An Economic Study of Institutions*. New York: Random House.

Vidal, John. 2015. "Amnesty Accuses Shell of Failing to Clean Up Niger Delta Oil Spills." *Guardian*, November 3. Accessed May 17, 2016. http://www.theguardian.com/global

-development/2015/nov/03/amnesty-report-accuses-shell-of-failing-to-clean-up-niger-delta-oil-spills.
Wainaina, Binyavanga. 2005. "How to Write About Africa." *Granta* 92:92–95.
Wenzel, Jennifer. 2017. "Introduction." In *Fueling Culture: 101 Words for Energy and Environment*, edited by Imre Szeman, Jennifer Wenzel, and Patricia Yaeger, 1–16. New York: Fordham University Press.
Wilderness Safaris. n.d. Accessed February 17, 2010. http://www.wilderness-safaris.com.
Wild Frontiers: Tanzania. n.d. Advertising pamphlet for Tour Company. Wild Frontiers: Halfway House.
Williams, Florence. 2016. "This Is Your Brain on Nature." *National Geographic* 229 (1): 48–69.
Williams, Gardiner F. 1902. *The Diamond Mines of South Africa: Some Account of Their Rise and Development*. New York: Macmillan.
Williams, Raymond. 1980. *Problems in Materialism and Culture*. London: Verso.
Working Group on the "Anthropocene." 2014. Accessed June 22, 2019. http://quaternary.stratigraphy.org/workinggroups/anthropocene.
Zurich Zoo. n.d. "Masoala Rainforest." Accessed June 22, 2019. https://www.zoo.ch/en/zoobesuch/anlagen/masoala-rainforest.

Index

abundance, 53, 98, 101, 152
    diamonds, 92, 95, 97
    fear of, 97–98
    nature, 44, 46, 49, 51, 63, 97
    wealth, 51, 104
administered society. *See* society
Adorno, Theodore, 1, 7, 16–17, 29–34, 50–51, 54, 59, 104, 125, 145, 147, 154, 167n5
    administered society, 59, 148
    Culture Industry, The, 8–9
    historical image, 29, 32, 37, 88
    Mammoth, 27–28, 33, 50
    Minima Moralia, 25, 29–31, 51
    natural history, 9–11, 155–56 (*see also* natural history)
    Paysage, 1, 25
    second nature, 10, 11–12 (*see also* nature)
    unintentional reality, 25, 50, 76, 83, 98, 101
    See also allegory; constellations
advertising, 15, 24, 64, 67–68, 129–30, 135, 146, 153–54
    diamonds, 93–95, 98
    Land Rover, 132–34
advice literature, 31, 48, 51, 151–52
Africa
    abundance, 5, 46, 101
    myths, 130–33
    the real of, 130, 132

wildlife, 39, 80, 101, 106, 109–10, 121, 125, 126, 141–43
    See also natural resources
Akeley Hall of African Mammals. *See* American Museum of Natural History
alibi of nature. *See* nature: alibi of
alienation, 11, 37, 44, 90, 131, 147, 148
alien flora and fauna. *See* species
allegory, 11, 35, 105, 158
American Museum of Natural History, 24, 39
    Akeley Hall of African Mammals, 24, 39–40, 42, 101–2, 106, 151
    Hall of Biodiversity, 24, 28, 37–39, 41–44, 50–51
    Roosevelt African Hall, 39, 101
Anglo-American, 88, 91–92
    See also De Beers
animals
    humans as, 119, 121
    metaphor, 106–8, 119–20, 145
    power, 102, 104, 113, 114, 123, 145
    science and, 105–8, 113, 122
    vitality, 102, 106
    wild, 102, 103–24, 125, 141, 143, 145, 153, 158
    See also hunting; violence
Anthropocene, 5, 14, 24, 55–56, 60–62, 69–70, 148, 152, 154–55

apartheid, 4, 21, 157
  government military experiments, 104, 105, 111–17
aphorism, 30–31, 37, 72, 158
Armstrong, Philip, 106, 167n21
authenticity, 44, 106, 128, 132, 134, 146, 155
a theory of everything, 8, 13

background-foreground, 56, 57, 71, 75, 100–101, 159
Baka, 40, 47
banana republics, 52
bananas, 24, 48, 51–53, 54–55
  Cavendish banana, 15, 51–52, 151
  Gros Michel, 52
Basson, Wouter, 112, 116, 167n8
Benjamin, Walter, 7, 31, 32
  allegory, 11
  See also constellations
biodiversity. See loss
biomes, 28, 41, 46, 48, 50, 80
  Mediterranean, 28
  Nama Karoo (semidesert), 80
  rain forest, 24, 28, 44–45, 46–47 (see also rain forest)
breeding, 24, 27, 103–5, 107, 111–17, 125, 141–43, 147, 148
Brown, Duncan, 108–9
Buck-Morss, Susan, 32, 162n10
buffalo, 110, 114, 141–43, 144
Bushmen, 110–11, 121, 156–58

CAIT Climate Data Explorer, 164n9, 165n12
Cameroon, 19, 39, 47
Cape Town, 82, 93
  "poo protests," 74
  water crisis, 1–4, 150–51
capitalism, 2, 5, 12, 19–21, 23, 59

"capitalist life as we know it," 15, 23, 55, 59, 70, 76, 149–50 (see also technique of life)
Capitalocene, 152
  estrangement, 11, 124
  growth, 59, 67, 73, 160
  mobility of capital, 13, 87
  moral, 97, 129
  production, 8–9, 36–36, 77, 97, 98, 101, 154
caracal, 125, 142–43
carbon, 76
  credit, 59
  dioxide, 13, 15, 61, 65
  emissions, 5, 7, 22, 55, 65–66, 70
Carruthers, Jane, 109–10, 140–41
cars, 1, 3, 7, 25, 34, 50, 58, 63–64, 66, 97–98, 132
  4×4 vehicle, 67, 131–34 (see also Land Rover)
cartel. See monopoly
Cecil, the lion. See under lions
celebrities, 93–94, 154
cell phones. See mobile phones
Central African Republic, 28, 38–39
Chakrabarty, Dipesh, 36–37
charnel house, 12
China, 5, 68, 70, 156, 166n7
cities, 72, 73, 97
climate change, 2, 4, 5, 14, 29, 33–35, 37, 60, 71, 141, 151–52, 155
  abstract knowledge of, 15, 56
  denialism, 14, 70
  science, 4, 8, 13–15, 55–56, 62–69, 70, 148, 152
cloning, 33, 34
  See also genetics
coal, 5, 76, 88, 150, 164n7
coffee, 48, 153
colonialism, 4, 5, 18–19, 21, 25, 39, 65, 74–75, 87, 132, 135–36, 141, 145, 147, 154, 157

colony, 5, 18, 48, 64, 75–77, 101, 126
   romantic notion of, 133, 136
   white male hero, 5, 101, 129, 134, 158
   See also elite; liberation
commodities, 15, 27, 65, 67–69, 124, 138, 148, 153
   circulation of, 5, 48, 56, 70
   diamonds, 87, 88, 94, 98
   introduction in Africa, 64, 163n21
   transfer of value, 67–69, 153–54
   See nature: commodification of
commons, enclosure of the, 4, 20, 77, 78, 97, 98, 101, 104, 156
compound, 24, 77, 87, 89–90
conduct, 30–31, 36, 45, 51
Congo, 39, 47
conservation, 39, 42, 125, 126, 128, 129–31, 141–42, 143
   practices, 109, 136–37, 153
   prison as, 124 (*see also* zoos)
conspicuous
   consumption, 16, 68, 82, 127
   leisure, 16, 82, 127, 153
constellations, 7–8, 11–13, 29, 31–33, 151, 153
   various, 14, 19, 25, 38, 54, 75, 105, 128, 146
consumer. *See* consumption
consumption, 5, 12, 61–71, 145, 152–55
   conspicuous, 16, 68, 82, 127
   culture of, 5, 7, 15–18, 23, 58, 61, 67–68, 69, 97
   refusing to consume, 69, 71
   uneven, 51, 61
   See also energy; society
contingent, the, 7, 32, 70
Cook, Deborah, 104
Cooper, Frederick, 64–65
corn, 52
   corn-starch, 153
Crutzen, Paul, 14, 60, 62–63

culture
   cultural tourism, 138–40
   industry, 8–9, 16
   notion of term, 9
   See also consumption; masculinity

day zero. *See* water: restrictions
De Beers, 75, 77, 84–89, 92–97, 100, 127
de Botton, Alain, 64
debris, 84, 88, 98
debt, 70, 153, 159–60
deep or geological time. *See under* time
deforestation, 23, 47, 48
design
   interior, 135–38, 140
   landscape, 43, 45, 50, 81–82
desire, 23, 50, 51, 83, 94, 134, 140
   consumer, 52, 126, 128, 142, 149, 153
   public, human, 29, 37, 94, 105, 120–23
   value and, 15, 16, 18, 67, 83, 152–54
detailing, 49, 55, 136–38, 140, 143, 147
development, 4, 19, 20, 21–22, 61–62, 64–65
   uneven, 64–65, 162n13
diamonds, 19, 21, 27, 74–102, 126, 141, 154, 155, 156
   conflict diamonds, 96–97
   diamond industry, 21, 78–81, 84–99, 101
   mythification, 77, 88, 92, 95–96
   symbolic value, 88, 92–95, 154
Dickens, Charles, 162n14
dinosaurs, 24, 30, 33–35, 42, 151–52
dispossession, 15, 19–21, 78, 83, 97, 101
dogs, 103, 107, 112–13, 117
   hunting dogs, 100, 158–60
   police or security dogs, 112, 113, 115
   wild dogs, 37, 108, 120, 142
   See also wolves
drudgery, 16, 74, 84

Index

Durning, Alan, 67–69
dwelling
    noun, 149
    verb, 104, 158, 163n3
Dzanga-Sangha rain forest. *See under* rain forest

earthquake, 72–73
East India Company, 87
Eden Project, 24, 28, 42–49, 50–51, 55, 124, 148, 151–53
    See also rain forest: Rain Forest Biome
education. *See under* environmental
electricity
    infrastructure, 5, 64, 72, 150
    supply, 73, 150–51
elephants, 39, 110, 123
elite, 20–21, 81, 83, 92, 95, 141, 149
    in Britain, 75, 78, 80
    celebrity, 154
    colonial, 4, 78–79, 80, 83, 84, 96, 104
    global, 68, 97
emissions. *See* carbon: emissions
emotional charge or investment, 25, 67, 94, 123, 126, 141, 145, 146, 149, 153–54, 160
enclave, 19, 95
    industry and market, 71, 76, 97, 162n20, 163n23
    nature, 23, 120, 124, 131, 147
energy
    consumption, 24, 36, 62–63, 165n12
    renewable, 150
England. *See* United Kingdom
environmental
    damage, 8, 13, 14, 19, 22, 28, 29, 48, 64
    education, 15, 28, 41, 42, 47
    transformation, 4, 8, 39, 59, 63, 66, 162n16

ephemeral, 7, 17, 56, 70, 105, 128
Epstein, Edward Jay, 75, 88, 94–95
Escobar, Arturo, 61–62
essay, 31
Esteva, Gustavo, 21
ethical judgment, 31
ethology, 106–7
Europe, 4, 5, 65, 70, 81, 106, 117, 120, 148, 166n19
everyday, 69–71, 73, 150
    experience, 14, 17, 23, 25, 51, 73, 102
exclusion and exclusivity, 50, 69, 79, 86–87, 91, 116, 135, 153, 155
exotic, 27, 41, 47, 51, 53, 82
expeditions, 39–41, 45, 102
experience, 6–8, 25, 30–31, 34, 37, 56, 136–37, 160
    See also everyday: experience
expert knowledge. *See* knowledge
exploit, the, 74–76, 79, 83, 84, 99, 100, 101, 127, 145, 146, 149, 158
exploitation, 98, 99, 149
    humans, 25, 78, 83, 98–99, 101, 153, 157
    natural resources, 4, 5, 21, 23, 25, 61, 74, 80, 84, 99, 149, 153
expropriation, 20, 78, 162n19
externalities, 23, 155
extinction, 28, 35–38, 41, 42, 44, 47, 63, 100, 104, 124, 141, 149
    voluntary extinction, 35–36
extraction, 19, 21, 23, 70, 77, 88, 89–98, 153, 161n6

fantasies, 6, 22, 24, 36, 51, 109, 128, 138, 143, 148, 155
    animals, 34, 108, 120, 122
    4×4 vehicle, 132, 134
    of violence, 111, 117, 119
Ferguson, James, 23, 131
fetish, 95, 145

film, 41, 94, 156–58
    set, 137
fire, 60–61, 108
foreground–background. *See* background–foreground
fossil fuels, 5, 60–61, 76, 97, 161n2, 164n7
Foucault, Michel, 118–19, 123
4×4 vehicle. *See* cars
foxes, 122, 125
fragments, 1–26, 27–29, 33, 149, 151
France, 65, 156
fruit industry. *See under* industry
future, 14–15, 18, 25, 29, 34, 35, 41, 42–49, 119, 124

game
    lodges, 127–28, 130, 134–40, 147, 153
    national reserves, 109–10, 126, 127
    private reserves, 23, 24, 125–49, 153
garden, 28, 42, 44, 80–81, 83, 98
    botanical, 27
    of Eden, 39, 42, 44
    See also zoos
GDP. *See* gross domestic product
genetics, 33, 35, 103, 113, 124, 128, 143
    See also breeding
gentlemen's club, 78–79
geography, 61, 66, 72
geology, 14, 55, 60
    See also time
Germany, 31, 58
global warming, 5, 8, 13–15, 55
    See also climate change
Gods Must Be Crazy, The, 156–58
Gould, Chandre, 112–15
Great Acceleration, 62, 68
    graphs, 14–15, 56, 62–63, 65–66, 68, 70–71, 152
greenhouse gas (GHG), 61, 63, 65, 77, 165n12
    See also carbon

Groote Schuur estate, 81–83, 88, 99
gross domestic product (GDP), 63, 140, 169n6
growth. *See* capitalism
guilt, 49, 144, 153

Hall of Biodiversity. *See* American Museum of Natural History
Haraway, Donna, 11, 39, 105, 120
haunting, 9, 14, 42, 50
Hawaii, East Island, 169n3
Hemingway, Ernest, 106
hesitation, 17, 54, 71, 73, 158
heterotopia, 118–19, 123
Himba, 132–34, 138–40
hippos, 110, 114
history, 9–13, 36–37, 57, 70, 81, 149, 151
    of diamond mining, 74–102
    See also Adorno, Theodore; natural history; time
honor, 16, 93
    honorific activity, 75, 84, 99, 127
    honorific costliness, 93, 94
Horkheimer, Max, 8, 74, 103
human enterprise, 56, 62, 63, 65, 68
humanity, 25, 36, 55, 61, 65, 70, 106, 152, 154
hunting, 5, 23, 39, 99–102, 104, 106, 158–59
    trophy hunt, 125–27, 140–48
Hwange National Park, 143, 146
hyena, 108, 114

IGBP. *See* International Geosphere-Biosphere Programme
income, 61, 68, 71, 129
    high, 62, 66, 71, 165n11
    low, 61, 62, 65
India, 58, 68, 78
indigenous
    flora and fauna, 82, 108, 109, 111, 119, 121

187

Index

indigenous (*continued*)
    population, 127, 133
    technique of life, 5, 47, 101
industrialization, 5, 21, 23, 28, 36, 59, 106
industrial revolution, 63, 97
    See also industrialization
industry
    fruit, 52 (*see also* bananas)
    hospitality, 161n5
    meat, 99, 101, 141
    notion of term, 9
    See also culture: industry; diamonds; nature; tourist industry
inevitability, 12
    myth of, 10, 13, 56, 71, 152
Inglis, Fred, 134–35
interior design, 135–38, 140
International Geosphere-Biosphere Programme (IGBP), 14, 56, 60
investment
    economic, 18, 71, 77, 87, 134, 160 (*see also* wildlife: investment)
    emotional, 25, 126, 146
    symbolic, 50, 95
invidious comparison, 16, 68, 91, 97, 107, 147, 152, 154, 157

jackal, 107, 125, 142–43, 149
Jameson, Fredric, 17, 32
jealousy, 156–58
Ju/'hoansi, 156–58
Jurassic Park, 34–35
juxtapositions, 1–26, 31–32, 38, 39, 65, 66, 72, 77, 129, 151

Kamil, Fred, 75, 91–92
Kapp, Karl William, 23, 98
Kimberley, 19, 75, 96, 127, 141
    Kimberley Club, 78–80, 83–84, 87, 96, 147
King Kong, 30, 33

knowledge, 7–8
    different orders of, 6, 15, 29–31, 34
    expert, 39, 56, 58–59
Kracauer, Siegfried, 54
Kruger National Park, 109–10

Lagos, 73
land, 20, 39, 77, 81, 101, 125–49
    See also commons, enclosure of the; dispossession; ownership; primitive: accumulation
Land Rover, 24, 132–34, 157, 158
landscape design, 43, 45, 50, 81–82
Latour, Bruno, 49–50
leisure, 78, 80, 97, 123, 127–28, 137
    conspicuous, 16, 82, 127, 153
liberation, 4, 5, 18, 39, 64, 65, 136–37
lifestyle, 17, 59, 137, 139–40
    consumer, 5, 21, 23, 35, 58, 67–68, 73, 152
lions, 110, 125, 143, 146
    Cecil, 25, 143–46
    Terry, 110–11, 121
lodges. *See* game: lodges
Lorenz, Konrad, 106–8
loss, 11, 13–14, 28, 48, 53, 149, 152–53, 155, 160
    biodiversity, 28, 36, 38, 41, 42, 52
    narrative of, 50, 56, 101
    of nature, 9, 13–14, 39, 46, 51, 53, 58, 63, 120, 124, 147
Lukács, Georg, 11–12
Luxemburg, Rosa, 20
luxury, 4, 27, 55, 76, 78, 80, 134, 137, 153, 155

mammoth
    woolly mammoth, 33
    See also Adorno, Theodore: *Mammoth*
Maori, 139–40

Index

marketing. *See* advertising
Marx, Karl, 19–20, 77–78, 98
masculinity, 39, 78, 84, 99, 101, 106, 109, 123, 132
  See also colonialism: white male hero
materialism, 17, 161n8
materiality, 9, 13, 55, 65, 70, 73, 120, 155
  animals, 105–6
Mbembe, Achille, 18–19, 22
McKibben, Bill, 56–58, 64
meat, 99–101, 141, 143, 158–59
Mediterranean Biome. *See under* biomes
Minima Moralia. *See* Adorno, Theodore
mining, 5, 75, 84, 162n20
  De Beers mine, 84–85, 88
  See also diamonds
Mitchell, Timothy, 76, 97, 161n2
Mitchell, W. J. T., 34
mobile phones, 15, 24, 63, 67, 70–71, 152–53
modernity, 2, 4, 5, 8, 106, 123, 130, 138–39, 151, 157–58
  confrontation with environmental limits, 4, 5, 8
  notion of, 4, 72
  See also technique of life: of capitalist modernity
Monbiot, George, 122–23, 148
monetary economy, 4, 51, 64, 94, 129, 150, 155, 163n21
monopoly, 20–21, 77, 87–88, 92, 95, 166n16
monument, 39, 74, 81
Mozambique, 150, 151
myths and mythification
  Africa, 130–33
  diamonds, 88, 92, 95
  dinosaurs, 34
  economy, 20
  mythic inevitability, 10, 13, 56, 71, 152
  nature as, 10, 81

wolves, 106, 108
  See also fantasies

Namibia, 132, 138, 140, 157
narrative
  conservation, 119, 129
  imperial, 24, 82–83, 133
  of loss, 50, 56, 101
  of progress, 4, 156
natural habitat, 39, 53, 118, 124, 139
natural history, 9–11, 69–70, 75, 104, 155–56
  See also American Museum of Natural History
natural installation, 28–30, 37–39, 41–49, 118
natural resources
  privatization of, 1, 125–49, 153
  resource curse, 19
  See also exploitation; primitive: accumulation; value
nature
  alibi of, 6, 48, 153, 155
  commodification of, 9, 18, 19, 106, 126, 149
  enclaved, 23, 120, 124, 131, 147
  end of, 13, 29, 56, 62
  health benefits, 49
  loss of. *See* loss
  nature industry, 6, 8–9
  notion of term, 6, 9
  preservation of, 23, 36, 39, 42
  pristine, 23, 58, 131, 136, 137, 138, 139, 147
  production of, 6, 24, 29, 39, 44, 101, 123, 126, 151, 155
  romantic notion of, 47, 111, 164n4
  second nature, 10, 11–12, 73, 152
  See also loss; natural resources
Newlands spring. *See* water
new safari. *See* safari

Index

Nichols, Robert, 20–21
Niger Delta, 23, 76, 153
Nixon, Rob, 22–23
Noah's ark, 35, 36
Norberg, Jakob, 31
North America, 4, 5, 52, 58, 64, 82, 105, 113, 119, 120, 166n19
  See also United States
nostalgia, 28, 53, 128, 137–38, 149, 151–52
nuclear
  bombs, 35
  deal, 150

ocean acidification, 63, 152
oil, 76, 153
  companies, 23, 98
  See also fossil fuels; Niger Delta
ownership, 3, 20–21, 23, 69, 79, 82, 84–92, 97, 116, 125, 126, 134, 159
Oxford University Wildlife Conservation Research Unit (WildCRU), 144, 145–46
ozone layer, 63

Panama disease, 52
parataxis, meaning, 6
particular, the, 7, 31, 32, 104, 157
Paysage. *See under* Adorno, Theodore
pecuniary emulation, 16, 83
Pensky, Max, 11–12, 162n11
photography, 43, 52–53, 75–76, 79–102
plastic waste, 165n13
population, rise in, 28, 41, 61, 63, 65–66, 162n16
positivism, 17, 101
postcolony, 6, 22–23, 58, 62, 69–70, 88, 104, 108, 123, 146, 153, 155–56, 160
  notion of, 5, 18–19
postmodernism, 17
postpolitical, 58–59
predators, 102, 104, 105, 111–25, 141, 142

primitive, 22, 139, 158
  accumulation, 19–21, 75, 77–78, 83, 90, 98, 156
privilege
  access to nature, 123, 137, 149, 153, 155, 159
  inherited, 127, 154
progress, 14, 21–22, 70, 98
  See also narrative: of progress
property. *See* ownership; primitive: accumulation
prowess, 99, 145, 146
pseudo-totality. *See* totality
publicity. *See* advertising
puzzles, 12, 30, 33, 151

racial discrimination and racism, 21, 39, 83, 115, 133, 135, 147, 157
  black diggers, 77, 86–87, 90–91
rain forest, 24, 28, 38–42, 47, 50, 51, 63, 118, 153
  Dzanga-Sangha, 11, 24, 28, 30, 38–39, 40–41, 118
  Masoala, 163n2
  Rain Forest Biome, 24, 28, 44–45, 46–47, 51, 118
real, the, 12–13, 17, 32, 35, 131, 157, 160
  of Africa, 130, 132
  loss of, 11, 52
realism, 15, 17, 51, 70, 158
reality, unintentional. *See* Adorno, Theodore
refrigerators, 52, 152
reification, 1, 12, 13, 48, 139, 155
resources. *See* natural resources
Rhodes, Cecil John, 74, 80–83, 87, 99–101, 127, 141
Rhodesia, 65, 83
Roodeplaat Breeding Enterprises, 112–14, 116
Rooipoort, 127, 141

safari, 39, 128, 131, 134–38, 147
sanctuary (term), 118
    See also wolves
sanitation system. *See* water
Satterthwaite, David, 61, 65–66
Sax, Boria, 105, 107
scarcity, 14, 73, 100–101, 104
    diamonds, 88, 95
science, 74, 101, 138, 148
    animals and, 105–8, 113, 122
    authority of, 55, 62
    natural installations and, 39–41, 44
    social, 60, 72
    See also climate change
scripted role, 31, 51
second nature. *See* nature
senseless necessities, 11, 12, 152
Serres, Michel, 56–57, 71–73
sewage, 4, 63, 149
    See also water: sanitation system
slow violence. *See* violence
Smit, Timothy, 42–46
Smith, Neil, 162n13
snakes, poisonous, 110, 116, 119
society
    administered, 59, 148
    consumer, 10, 16, 25, 51, 55, 64, 66–71, 131, 147 (*see also* consumption)
    feudal, 147
South Africa
    access to water and sanitation, 1–4, 74, 149
    blacks, 21, 40, 74, 85, 100, 101, 113, 115, 147
    carbon emissions, 5, 73, 77
    history, 4, 5, 24, 119 (*see also* apartheid)
    South African Defence Force (SADF), 110–14, 116, 120, 121, 157
    whites, 2–3, 21, 74, 105, 109–11, 114–15, 120, 121, 127, 129, 157
South America, 28, 52
species, 27, 35, 36, 37
    alien, 82, 104, 105, 108–9
    endangered, 52, 120
    See also extinction; loss: biodiversity
Spengler, Oswald, 82–83
spiritual, 110, 134, 135–37, 148
standard of living, 5, 14, 61–62, 67, 70, 105, 149
status, 16–17, 23, 69, 74, 127, 147, 153
    diamonds, 92, 93
    hunting, 16, 99
style, 24, 129, 135, 137
    See also lifestyle
subjunctive mood, 14, 29, 54–73, 151
surplus, 20, 153
    value, 98, 145
survival, 3, 4, 16, 47, 146, 149
    wolf, 103, 120
Suzman, James, 157–58
Swyngedouw, Erik, 49, 59
synecdoche, 6–7, 18, 28, 52, 54, 56, 67, 104, 151

Tanzania, 130–31, 158
taxidermy, 39, 43, 101
technique of life, 1, 18
    alternative, 12, 24, 71
    of capitalist modernity, 4, 55, 57, 59, 64, 98, 102, 128, 149, 150, 153, 157–58
    geographical location, 18, 140, 161n1
    indigenous, 5, 47, 101
    phrase, 161n1
technology, 23, 28, 43, 71, 73, 75, 152–53, 161n1
    communication, 52, 131, 150–53 (*see also* mobile phones)

technology (*continued*)
    ecotechnology, 59, 163n2
    transport, 3, 5, 52, 131, 132 (*see also* cars)
    violence, of, 116, 148
temporality, 22, 54, 60

Theron, Charlize, 93
time
    deep or geological time, 35, 36, 60, 69–70
    dream time, 81
    historical time, 32, 37, 56, 57, 69, 124
    slices of, 119, 123
totality, 71, 105, 162n11
    Anthropocene as, 24, 55, 69, 73
    pseudo-totality, 32
tourist industry, 23, 126, 134–35, 138–40
tradition, invention of, 80–81, 84, 88, 89, 94, 97
transformation
    social, 4, 44, 50, 59, 61–62, 64, 66
    See also environmental: transformation
transience, 70, 73, 75, 146, 155–56
Truth and Reconciliation Commission (TRC), 24, 105, 112–13, 116
Tsitsikamma Wolf Sanctuary. *See under* wolves

uncertainty, 7, 14, 15, 29, 56, 59, 71
United Kingdom, 4, 9, 13, 19, 77, 78, 81–82, 94, 122, 126, 127, 135, 148
    colonial regime, as, 65, 77, 81, 110
United States, 19, 31, 41, 70, 94, 156
    See also North America
unpredictability, 2, 4, 14–15, 29, 54, 73, 151
utility, 93, 145
utopia, 2, 9, 44, 118, 124, 145, 148, 156, 168n13

value, 15–16, 18, 22, 67, 83, 107, 138, 141, 149, 153–55, 160
    aesthetic, 94, 135, 137, 143
    emotional, 25, 94, 126, 145
    fantastic(al), 21, 76, 96, 98, 142–44
    geographical movement of, 76, 86, 162n13
    inflation of, 141–43, 155
    moral, 130, 135, 137, 141
    nature, 5, 6, 9, 19, 58, 95, 130, 155
    regime of, 86, 91, 128, 141
    social, 83, 106, 157
    surplus, 98, 145
    symbolic value, 50, 88, 92, 95, 117, 154
    use value, 15, 132, 143, 145, 152, 154, 156, 159
    value extraction, 21, 76
Veblen, Thorstein, 16–17, 68, 74, 92, 93–94, 99, 127, 146, 152, 154–55
violence, 4, 5, 22, 116, 123, 134, 141, 155
    animals, 104, 105, 111–21, 124
    diamonds, 88, 91, 96–97
    dispossession, 15, 19–20, 78, 83, 97, 101
    fantasies of, 111, 117, 119
    postcolony, 15, 19, 22, 99, 160
    slow, 22
    technology of, 116, 148
    See also hunting; industry: meat
Voluntary Extinction Movement, 35–36

waste disposal, 55, 153
water
    municipal water, 2, 4, 149
    Newlands spring, 1–4
    restrictions, 2, 150–51
    sanitation system, 4, 74, 149
    usage statistics, 63
wealth
    abundance, 51, 104

uneven distribution of, 4, 5, 61, 69, 78, 129, 158 (*see also* dispossession; exploitation: humans)
weather, changes in, 2–3, 57
whites, 4, 39, 110, 129, 133, 145, 147
    diggers, 86–87, 90
    white men, 39, 84, 133, 144, 146 (*see also* colonialism: white male hero)
    See also South Africa
WildCRU. *See* Oxford University Wildlife Conservation Research Unit
wildlife
    African. *See* Africa
    conservation, 109, 123, 130, 142, 144 (*see also* conservation)
    investment, 141–43

wildness, 1, 106–9, 114
    rewilding, 120, 122, 148
    wilderness, 21, 101, 130–31, 134, 138, 146
    See also animals
Williams, Raymond, 126, 161n6
Wit Wolwe, 114–15
wolves, 103–24
    myths, 106, 108
    survival, 103, 120
    Tsitsikamma Wolf Sanctuary, 103, 111, 119, 121
    wolf dog, 24, 105, 111–17
women, 47, 84, 95, 110, 132–34, 159–60

Zimbabwe, 123, 143–44, 146
zone of contact, 140
zoos, 27, 30, 35, 36, 50, 163n2

CPSIA information can be obtained
at www.ICGtesting.com
Printed in the USA
LVHW091952140420
653438LV00002B/3